61 LESSONS FROM THE SKY

MILITARY HELICOPTERS

FLETCHER MCKENZIE

SSP

61 LESSONS FROM THE SKY

STORIES & LESSONS FROM
61 PILOTS & CREW FROM NINE MILITARIES
AROUND THE WORLD

RAF, RCAF, RAAF, UK ARMY
USAF, USCG, USN, USARMY, USMC

This edition published 2023 by Squabbling Sparrows Press

ISBN 978-0-9951421-38 (Paperback edition)
ISBN 978-0-9951421-21 (Ebook edition)

Published by Squabbling Sparrows Press
PO Box 4213, Marewa, Napier 4143
New Zealand

Squabbling Sparrows Press

ALSO BY FLETCHER MCKENZIE

I dedicate this book to Ben Pryor and Scott McKenzie.
Thanks for being you.

Blue skies.

"The fact that... helicopters are eagerly sought in large numbers by air forces, armies and navies all over the world serves to underscore their value."

Bill Gunston and Mike Spick
Modern Fighting Helicopters
1998

CONTENTS

FOREWORD
PAUL 'FOO' KENNARD

"The combat frequency was to be kept clear of all but strategically essential messages, and all unenlightening comments were regarded as evidence of funk, of the wrong stuff. A Navy pilot (in legend, at any rate) began shouting, "I've got a MiG at zero! A MiG at zero!"—meaning that it had manoeuvred in behind him and was locked in on his tail. An irritated voice cut in and said, "Shut up and die like an aviator."

Tom Wolfe – 'The Right Stuff'

Military aviators are, well, just different.

We try to constantly juggle the challenges and physics of flight itself with complex, hazardous and capacity sapping missions, often flying platforms with crippling workload issues due to lack of investment and invariably away from the comforts of home for extended deployments. We're also inheritors of a long and proud tradition of being taciturn and confident; the choice of that quote from 'The Right Stuff' at the top of this forward is deliberate. As military aviators we're supposed to be made of 'The Right Stuff', as fearless as a Bader, Olds or Steinhoff and as cocky and irreverent as a Pete 'Maverick' Mitchell or a Kara 'Starbuck' Thrace. Whether we like it or not, there is a public image of our trade which brings with it implied and perceived pressures. It's a caricature that's often difficult or even impossible to live up to.

"You're not pretty, but you're safe…"
Tony Muncer, QFI, on sending 17-year-old me solo…

For the first half of my flying career, flying the CH-47 Chinook, I was guided by the senior 'shags' on the squadron, invariably to be found in the crew room drinking coffee and reading a paper (or outside smoking). Aviators of comparatively junior rank who seemed implausibly old to still be flying operational sorties, had acquired deep reservoirs of knowledge and were either skilled or lucky simply because they were still 'here' and not a name on a memorial wall. When they spoke, we listened. Often, they would make a semi-opaque reference to an accident or incident from which lessons could be extracted – giving us tyros the opportunity to seek out and read the Accident Report. We contented ourselves with a 'well that won't happen to me!' mentality, yet the same accidents seemed to keep happening…

The second half of my military service saw a fundamental change. Firstly, the 'old and bold' aviators disappeared from crew rooms with almost indecent haste. Many simply worn out by seemingly endless deployments to Iraq and Afghanistan. There came a tipping point where their love of the flying and the Service was overtaken by the needs of the self and the family. The value of these 'oracles' has been recognised by the RAF, who now advertise for former aircrew to return as non-flying 'Squadron Uncles' to advise the new crews, 'Junta', and middle/senior management, in the hope of passing down valuable lessons of the air, and, indeed, of the ground, as many have been Flight and Squadron commanders in their previous service.

Secondly, our approach to open reporting and a 'Just Culture' has been transformed. In the late 90s, I learned about flying from boozy tales of 'near misses' in the weekly 'Happy Hour' in the Officers' Mess – loquacity being significantly enhanced after a few pints. The decline of the 'Drinking Culture' has meant that these, often hushed, conversations are now rarer. Fortunately, the Open Reporting System has taken up much of this slack. Individuals are now inculcated during their flying training into the need to report honest mistakes, without fear of heavy censure unless they committed a deliberate nefarious act for personal gain.

And this is the rub.

We're not all Baders or Mavericks. We're just humans with human failings. As military aviators, in flight safety, as in combat, we should be watching each other's 'sixes'. We should put our hands up when we make an error, and not feel fear in calling out a dangerous trend, tendency or action if we see it. With fewer aircraft we simply cannot afford the attrition that previous generations grudgingly acknowledged as being 'part of the job'. We can, and must, do better.

Fly and fight safe.

Paul 'Foo' Kennard

Paul Kennard served 22 years in the Royal Air Force as a helicopter pilot, flying the CH-47 Chinook in Northern Ireland, Bosnia, Kosovo, Iraq and Afghanistan. He was a Qualified Helicopter Tactics Instructor (QHTI), Electronic Warfare Instructor (EWI) and served for 5 years on the Rotary Wing Operational Evaluation and Training Unit as both an Operational Test and Evaluation Pilot and Staff QHTI. He also served as a Capability Requirements Manager for the Chinook and as a Technology Manager for the Air Domain, specialising in Helicopter Degraded Visual Environment (DVE), Aircraft Survivability Equipment (ASE), UAV technology and aircrew protection systems. Upon leaving the RAF in 2015, he established Ascalon Defence Consultancy Ltd, where he provides specialist technical advice and project support into industry and assorted government and NATO agencies. He is a contributor to Forbes.com and contributing editor to the Heli-Ops family of magazines.

PROLOGUE
FLETCHER MCKENZIE

I'M lucky enough to work with or on helicopters almost everyday of my life, mainly with machines based in the military or being ex military machines or parts — from Allison M 250-C20b engines, Safran fuel injectors to overhauled Breeze Eastern winches. I also have been very lucky to be able to commercialise military technology and licence military design intellectual property, giving us the ability to add value and innovate these designs for various helicopters in service with militaries around the world. We have been able to innovate and market an ultra light armour floor for the NH90 and AW109 helicopters. I get to work with current and ex military helicopter pilots and engineers, one of which I asked him to do the introduction, thanks 'Foo'. You can read more from him in HeliOps Magazine.

Being able to work within this arena in my day job is exciting and my days are never boring. Being able to supply much needed parts and to help protect pilots, crew and people and the helicopter itself makes me believe that I am helping this global industry.

I am not a helicopter pilot, but I operate a banner towing company. Usually we tow banners from a fixed wing aircraft and undertake the occasional sky writing job. However, for one job, we required the need for helicopter banner towing, as the banner we were provided was a massive banner that was usually hung from a crane outside each of the Super 15 rugby stadiums. The banners we usually tow are manufactured from sailcloth, but these were not, and proved to be a lot heavier and harder to "fly". The job consisted of towing the flag for the regional Rugby Waikato team the Chiefs, we used a Schweizer 300 based in the Waikato and then for the Canterbury Crusaders, we used a Aérospatiale AS 355N Ecureuil 2 based in Christchurch. As part of this process I decided to undertake helicopter flying training in the Schweizer 300 - it was surprising, taking nine minutes to hover, however I still felt out of control, it took me back to when I first jumped in the glider at age 16. The sudden change of situational awareness was incredible, my mind had been normalised into wanting to look at the airspeed indicator and see that I was flying over the stall speed, of course this was mentally somewhat of an issue to have a "o" airspeed but still I was flying. I realised how much harder it is to fly a helicopter and my respect increased markedly for helicopter pilots.

For this introduction I have concentrated on the helicopters that I have been involved with, which you'll see is more eclectic than most. And I wanted this book to have an equally diverse mix of lessons from various military operators — and we do, with lessons from nine different organisations.

The history of vertical flight began as early as about 400 CE; there are references to a Chinese kite that used a rotary wing as a source of its lift. Toys using the principle of the helicopter — a rotary blade turned by the pull of a string were around in the Middle Ages.

That history reminds me of my visit to the Hiller Aviation Museum in San Carlos (San Francisco). I knew Hiller was part of helicopter history, but I didn't realise how many inventions by Hiller are similar to those available today, like the their first flying platform contracted in 1953 by the Office of Naval Research (ONR) for a one-man flying platform, featuring two contra-rotating rotors spinning inside a duct. While at the museum I bought a plastic helicopter toy blade from my young daughters — produced for a few cents out of plastic and in bright colours with the Hiller Museum branding logo on each blade. Putting the plastic stick (that is joined to the middle of the blade) between your hands you simply push one hand and pull the other creating the force to turn the blade — the result of course is flight.

In the 15th century, Leonardo da Vinci drew several aviation concepts including a helicopter that used a spiral airscrew to obtain lift. In 1784 a toy, using rotors constructed of feathers from birds, was presented to the French Academy of Science by artisans Launoy and Bienvenu. Later in 1870 Alphonse Pénaud created a more successful model. The word helicopter is adapted from the French word hélicoptère.

The name of Sir George Cayley surfaced in my research. Regarded by many as the father of fixed-wing flight, his scientific exposition of principles in 1843 ultimately led to the successful helicopter. From then on, a number of helicopter ideas were spawned by numerous inventors, usually in model or sketch form. Many ideas did not progress any further. There were two main trends in vertical flight. One was the widespread of minor successes with helicopters; the second was the appearance and apparent success of the autogiro (also spelled autogyro).

In 1921, the US Army Air Service hired George de Bothezat to build a prototype helicopter. In 1922, the quadrotor helicopter, de Bothezat designed, lifted off the ground for less than two minutes. I feel there is a very similar look to the mass produced public UAVs available today.

In Spain 1923, Juan de la Cierva made the first successful flight of an autogiro — having the advantage of a relatively short takeoff and a near vertical descent.

Heinrich Focke at Focke-Wulf produced the Cierva C.30 autogyro in 1933 (under license). He designed the world's first practical transverse twin-rotor helicopter, the Focke-Wulf Fw 61, flying in 1936. In 1937 it broke all of the helicopter world records demonstrating a flight envelope that had only previously been achieved by the autogyro. The technology of the rotor head and rotor blade developed for the autogiro contributed to the development of the helicopter, which in time made the autogiro obsolete.

Use of the helicopter during World War II was varied. Nazi Germany used helicopters in small numbers for observation, transport, and medical evacuation. The Flettner Fl 282 Kolibri synchropter — using the same basic configuration as Anton Flettner's own pioneering Fl 265 in the Mediterranean theatre, the Focke Achgelis Fa 223 Drache twin-rotor helicopter was used throughout Europe. Extensive bombing prevented Germany from manufacturing helicopters in large quantities.

Igor Sikorsky and W. Lawrence LePage competed to produce the US military's first helicopter. Russian-born engineer Igor Sikorsky settled on a single rotor design, the VS-300, the first practical single lifting-rotor helicopter design. He experimented to counteract the torque produced by the single main rotor, settling on a single, smaller rotor mounted on the tail boom. It is what we know as the helicopter today. The VS-300, termed world's first practical helicopter, took flight at Stratford, Connecticut on September 14, 1939. The VS-300 led to a long line of Sikorsky helicopters, and it influenced their development in a number of countries, including France, England, Germany, and Japan.

1944 saw the world's first mass-produced helicopter, the Sikorsky R-4. The Sikorsky R-4 was developed from the VS-300 - the R-4 was the only Allied helicopter to serve in World War II. It was used primarily for search and rescue (by the USAAF 1st Air Commando Group) in Burma, in Alaska, and in other areas with harsh terrain. Total production reached 131 helicopters before the R-4 was replaced by the R-5 and the R-6 Sikorsky helicopters. Sikorsky produced over 400 helicopters before the end of World War II. In my travels I found the XR-4, at the Smithsonian, on display in the World War II Aviation (UHC) at the Steven F. Udvar-Hazy Center. This machine helped usher in new training practices and procedures that became the standard in future rotary winged operations in the USA.

After World War II the commercial use of helicopters developed rapidly in many roles, including fire fighting, police work, agricultural crop spraying, mosquito control, medical evacuation, and carrying mail and passengers.

This expanding market brought additional competitors into development and each competitor bought a different approach to the problem of vertical flight. The Bell Aircraft Corporation, with a series of prototypes launched the Bell Model 47, one of the most significant helicopters, it incorporated an articulated, gyro-stabilized, two-blade rotor. Entering US military service life in 1946, it was operated over thirty years in various versions and under different designations. Designated the H-13 Sioux by the US Army, operated during the Korean War, it served a variety of roles, including reconnaissance and scouting, search and rescue, and medevac.

While filming for *FlightPathTV* we met Phill Hooker from Tauranga, New Zealand, who operated a fixed wing training school and had a number of helicopters, including a Bell 47 in MASH colours, a Kawasaki 369 (a MD500 made under licence) painted in US livery from the Vietnam war. We used both helicopters for the shooting sequence. We also worked on a filming sequence with the K369 and troops on the ground to do a Vietnam reenactment for the airshow that was coming up in the following weeks. We also filmed the RNZAF's Souix Blue, a double helicopter act for local airshows. The Souix were still being used for training by the RNZAF until their retirement in 2012.

Jet-engine helicopter technology arrived in 1951 in the form of the Kaman Aircraft Corporation's HTK-1. Kaman's patented aerodynamic servo-controlled rotors in a "synchropter" configuration this means side-by-side rotors with intermeshing paths of each blade. The Kaman Kmax is still in production seventy years later - this has recently been converted to a drone for fire fighting. Jet engines had many advantages for helicopters as it was smaller, it weighed less but with comparable power, had far less vibration, and used less expensive fuel. In 1952 a US Army requirement for a medical evacuation and utility helicopter was released - Bell answered with the first born of Huey family, the UH-1 Iroquois that first flew in 1956.

The first time I ever stepped up into a helicopter — it was an Royal New Zealand Air Force (RNZAF) Bell UH-1 Iroquois (nicknamed "Huey") - a utility military helicopter powered by a single turboshaft engine designated as a T-53 engine, originally designated HU-1, hence the Huey nickname, which has remained in common use, despite the official change to UH-1 since 1962, UH standing for utility helicopter. More than 16,000 have been built since 1960). It was big, grey, and had been operating and flying for over 30 years. I on the other hand was small and had only operated for 14 years. And I was in awe of this loud flying machine that made an awesome thumping sound. Ever since that moment, I have been fascinated by helicopters.

That Huey was the first helicopter I got to see up close, as a 14-year-old with the Air Training Corps, whilst attending a NCO (non commissioned officer) Course on a military base where both the Air Force and Navy helicopters were stationed for training.

For a young teenager it was beyond exciting watching the Iroquois fall from the sky one after another as they practiced autorotations, coming in fast and flaring just before hitting the ground and then running onto the grass on their skids. I remember one of our classes distinctly, due to the great view from the windows overlooking the grass runway. The whole day we watched the aircraft coming in and flaring, worried that they would crash due to the very high angle and the speed of the aircraft relative to the ground. Sometimes we'd all stand up to watch, occasionally running towards the window thinking one would hit the ground. I don't recall learning anything that day given how distracted we were by the free airshow outside.

Since then I've been lucky to fly as a passenger in a number of civilian helicopters around the world, I have also been flown with militaries on various exercises. The most terrifying experience was in Cape Town on a ex military Huey that flew in the Vietnam conflict. I had started to understand the limitations helicopters and pilots had, building up knowledge of how air forces operated (usually operating with built in margins for error). While the Cape Town experience was exciting, to be honest, there was little margin for error as we flew towards trees and other local fauna at low level, afterwards I spoke with the pilot who turned out he was a very experienced crop-duster pilot with around 20,000 hours. While writing this introduction my curiosity got the better of me and I decided to do a search for the company, I still see they are operating. Great to see nothing has happened, although I note floatation devices now on the machine...

The Air Training Corps (ATC) were first part of the Air Force (set up in 1941, to train potential airmen in basic airmanship and to provide an insight into Air Force work), becoming its own organisation under the Chief of Defence Force in 1971. As part of the ATC, I spent many weekends learning to fly gliders on that same Air Force Base — Base Hobsonville. I went on to staff gliding courses for the cadets.

Occasionally we would see the Royal New Zealand Navy's Wasp helicopters doing test flights, these helicopters served on the Navy's Frigates. The Westland Wasp was a small 1960s British built turbine powered, shipboard anti-submarine helicopter. With its very distinctive sound, it looked and sounded like a wasp.

With my filming and production experience and working on an online fitness project, I met up with an associate from the Air Training Corps, and over a coffee we decided to build an aviation television series, called *FlightPathTV*. We sold it to Discovery Channel and it was here where I really started working closely with helicopters and the military.

Our first up close encounter with military helicopters was at the Royal New Zealand Air Force (RNZAF) Dip Flat training camp for the RNZAF's Exercise Blackbird, mountain flying at its best. We arrived at camp late in the afternoon and we had a briefing with various offices and media liaisons - the weather was good for filming and we had the chance to try out our camera gear on a flight picking up a crew member from a valley. It was a shakedown flight for us to ensure we were ready for the next day. We were flying with the same Iroquois squadron (and same helicopters) I saw at age 14 - some 20 years later. Away we flew, it was blue skies in the mountains however as we got closer to the valley the weather closed in. It started snowing, and for us we thought that would just add to the footage. They dropped us off and flew out so we could get some approaching shots from the Valley floor... we spoke with the crewman and then the snow started falling heavily and the Iroquois approached several times in the valley to pick us up (we thought they were just giving us lots of footage), turns out it was becoming harder to get in to pick us up due to the snow fall. They finally got in and as we flew away, we heard how close they had been to leaving us on the mountain with the crewman and the small shelter that was available.

In 1955 a French SNCA-S.E. 3130 Alouette II made its first flight, it was powered by a Turbomeca Artouste II turbine. The Alouette II has been a very influential helicopter in the world and started a trend toward jet-powered helicopters. It was predominantly for military carrying out various roles, observation, photography, air-sea rescue, liaison and training, and it has also carried anti-tank missiles and torpedoes.

The first military contract that I secured was in 2008 when we looked into filming a number of stories for *FlightPathTV* with 6 Squadron, an RNZAF Squadron, but all helicopters are flown with RNZ Navy pilots. We were flying in the Kaman SH-2F Seasprite (ex-US Navy) that had replaced the Westland Wasps.

We flew with the squadron on a number of occasions. The first (and then contracted by the NZDF) was flying in the Seasprite to capture the first ever live New Zealand deployment of a AGM-65 Maverick missile fire from the Seasprite. The project required dealing with a team of officials who were very positive and wanted the project and the filming to go well. We hit a number of challenges with wiring up the helicopter with cameras (back then we used mini lipstick cameras (before GoPro). After much perseverance, we were ready, and on the day the missile fired and hit the target, we captured the missile up close (with a few interesting messages on the side of the missile). All-in-all, it went well.

The first night firing was nearly a year later in March 2009, and we wanted to capture the footage with both night vision IFR and regular camera equipment. With no budget to pay additional camera operators, it was decided that I should accompany Malcolm on the chase Seasprite to film the firing with normal camera equipment. It should be easy... all I needed to do was point and shoot. Not quite, given it was at night and auto focus wouldn't work as it would try to focus as the missile fired.

This opportunity required HUET training — Helicopter Underwater Escape Training. An experience which was somewhat harder than I expected. Here are the basics: sit in a simulation of a helicopter with doors, fully clothed, strapped in, as you're slowly pushed into the cold water. You must refrain from opening the door or exiting, until the aircraft is fully upside down, all while your body is gasping for air. A slow, painful, non-breathing experience. The reasoning behind the training is that as the engine is located above your head and the helicopter blades are maybe still turning after the aircraft lands in the water, the helicopter will turn turtle due to the weight of the engine(s).

The night fire was successful, and we flew in the chase/back up Seasprite to Whitianga Airfield on the Coromandel coast of New Zealand's North Island in the evening, where an Air Force fuel tanker was waiting for us to fuel up before heading out up to the deep blue sea out off Great Barrier Island. After locating the frigate HMNZS Te Mana, we circled, filming the ship with NVG's and then filmed the missile aircraft taking off to simulate an actual launch, filming the first live AGM-65 air-to-surface Maverick missile to destroy a floating target, filming the helicopter as it fired the missile east of Great Barrier Island - our support was an RNZAF Orion flying overhead to monitor the area for shipping and to also film with their surveillance equipment.

We did a follow up visit with *FlightPathTV* to RNZAF Dip Flat to film the RNZAF training with the new NHIndustries NH90 that was chosen as the primary replacement helicopter for the Bell Huey and the new Leonardo AW109 at Exercise Blackbird once again. Flying in these newer machines was obviously far more complex and sophisticated, but breathtaking all the same with the snow capped mountains in the background.

Military helicopters are exciting but complex flying machines, operating under huge demands, adding huge value to their organisations, and play an integral part in sea, land and air operations.

These helicopters play various roles from attack, observation and anti-submarine warfare, while the most common use is transport of troops (which now includes the Osprey tiltrotor aircraft — incorporated into this book) these helicopters and tiltrotors can be modified or converted to perform other missions such as combat search and rescue (CSAR), medical evacuation (MEDEVAC), airborne command post, most modern helicopters have modular systems which allow the same airframe to be configured for different roles.

I have attended the HAI (Helicopter Association International) Heli-Expo a number of times and at the last show a good friend of mine (and ex NH90 pilot who wrote the introduction for *81 Lessons From The Sky*) introduced me to Claude Vuichard, any experienced mountain rescue pilot based out of Switzerland. I interviewed Claude to hear what he had to say about the Vortex Ring State (VRS) recovery technique. A young man stood listening to the discussion, and later introduced himself as a young pilot in the US military, saying he had just been trained on the recovery technique and said thank you for helping him be a safer pilot. It was great to see the gratitude and safety focus coming from such a new pilot. The US Navy in Chapter 2 covers this recovery technique.

I want to share powerful stories and lessons from other pilots. Many of the stories in this book (even though I am not a military pilot) made me think about how I would approach the same situation that the pilot was confronted with. Which brings us to the concept of the "Swiss cheese model" - which is about accident causation - I am sure you know it. It is a model used in risk analysis and risk management, including aviation safety, engineering, healthcare, emergency service organisations, and as the principle behind layered security (also in computing). The Swiss Cheese Model of accident causation illustrates that, although many layers of defence lie between hazards and accidents, there are flaws in each layer that, if aligned, can allow the accident to occur.

Therefore, in theory, lapses and weaknesses in one defence do not allow a risk to materialise, since other defences also exist, to prevent a single point of failure. The model was originally formally propounded by Dante Orlandella and James T. Reason of the University of Manchester, and has since gained widespread acceptance.

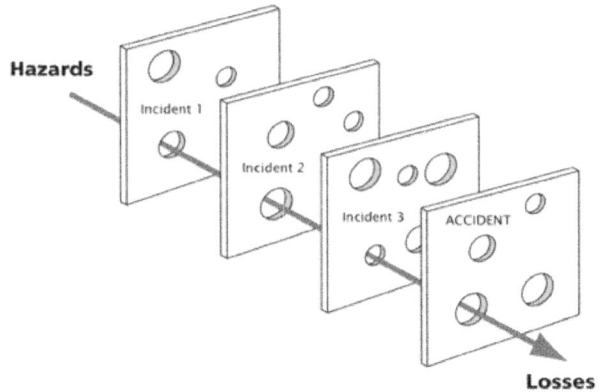

Adapted from the Swiss cheese model of accident.
Created: Creative Commons - Davidmack

I hope that when you read these stories, you are able to make notes and look to remove a few holes from the layers (of cheese) in your planning, flying and operations, building up new habits to ensure that we all fly safer. What further lessons will be learned and shared with the future pilots of tomorrow?

Helicopters and fixed wing aircraft differ in form and function, but the basic principles of safe operation apply to the operators of both types. No matter what sort of aircraft you fly, everyone should be able to learn a number of lessons from this collection of 61 lessons from the sky.

Being able to work with military helicopters in my day job makes it fun and exciting. Being able to help keep them in the air and possibly protect pilots, crew and people and the helicopter itself makes me think that I can make a difference in this ever changing industry.

Be safe and blue skies.

Fletcher McKenzie

HOW TO USE THIS BOOK

Each lesson has been replicated in the pilot's or crew member's words, without any editing other than minor grammatical corrections. You may notice some errors. We have purposely not amended the original reports.

A glossary of terms is included at the end of this book for your reference. Please note that this book may contain a mixture of both American English and British English, depending on who is telling the story.

If you find a term or an acronym in this book which isn't in the glossary, please email Fletcher:

fletch@avgasgroup.com

Each lesson has space for you to make your own notes if you want to. I recommend doing this to cement the learning.

Writing a short review of this book on your favourite digital platform, or on your personal blog or Facebook page, will help spread the word about aviation safety. Saving lives is the primary goal of this book.

AUSTRALIA

Flight Safety Australia:
Civil Aviation Safety Authority
CASA

CASA's flagship aviation safety magazine. Topical, technical, but reader-friendly, articles cover all the key aviation safety issues – safety management systems, maintenance, runway safety, human factors, airspace, training, aviation medicine and more.

Flight Safety Australia, and its predecessor the Aviation Safety Digest, have provided the Australian aviation community with credible and comprehensive aviation safety information since the early 1950s.

From its beginnings as a printed monochrome booklet published only a few times a year, Flight Safety Australia has evolved into an interactive and content-rich publication available across multiple digital platforms.

Flight Safety Australia is produced by a small, dynamic team of writers, designers and contributors based out of the Safety Promotion branch of Australia's Civil Aviation Safety Authority.

RAAF:
Defence Aviation Safety Authority
(DASA)

The DASA is responsible for enhancing and promoting the safety of military aviation. This is achieved through a Defence Aviation Safety Program (DASP), which supports compliance with statutory safety obligations and assures the effective management of aviation-safety risks.

The Defence Flight Safety Bureau is accountable to the Chief of Air Force in his capacity as the Defence Aviation Authority for the strategic management of flight safety in Defence. The Bureau provides Defence with independent aviation investigation, research and analysis, safety training and safety promotion capabilities. Accordingly, DFSB is the centre of expertise for flight safety within Defence.

DASA Publications include, Aviation Safety Resources, Aviation Safety Spotlight, Focus Magazine and RAAFSAFE Magazine.

UNITED KINGDOM

Confidential Human Factors Incident
Report Programme for Aviation
CHIRP

Known by the acronym CHIRP, its aim is to contribute to the enhancement of flight safety in the UK commercial and general aviation industries, by providing a totally independent confidential reporting system for all individuals employed in or associated with the industries.

The Programme is available to engineers and technical staff involved with the design and manufacturing processes, flight crew members, cabin crew members, air traffic controllers, licensed engineers and maintenance/engineering personnel and individual aircraft owners/operators.

CHIRP complements the UK's CAA Mandatory Occurrence Reporting system and other formal reporting systems operated by many UK organisations, by providing a means by which individuals are able to raise safety-related issues of concern without being identified to their peer group, management, or the Regulatory Authority.

CHIRP is a totally independent programme for the collection of confidential safety data, and when appropriate, acting or advising on information gained through confidential reports. Independent advice is provided on aeromedical and Human Factors aspects of reports, involving such topics as errors, fatigue, poor ergonomics, management pressures, deficiencies in communication or team performance. The sensitivity of these topics requires that the anonymity of the reporter must be, and always has been, fully protected.

Royal Air Force Safety Centre
(RAFSC)

VISION: A safety organisation which delivers effective Total Safety Management and leads on intelligent application of critical thinking.

MISSION: To provide independent assurance of the RAF Safety Management System underpinning CAS' commitment to Total Safety in order to maximise the delivery of RAF capability.

Based at HQ Air Command, RAF High Wycombe, Buckinghamshire, HP14 4UE

CANADA

Royal Canadian Air Force
Flight Safety

Aviation accidents and incidents have the potential to cause the loss of lives and of valuable resources. It is therefore important to investigate such Flight Safety occurrences with the objective of quickly identifying effective measures that will either prevent or reduce the risk of similar occurrences.

Flight Safety reports are prepared solely for the purpose of accident prevention. The occurrence investigation class and report type are determined by the aircraft damage level, the personnel casualty level, and the safety of flight compromise level.

Within the Department of National Defence, the Director of Flight Safety is appointed as the Airworthiness Investigative Authority, and is charged with investigating all matters concerning aviation safety (independently of the chain of command). The powers of the Airworthiness Investigative Authority are delegated from the Minister of National Defence, pursuant to the Aeronautics

Act. The Chief of the Air Force Staff is responsible for flight safety policy in the Canadian Armed Forces.

UNITED STATES OF AMERICA

Aviation Safety Reporting System
ASRS

ASRS collects voluntarily submitted aviation safety incident/situation reports from pilots, controllers, and others. It then analyses, and responds to the voluntarily submitted aviation safety incident reports in order to lessen the likelihood of aviation accidents.

ASRS acts on the information these reports contain. It identifies system deficiencies, and issues alerting messages to persons in a position to correct them. It educates through its newsletter CALLBACK, its journal ASRS Directline and through its research studies. Its database is a public repository which serves the FAA and NASA's needs and those of other organisations world-wide which are engaged in research and the promotion of safe flight.

ASRS data are used to identify deficiencies and discrepancies in the National Aviation System (NAS) so that these can be remedied by appropriate authorities. Support policy formulation and planning for, and improvements to, the NAS and strengthen the foundation of aviation human factors safety research.

US Navy & US Marine Corps:
The Naval Safety Centre
(NAVSAFECEN)

A continuously improving command that develops leading indicators of risks and hazards to empower all Sailors, Marines, civilians and their families to embrace a proactive culture of risk identification and management to achieve zero preventable mishaps.

The Naval Safety Center was established in 1951 at the Naval Air Station, Norfolk, Virginia. The staff collected, evaluated and published information about aviation safety, and also advised the Chief of Naval Operations and the Commandant of the Marine Corps on all phases of the aviation-safety effort.

Today, the Naval Safety Center is organized into four directorates: aviation, afloat, shore, and operational risk management/expeditionary warfare. Six departments and five special staff divisions provide support to the core operations of the command. The Naval School of Aviation Safety in Pensacola, Florida, is also a NAVSAFECEN detachment consisting of civilian and military staff, which includes Marine Corps personnel. As an Echelon II command, NAVSAFECEN provides oversight of its single Echelon III command, the Naval Safety and Environmental Training Center in Norfolk, Virginia.

To preserve warfighting capability and combat lethality by identifying hazards and reducing risk to people and resources.

US Air Force:
Air Force Safety Center
Aviation Safety Division (SEF)

The Air Force Safety Center resides on Kirtland Air Force Base, located in the high desert of north-central New Mexico and it occupies a majority of southeast Albuquerque.

The Aviation Safety Division (SEF) consists of safety-trained professionals spanning the domain of flight. The division preserves warfighting capability by establishing Air Force aviation safety policy, promoting mishap prevention programs for all aviation assets and through the establishment of proactive safety programs. It oversees the aviation mishap investigative process, the collection and accuracy of flight safety data and the disposition of risk-mitigating actions. It provides proactive and reactive engineering and operational analyses of flight safety issues. In the 1950s when the Air Force became a separate department, the Air Force Chief of Staff designated the Office of the Inspector General to oversee all inspection and safety functions. These functions were consolidated in an inspector general group at Norton AFB, California.

On Dec. 31, 1971, the Air Force Inspection and Safety Center was activated, replacing the 1002nd Inspector General Group. The center was then divided into the Air Force Inspection Agency and the Air Force Safety Agency in August 1991. Reorganization of the air staff in 1992 created the Air Force Chief of Safety position, reporting directly to the Air Force Chief of Staff. The Chief of Safety became dual-hatted as the commander of the Air Force Safety Agency. In July 1993, the agency moved to Kirtland AFB due to the closure of Norton AFB.

Following The Blue Ribbon Panel on Aviation Safety in 1995, the Air Force Safety Center was activated on Jan. 1, 1996.

U.S. Army:
U.S. Army Combat Readiness/Safety Center

With origins dating back to the Korean War, the U.S. Army Combat Readiness Center has become a Department of Defense leader in safety and occupational health training, policy, and accident investigation expertise.

The late Vietnam years and postwar era were a time of marked change for the organization, with redesignation in 1972 as the U.S. Army Agency for Aviation Safety, necessitating an expansion of scope to include accident prevention education, safety assistance visits, establishment of aviation safety policy, comprehensive collection of aviation accident data, promotion of systems safety doctrine, and support of selected aspects of the Army's ground safety program.

Through more than 60 years of existence, the USACRC and its various iterations have all been focused on the singular goal of preventing needless loss, preserving the lives of Soldiers and Army civilians, and maintaining the Army's status as the world's most ready and capable military force. Change may be constant, but that commitment remains unwavering.

U.S. Coast Guard:
Office of Aviation Forces

CG-711's mission is to provide Coast Guard aviation with capability in the form of resources, doctrine, oversight, and training programs to support safe and effective execution of Coast Guard missions.

CHAPTER 1

SITUATIONAL AWARENESS, COMPLACENCY & FATIGUE

"...keep your hands close enough to the controls so that you can prevent the student doing anything which may become dangerous – however unlikely that thing may be in your mind".

RAF Squirrel Instructor, name withheld

THE NIGHT OF THE MISSING CREW MEMBER

HH-46E SEARCH AND RESCUE, UNITED STATES MARINE CORPS, UNIT WITHHELD

1st Lt. Jennifer Smith, Summer 2011

On the last day of flight operations, a ship was steaming back to port. The aircraft commander (AC) of an HH-46 helicopter, who also served as the maintenance officer as an additional duty, was spending the last few hours of a three-week deployment reflecting upon the hard work of his maintenance crew. The maintainers had worked hard on this particular trip and invited the AC to play a game of poker that evening.

I'll go ahead and throw it out there that alcohol wasn't involved in this story. In fact, it wasn't even permitted on board. The ship had started back at about sunset the night before, and the time was now 3 p.m. Everything that needed taken care of was, and the poker game was well under way. The thought of having been awake for more than 22 hours never crossed the AC's mind when a "man overboard" announcement was made over the public address system.

Shortly after one helicopter launched in the search effort, the decision was made to put another crew in the air. Having only four ACs and four co-pilots on this deployment, there were now only three ACs and three co-pilots from which to choose. The AC playing poker was not the designated pilot on duty that night; however, having more experience than the other AC, and wanting to avoid making the skipper fly, he volunteered to take the mission.

The AC, having about 800 hours in the HH-46, and a relatively new co-pilot briefed and began the search with a crew chief and rescue swimmer in the back. There were no night-vision goggles at this time, and they were flying search patterns on instruments at night about 500 feet above the water.

One of the crewmen thought he saw something, so a flare was dropped in the water and a search pattern was set up above the light. It was long towards morning, and a little sliver of moon was just coming up.

Since the inexperienced co-pilot wasn't responding to the AC's directions, the AC said, "I have the airplane," without hesitation.

Having been looking for the missing person in all directions with eyes inside and outside of the helo, spatial disorientation quickly overcame the crew. The aircraft was swinging violently with a motion similar to that of a pendulum. The AC looked at the flight instruments, pulled in the power and was overcome by vertigo as the helicopter swayed back and forth. After what seemed like forever, the helicopter climbed to nearly 2,000 feet and finally regained control.

Close to the same time, word came in that the missing crew-member had been found. They returned to the ship just as the sun was rising.

Lessons Learned:

Years later, the helicopter pilot from that mission reflected upon those events and was reminded how fatigue played a critical role in his decision-making abilities that night. It wasn't a matter of falling asleep at the controls that put him searching for straight-and-level flight, but after being awake for nearly 24 hours, diminished physical and mental function were definitely factors. He had made three or four poor decisions that night, largely due to fatigue.

The moral of the story is to not act brashly. That AC should've never flown the rescue mission and is lucky that his whole crew didn't end up in the water that night.

NOTES:

THE RISKY FLASK

H-U1, ROYAL AUSTRALIAN AIR FORCE VIA CASA, UNIT WITHHELD

Lloyd Knight, April 2008

Here's a story about incorrectly stowed gear. The closest I ever came to crashing a helicopter in Vietnam was not because of enemy action. Nor was it because of equipment failure or even crew error per se.

It was one of those subtle events that do not have the usual checks and balances one finds when applying the Reason Model to accident prevention. An occasion when a bit of luck, and some coarse handling overcame the problem.

A four-ship formation was flying into a fire support base in the tall timber. We were number three. Number one had terminated in the middle of the landing area and taxied forward to park near the edge of the pad. Number two was about fifty feet up and just about to terminate. He would then move forward and set down next to number one. I was about fifty metres behind him and was just starting to increase power to complete the approach.

Unlike an aeroplane, in which the pilot takes all power off as it touches down, a helicopter gradually increases power as it terminates in a hover. The power required is approximately the same as that used for take-off, and is often higher, depending on the type of approach and the termination area. The pilot increases the power by pulling up on the collective pitch lever. That's the one in his left hand.

As I raised the lever to about half travel, it jammed. I lowered it slightly then raised it again with the same result. I yelled out, 'Collective jamming,' and looked for somewhere to put down with a run-on landing. This requires less power. There was nowhere to go and we were coming down on top of number two. I hit the radio button and called something like, 'Numbers two and four go around, number three has jammed collective'. I think number four behind me got the message and went around. However, number two just continued with his termination. He hadn't heard my call, or was slow to respond. I pumped the lever one more time as I tried to steer clear of the helicopter beneath me. I pulled up real hard and something gave as the obstruction was overcome, and I had full control again.

We were descending quite rapidly now so I just about stood the bird on its tail and pulled maximum power to terminate in a high hover. We were too low to go around.

Number two taxied off, and I descended to a respectable height, moved to our pre-planned parking area at the back of the pad and landed. That was a lucky escape from what would have been a nasty accident.

I wiped the sweat from my brow and yelled, 'What the hell was that?' I looked over at my co-pilot, as he sheepishly held up a rather mangled silver whisky hip flask. I think it may have been a family heirloom that he used as a water bottle. We probably all could have done with a swig of the real stuff.

During the flight, the weight of the flask had caused his pocket to slip down the outside of his leg. This placed the flask just in front of the armour plate extension on the side of his seat, and directly above his collective lever. When I raised my lever, his followed and jammed the flask against the armour.

Lessons Learned:

Nothing should be placed so that it can become an obstruction to the flight controls, given that in flight, things can move about. I recall often seeing H300 pilots flying with all manner of gear, on the deck in front of the pedestal (and the pedals).

I suppose the same principle should be applied to handbags and briefcases placed between a car driver's legs. They can slip forward on braking and obstruct the foot pedals. I know someone who had that happen to them.

NOTES:

PRACTICE ENGINE FAILURE GO!
SQUIRREL HT1/2 AS-350BB, ROYAL AIR FORCE, UNIT WITHHELD

Name Withheld, October 2009

Assumption is the mother of all...

One flying instructors close shave with communications, flying and a healthy dose of, "I thought he understood".

"Practice engine failure go..."

How many times have you heard that? How many times have you said it? It usually results in the student making their way through some form of emergency drill and then we all go home for tea and buns. In an attempt to maintain that happy status quo I have been asked to write this piece about an incident which happened to me and which almost did not result in us going home for tea and buns.

Some background will be of use to non-helicopter specialists.

The Squirrel HT1/2 is a single engine conventional rotor helicopter used for basic and advanced helicopter flying training; we also use it here at Central Flying School CFS (H) to teach experienced helicopter pilots how to become Qualified Helicopter Instructors (QHIs).

In common with many other single engine helicopters it is inadvisable to hover the Squirrel much above 5 feet because if the engine were to fail, it is unlikely that a successful landing could be made from up there. Successful landings can be made from around 5 feet without the benefit of the engine, and indeed they are practised regularly by staff QHIs. To make this practice more realistic the throttle may be retarded in the hover so that the engine plays no part in the subsequent landing. The throttle is operated by a twist-grip on the collective lever. When the throttle is retarded in the hover it is done so in one swift movement. The main rotor will begin to slow down immediately as it is no longer being driven, but because it still has a certain amount of inertia, a well timed application of extra pitch will slow the rate of descent sufficiently to allow a soft landing; but the higher you are the further there is to fall, and from much above 5 feet the rate of descent will have built up so much that even the most well-timed application of extra pitch is unlikely to be effective enough to prevent a heavy landing. It is not possible to re-engage the engine until after the aircraft has landed. These practices are known as engine-off landings. However, this closing of the throttle is only ever done after a number of careful briefings both on the ground and in the air, and only then under specific circumstances, and even then the throttle is only ever closed by the person acting as the instructor. Other types of practice engine failures may be initiated by the same phrase "Practice engine failure go..." but the throttle is never closed unless this careful and protracted sequence of briefings have been carried out. I knew that, and I assumed that everyone else did...

Can you see where this is going yet?

The incident itself was relatively quick, as these things often are, and the outcome was relatively benign, as these things so often sadly are not. The student was flying the aircraft at a relief landing ground (RLG); he had just completed an approach to the hover and was briefing the next manoeuvre. He inadvertently allowed the aircraft to drift upwards in the hover to about 30 feet. In order to draw his attention to this fact, I called "Practice engine failure go..."

Fully expecting him to simply lower the collective slightly and conduct a powered run-on landing straight ahead, making a mental note as he did so to monitor his hover height more carefully in the future. But he didn't; he closed the throttle instead. I took control and cushioned the landing as well as I could. It turned out that no damage had been done and we subsequently flew the aircraft back to base after an engineering inspection.

So, what was the problem? Well, I allowed the aircraft to be placed about 22 feet or so above the height from which a successful engine-off landing is likely to be made; I then said something which inspired the student to close the throttle, and I was neither able to stop him doing so, nor was I able to re-open the throttle before landing.

A little of the non-technical background to this incident may now be of interest. The student in this case was actually a very experienced helicopter pilot recently returned from the latest of a large number of frontline detachments. He had also been a fixed wing instructor. Between the two of us in the cockpit that day we had over 15000 flying hours and over 50 years of experience in the military. Surely he must think the same way I do? He was learning to be a helicopter instructor. The previous day we had been practising hover engine-off landings as part of the course. As part of that previous sortie the student instructor is encouraged to use the throttle himself to initiate the engine-off landing, as he would have to if he had a real basic student on board with him. The engine-off sortie is carefully briefed on the ground beforehand, so that both crew members know exactly what will happen, who will initiate and who will carry out each engine-off landing. The engine-off landing sortie may only be carried out at certain airfields. Before each engine-off landing is carried out during the sortie, a further brief is conducted in which specific mention is made of the entry height, type of engine-off to be practised, who will close the throttle and who will carry out the engine-off landing. Each engine-off landing is initiated by the phrase, "Practice engine failure go...".

This previous sortie had been carried out uneventfully. Today's sortie was not to include engine-off landings. They were not mentioned in the pre-flight brief, and were not authorised. We were at an RLG where they are not permitted, and no engine-off landing checks were mentioned at any time during the flight. Would you therefore have expected your student to initiate an engine-off landing in response to the phrase, "Practice engine failure go..."? I didn't. But I should have been ready for it, just in case...

Lessons Learned:

Firstly, "Expect the unexpected". I've never thought that was a particularly helpful phrase. But in this case it could be interpreted as, "Keep your hands close enough to the controls so that you can prevent the student doing anything which may become dangerous – however unlikely that thing may be in your mind". The more potentially dangerous the situation, the closer your hands should be to the critical control; and if you may need to prevent a swift movement of the throttle, your hand needs to be already on it. In this case, whilst I was able to take control quickly, I wasn't able to prevent the throttle being closed.

Secondly, of the options available to me to highlight the student's error, was calling, "Practice engine failure go..." the best one? Probably not. I did wish to make the point rather more memorable to him than just murmuring, "Height", but perhaps not quite as memorable as it now is.

Thirdly, this is yet another example of two people in the same cockpit having totally different interpretations of the same situation. Ask yourself, "Is what I have just said to the student totally unambiguous — is the student thinking what I am thinking – will he do what I think he will?". Speak to your shiny new Aircrew Performance Coach, they will explain all about Neuro-Linguistic Programming.

Finally – it's always the instructor's fault.

Whatever the student should, or should not have done, is irrelevant. I allowed the aircraft to end up in a position from which I was lucky to recover. A superior instructor would have used his superior judgement to prevent him from being there in the first place.

Christmas comes early for one instructor, and hasn't he been a good boy? For Santa brings him the greatest gift of all... hindsight. In all seriousness, what this experience does highlight for me is the danger that we all face, regardless of branch, when we begin to get comfortable. You know what I mean; when you hear yourself saying things like ......'Oh this is just a routine flight,' or, 'I don't need the MPs; I've done a ???? so many times I can do it in my sleep'.

Complacency as we have seen elsewhere in this fine publication can be just as dangerous as inexperience. If there is one thing I have seen throughout my career is that the best people often make the worst mistakes; and 9 times out of 10 this is as a result of becoming blasé about the job.

The Service asks us to give our best in situations that are often extremely demanding and unforgiving of even the slightest complacency. The challenge lies in identifying how we prevent complacency developing in the first place. I don't pretend to know the answer, but I daresay you bright sparks out there do, so put pen to paper and give the gift of hindsight to others before the event!

NOTES:

MARK, MARK

UH-1Y VENOM, UNITED STATES MARINE CORPS, MARINE LIGHT ATTACK HELICOPTER SQUADRON 269

CAPT Dan Bowring, June 2014

The flight was a textbook, night escort with close-air support provided to a ground force and delivered by two MV-22 Ospreys.

The weather was clear. The combined brief with the Osprey and skid crews went well. The instructors from both platforms had developed a solid, safe, and tactically relevant game plan for the pilots-under-instruction. I would be flying the UH-1Y Huey as Dash 2 to an AH-1W Super Cobra. The lead Cobra's student was receiving his last night-systems-instructor, pre-certification flight, and my copilot was receiving a series-conversion flight to complete her conversion from the legacy UH-1N to the upgraded UH-1Y.

UH-1N pilots transitioning to the UH-1Y have to complete a conversion syllabus prescribed by the UH-1Y Training and Readiness Manual. Flights from the Core, Core Plus, and Instructor syllabi must be flown based on qualifications and designations previously held in the UH-1N. My copilot was nearing the end of her conversion syllabus.

Our goals for the flight were to continue to increase systems proficiency and use, and deliver effective rockets under low-light conditions.

The UH-1Y is generally easier to fly than the UH-1N; however, the systems interface and cockpit management differences associated with 1970s "steam gauges" compared to state-of-the-art technology and a glass cockpit present the biggest challenge for conversion pilots.

The section's launch from MCAS New River to MCAS Cherry Point, where we would upload ordnance and fuel, was slightly delayed due to maintenance. However, there was plenty of extra time built-in to our timeline to deal with these sorts of delays, which are common during off-site ordnance operations.

Once on deck at MCAS Cherry Point, we discovered our second issue of the evening. The crew-served ammunition for our crew chief's guns to Cherry Point was still at MCAS New River. We got the ammunition to the Ospreys and delivered it to MCAS Cherry Point's combat arms loading area (CALA). This second delay resulted in a shift of our intended timeline. After quick coordination over the radios while on deck at Cherry Point, the L-hour was slid right and the mission was back on track.

Entry into the R5306A and BT-11 range complex was uneventful. The weather still was beautiful, and we had a no-moon, low-light night over the coastal marsh island. My copilot was focused on working the aircraft systems and using the FLIR to locate the landing zone, scan for enemy, and provide initial terminal guidance (ITG) for the MV-22s via an IR laser pointer delivered from the FLIR. We joined-up on the MV-22s and provided fires on the zone to neutralize the notional threat.

Following the planned insert, the Ospreys departed for contingency holding, and we began providing close air support to the ground forces. With 13 of the 14 2.75-inch inert rockets remaining on our aircraft, I asked my copilot to set up for the transfer of controls. This would allow her to deliver the remaining rockets for her training. We executed a three-way change of controls, backed up with a shoulder tap as briefed, and she assumed control of the aircraft.

As planned, we set up to deliver rockets and guns on the airfield from a medium-altitude profile. A quick attack brief was given by the lead aircraft, and we rogered-up to a trail attack. As we were maneuvering to run-in for the attack, I heard a loud bang come from the cabin area. My reaction was to ask if the crew chief was working to clear a jam on the .50 caliber GAU-21 or if he had a round discharge while working on the gun.

Before I could ask the question, our crew chief frantically relayed that our rocket pods had just fallen off the aircraft, with a couple of expletives added for emphasis. This was immediately followed by a "Mark, mark" call from our senior crew chief instructor. I marked our location as I began to digest what exactly had just occurred. My copilot immediately said she had accidentally hit the emergency jettison.

We quickly called terminate to our lead and notified range control of our jettison. Although we had an eight-digit grid, the pods were dropped from approximately 1,000 feet AGL and 100 knots. We had been in the middle of the range, and there was no chance the pods could have departed the range or hit any structures on the complex. The next 30 minutes was spent trying to recreate the expanding-box search pattern that I dimly remembered from flight school HTs. But, locating two green LAU-68 rocket pods in a dark swamp is nearly impossible.

At the conclusion of our range time, we returned to MCAS Cherry Point, and then to MCAS New River. Knowing that the jettison was a commanded jettison and there was nothing wrong with our aircraft, our commanding officer was comfortable with me bringing the aircraft home. The transit times back provided sufficient time to discuss the jettison and the conditions at the time of the event — specifically flight time in the last 30 days and total flight time in the UH-1Y aircraft. Although both of these numbers were low, they were average for a conversion pilot in our squadron.

Lessons Learned:

As mentioned, the redesigned UH-1Y cockpit incorporates a hands-on collective and stick (HOCAS) set-up on the cyclic and collective. This allows the flying pilot to switch radios and MFD displays, select weapons systems, and perform a multitude of other functions without removing their hands from the cyclic or collective. The HOCAS switches are slightly different in design and feel to aid in identification; however, a pilot with limited flight time in the aircraft and even less flight time in the past 30 days can get mixed up. Specifically, the collective has eight switches with the radio transmit and emergency jettison next to each other. Although the jettison has a raised guard around the switch, a pilot could mash the jettison switch down while searching for the radio transmit switch.

As an instructor it is my job to identify potential missteps of students. At a minimum, I need to discuss and implement control measures that will help a less experienced pilot avoid a hazardous mistake. Simply discussing the placement of the emergency jettison switch, feeling the switches around it, and moving your thumb left and right across the switches to identify vice mashing straight down could have helped prevent this jettison. Preflight blindfolded cockpit drills and systems discussions are tools that can be used and refined before ever strapping into the cockpit.

A second set of conditions is harder to quantitatively evaluate: the intangibles of instructorship and CRM between instructor and student. After reviewing the flight, I believe there was a point where we had reached diminishing returns on my copilot's systems learning objectives, and I should have shifted to her flying and familiarization with the low-light-level environment. I could tell she was struggling with the sensor and remaining oriented in the objective area. This is common when spending a significant amount of time heads-down in a new aircraft. As the instructor, I should have recognized the degradation in situational awareness (SA) and made a control change to help build her SA back up. Hindsight is 20/20, but perhaps if her

SA had been higher prior to pushing in for an attack, the misidentification of the HOCAS switches would not have occurred.

An instructor is part mentor, part psychologist, part cheerleader, and part hammer as the situation dictates. Identifying what role is necessary and how to instruct the multitude of different personalities in the fleet are the attributes of a good instructor. My evaluation of the overall situation and the real-time learning that was or was not occurring could have been an additional control measure.

Our jettison occurred in a restricted area, on a range, over a swamp. No one was injured, and no property was damaged, except the two rocket pods. However, this situation could have been catastrophic had it occurred over the numerous residential areas we fly over en route to the range complex. Our jettisons are armed from liftoff to landing, anytime we are carrying ordnance. Like everything in aviation, a simple mistake can result in a real disaster.

NOTES:

SNOW LANDINGS
AW101 MERLIN, ROYAL AIR FORCE, MERLIN FORCE

Name Withheld, November 2010

Landing a helicopter is like parking your car. The more practice you get the better you are at it. Ultimately though, when you have found a space, in order to know what steering, brake and accelerator inputs to make, you need to reference your car's position to the open space or the cars between which you intend to park. References are also the secret to hovering and landing a helicopter. In normal UK conditions this is relatively easy, but when these references become obscured by the environment, landing without specific training becomes a serious flight safety concern.

The weather last winter was changeable, giving sudden, often heavy snow showers. With it came poor visibility due to low cloud bases caused by the cooler snowy surfaces, similar conditions to those found in the Arctic. Being able to delineate between white cloud and snow covered surfaces becomes more difficult, especially as the visibility deteriorates. The disorientation caused by this phenomenon manifested itself as a serious flight safety concern at RAF Benson. For several years, the Puma, Merlin, Chinook and Commando

Helicopter Forces have sent detachments to RNAF Bardufoss, Norway inside the Arctic circle to train in just these conditions, and just as well; landing an aircraft in snow is one of the most testing techniques which Support Helicopter (SH) aircrew are taught, and here's why.

Lessons Learned:

As the helicopter gets near the ground and slows, its downwash (a 70 knot wind, keeping the aircraft airborne) hits the surface, and creates an enormous blowing cloud of snow. "White-out" ensues, creating a very disorientating experience and without reference to anything on the ground, landing is extremely hazardous. A similar situation results when operating in the desert, and it's often referred to as a limited visibility landing. So the art is to win the battle, helicopter vs. snow. By picking a marker on the ground (something sticking out of the snow), the aircraft is manoeuvred from transit to the ground reducing speed and height to zero, at the same time, before the snow cloud has an opportunity to obscure the reference. Easy, provided that you bear a few things in mind.

Firstly, size loses its context in the snow. Picking a marker in snow conditions is a challenge itself. It needs to be something chunky enough to stand out but small enough to get under the rotor disc, bearing in mind, the blade tips are spinning at nearly 400mph! The other major considerations are the thickness of the snow and what is under it. Often in deep snow the aircraft wheels will never actually reach the ground and it will sit on the snow after landing on its belly. But you just don't know. In the battle, helicopter vs. snow, the speed and height must be zero at touchdown, or a sub-snow level boulder that you had not seen might damage the aircraft undercarriage or belly skin. There are many different considerations that go into perfecting this technique and with practice it becomes an essential skill for SH squadrons to maintain.

Some may argue that this type of approach in these times of

desert warfare is the mainstay of helicopter aircrew skill sets, with limited visibility landings being flown daily in Afghanistan, and other environmental training deployments. The techniques are similar, but not the same. The smooth monochromatic nature of snow cannot be understated, and consequently the importance of a predetermined, crew-agreed marker is paramount before the start of an approach. With dust, however, the undulations and texture of the ground allow the crew to modify their marker late in the manoeuvre, making it a more flexible approach profile, even when in the heaviest "brown-out" conditions. So landing a helicopter in Arctic conditions is much more involved than a normal hover landing, which is practiced and taught daily, and subtly different to landing in the dust. To be competent to deal with Arctic conditions and safely land a helicopter in the snow, involves a specific qualification and training of its own as a result.

The decision was made at RAF Benson, during the heavy snow conditions earlier this year, that only Arctic qualified aircrew would cascade training to those without snow experience rather than falling back on the fleets' unquestionably vast "limited visibility" operational experience. The Merlin Force had suffered a period of serviceability issues around this time with many crews were on the edge of currency. There was therefore a risk balance to be contested, between the continuation of routine currency training and the difficult decision to qualify crews in the difficult conditions. With the exception of operations and their kinetic threat, approaches into limited visibility landings, especially snow are dangerous, especially without training and practice. Advantage was taken to train more crews and share this Arctic experience, although it was a hindrance to normal training and tasking. This decision wasn't taken lightly but was one that would be repeated on flight safety grounds if, and when, these conditions return again this year.

Whilst on the subject of low visibility landings I thought it may be of interest to provide you all with an update on the latest technological solutions to the problem. As such I have consulted the boffins at Defence Science and Technology Laboratory (Dstl) to see what they are working on; so here comes the science bit...

"Accidents due to brown/white-out can be broadly divided in to two causal areas; loss of situational awareness and unseen landing site (LS) obstacles. With dust-penetrating sensors, which can identify LS hazards, still some way off, Dstl have been working on the situational awareness problem. Dstl scientists and engineers initially carried out a rapid technology assessment of several proposed solutions, which resulted in a Ferranti Technologies Limited conformal symbology solution being taken forward to simulator and flying trials. The system utilises an Advanced Signal Display Computer, with feeds from a high grade EGI, millimetric wave RADALT and aircraft RADALT to generate symbology. The symbology is presented on a helmet mounted display, and provides the crew with a virtual 3D representation of the LS that stays fixed to the earth as the pilot flies his approach. The LS symbology provides the pilot with enough cues to fly visually, even when the outside world is completely obscured by dust or snow. The system can be used with helmet mounted day HUD for daytime operation, with the symbology fed through current night vision goggles to provide a night time capability. Currently LVL is undergoing de-risking activities prior to hopefully achieving UOR status in early '11."

NOTES:

FANGS OUT!

CH136 KIOWA, ROYAL CANADIAN AIR FORCE, 427 SPECIAL OPERATIONS AVIATION SQUADRON

Captain Gary Fleming, 1984

As I look back over a 5,000 hour flying career spanning 38 years and counting, my mind often slips back to a traumatic, albeit formative flying experience. Not many aircrew get the chance to experience a near-catastrophic accident that shapes their view on flight safety so early in their career. Although I didn't feel it at the time, I was lucky to go through this misadventure and emerge unscathed and wiser.

Flying the mighty CH136 Kiowa in 1984 was an amazing experience. From your aerial perch, you controlled artillery fire and fighters, guiding bombs and howitzer rounds onto target with deadly precision. Your only protection was your ability to fly low... really low. Keeping your aircraft four feet above the terrain, you were able to stay hidden from the many weapons systems that could shred your soft aluminium skin. These "Nap-of-the-Earth" flying techniques were demanding, especially for a 22 year-old flying solo with just 200 hours under his belt!

The halcyon days of 1984 were marked by a fast-disappearing cadre of experienced pilots, being replaced by fresh "pipes" from the training system (fast-forward to 2018... sound familiar?). In the single pilot arena, much needed cockpit leadership was provided by a slightly more experienced section lead. On my fateful day, I was flying wingman for my deputy flight commander. We decided to finish off our standard training flight with the Kiowa reconnaissance skills exercise called "Hounds and Hares". We split the section and flew to opposite corners of a 6 Km x 3 Km box. The objective was to approach the other aircraft's location and spot them before they saw you. You would then call in their eight figure grid via the inter-plane frequency. If the target grid was within 100 metres, then the game was won. On this occasion, both my observer (combat arms NCM) and I felt our "fangs go out." We were determined to beat lead, so employed all of our limited flying skills. We aggressively flew to the absolute clearance limits of our craft, using every fold in the terrain and tree cover to mask our approach. Then, we saw the "enemy"... a glint of rotor flash along a tree line, they were dead meat. We were both so focused on calling out the grid, until... BANG! A definite thump and a subtle change in rotor pitch...

We quickly realized that "something" had happened to our Kiowa. Realizing that we were less than two minutes away from the squadron helipad, we opted to fly directly home. Congratulating ourselves on our derring-do and quick decision making, our hearts sank as we shut down. There was a definite whistling noise coming from the rotor system. Instead of the beautiful swept rotor tips at the end of the blade, there was now just a shorter, blunt end with the internal structure of the rotor clearly visible. Maybe our quick decision to come home wasn't the right move? Maybe saving the aircraft (and consequently our lives) by landing right away was the cautious approach? After all, the technicians would only have to drive 15 minutes to our location. Was winning the game so important that I was willing to risk damage and injury? I felt very sheepish as my Flight Commander pointed these things out to me and what might have gone terribly wrong.

I flew again the same day, then twice the next day. Quickly, the incident was forgotten and forgiven by my squadron mates. The aircraft was repaired and returned to service. The Flight Safety report was filed. Compared to the detail and analysis seen in today's flight safety reports, mine was pure vanilla. "Personnel/Pilot/Inattention... unit briefed to maintain obstacle clearance".

However, those personal lessons stayed with me for the next 4,800 hours. As a flight commander, I used my story on many occasions to mentor the next generation of aviators. While I had many other in-flight emergencies over my career, this first one gave me my most valuable lessons:

Lessons Learned:

When the aircraft is telling you something — listen!

If you think you should land — land!

Never get too wrapped up in the game — flying the aircraft always comes first!

<u>NOTES:</u>

TIP STRIKE

PUMA HC MK2, ROYAL AIR FORCE, UNIT WITHHELD

Name Withheld, July 2011

I did not wake up thinking ,"Today I'm going to fly into a tree, then ignoring all the obvious clues, carry on flying regardless." But that is exactly what happened. Weeks have gone by and the incident has rarely left my thoughts. My memory of what occurred has been infused with the inevitable post-incident feelings of gut-wrenching guilt and incredulity. It has become increasingly difficult to distinguish between my feelings during the incident and the variety of emotions storming around my head ever since. I am certain that I never believed that my aircraft or crew were in danger but beyond that the boundaries blur.

It was a dust training sortie on the savannah surrounding Archers Post, Kenya. Recent rainfall had bound the soil and precipitated vegetation growth, so most of the dust training areas were relatively benign. That said during previous sorties several suitable areas had been identified that allowed a natural progression of dust intensity to be experienced during dust approaches. My co-pilot/student had flown good approaches to all of these areas before we graduated to a track which was known to have more 'senior dust'. The track was rutted and surrounding vegetation meant one had to choose the Landing Point (LP) carefully. He flew several approaches and overshoots without incident. We then elected to change the LP to a point slightly further up the track. It's normal to adjust the LP during dust training to ensure the dust is fresh and allow the crew to reset slightly. The recce was updated. We were all aware of the tree on the undershoot that was on the left hand side of the track, but were content that our approach path kept us clear. In retrospect I can see that the new LP was too close to the tree. Error number one. On the approach itself, being in the Left Hand Seat (LHS), I noted the tree on the left hand side prior to entering the dust cloud. Though it was close I judged that we were sufficiently clear so I chose not to mention it. Error number two. After the dust had cleared on landing however, I noticed that there were leaves and debris hanging off the branches. I called the rest of the crew's attention to this. Nobody had felt or heard anything unusual in the latter stages of the approach. The aircraft handled perfectly normally. We felt there was no danger to the aircraft and that the incident was minor. We lifted. Error number three. Once airborne we made a further damage assessment. Again, no unusual vibration or noise. We were content that the aircraft was not damaged. We elected to continue training, which we did without incident and only became aware of damage to all four blades tips when we shut down. Error number four.

What puzzles me now, is not that we hit the tree, but why we all decided it was a good idea to carry on, rather than shut down and inspect the blades. When we shut down and saw the damage to the blades I was utterly dismayed. How could I not have known this was coming? We all saw the damage to the tree — a pretty big clue that something had impacted it. How come we failed to realise the gravity of the situation and the potential damage this could have done? These questions have plagued my thoughts. Since nobody in the crew ever voiced any doubt about what we were doing I can only imagine that any niggling concerns that one might reasonably expect us to have had were subconscious or non-existent.

When I saw the damage to the tree I imagined that this could have been done by down-wash. It didn't seem possible that the aircraft had hit the tree because if it had I felt sure I would know. The world outside the cockpit didn't match the world inside the cockpit. That said, why risk it? Why not shut down and check? There was, after all, compelling evidence outside the cockpit that the aircraft could be damaged. I think I matched the in-cockpit reality to the desired reality, being hopelessly optimistic, perhaps willing the situation to be less serious than it was. The fact that the crew appeared equally unperturbed seemed to validate my judgement. You can usually rely on the crewman, the only person without his hands on the sticks, to tell the guys up front when they're doing something daft. The crewman on this day was something of a Puma veteran. Yet he too was more than content to carry on. Don't think that I wasn't concerned by what had happened. I was, but I believed, or wanted to believe, that it had been 'a close one' and something we could 'talk about on the ground'. Could it be that years of flying tests and learning to put a poor performance behind me and carry on with the sortie, had conduced me to virtually ignore a serious flight safety incident in order to finish the training I had set out to do? I don't remember feeling any press-on-itis. I was cross with myself for not calling an overshoot when I'd had the chance but had resolved to not let it detriment the rest of the trip. I was asked later if I hadn't had some notion, in my gut, that we were doing the wrong thing. I honestly don't think I would have flown an aircraft that I thought was damaged. I'm not that brave. The only anxiety I remember feeling was about my failure to call the overshoot. I genuinely never felt in danger and neither did the rest of my crew.

On seeing the damage to the blades, the bewildering stupidity of my actions became painfully obvious. That knot in my stomach, which I should have felt at the time, has gnawed away at me ever since.

The crewman on board, offers this record of events:

"As I'd completed over a dozen approaches to this LS over the last few days, I don't know if any complacency or over confidence had set in; I was aware of the obstructions, and even though they were close I was satisfied that they were sufficiently clear of the aircraft.

During the approach in question, I was operating from the starboard door, which is standard for the ac being flown from the right hand seat. Once the aircraft was fully enveloped in the dust cloud, it was very difficult to determine whether we were at the same position on the track as before; once the dust cloud had dissipated, it was evident that we were slightly aft of the desired landing position, even so I was still content with the clearance.

I was unaware of the tip strike during the latter stages of the approach, and it wasn't until the medic brought the floating debris to my attention that I realised we'd probably had a tip strike. I asked the rest of the crew whether they'd felt anything through the controls during the latter stages of the approach. When they said no, and due to the size of the debris, I believed that the disc had just clipped the tree's extremities; and because no vibration had been felt, I supposed minimal, if any, damage had been done. On lifting to the hover, I asked whether there was anything felt through the controls and if it all felt normal; with the reply that it did feel normal I was content with the rest of the crew to continue. The only slight anomaly I recall was the slight 'swishing' sound which was reminiscent of a Wessex when it starts to lose its blade tape.

On shut down on the HLS when I saw the damage to the tips, I realised how stupid we'd been to continue. I believe the austere location of the LS and the fact that the debris consisted of just small twigs influenced my thought processes and convinced me that it was ok to continue and not to shut down. Furthermore, I don't think a recovery team would have been able to complete the blade change and rectification work in the LS as it would have been unsuitable for the lifting gear required and I think this may also have been in the back of my mind".

Lessons Learned:

I have tried to understand why we all failed to appreciate the seriousness of the situation and over time my feelings have mellowed to a puzzled acceptance of what's been. What precipitated me to carry on flying a damaged aircraft after witnessing damage to the tree that it had struck? How did we manage to convince ourselves that the 'swishing' sound from the blades was perfectly normal? Could it be an indoctrinated resolve to remain unfazed when things don't go to plan? Perhaps. Or maybe the subconscious feeling that we couldn't all be wrong so our decision to carry on flying must have been a reasonable one? Quite possibly. But my deep down feeling is that I made the picture fit what I wanted to believe. So take it from me — be careful what you wish for.

RAF comment:

An honest and brave report where the author highlights a number of human factors issues. There would undoubtedly have been some element of perceived pressure to not leave an aircraft in the wilderness, for something seen initially as 'trivial', particularly if the crew thought that they should not have allowed themselves to get into this condition and that other crews possibly would not have. Overwhelming plan-continuation bias encouraged the crew not to deviate from the original intentions and to ensure that all subsequent observations confirmed that decision. While we are all fallible to human error, aviators must be aware of the potential consequences of all decisions and work to ensure the safest conduct of every sortie.

NOTES:

NOT SEEING THE FOREST FOR THE TREES

MH-60 SEA HAWK, UNITED STATES NAVY, HELICOPTER MARITIME STRIKE SQUADRON 49

LT Nathan Rice, June 2015

Things were smooth during the fourth month of my HSL-49 Helicopter Aircraft Commander (HAC) cruise. It was a 4th Fleet Counter Transnational Organized Crime (CTOC) deployment embarked in USS Gary (FFG 51), and the detachment was running astonishingly well. Our officer in charge (OIC) had recently called everyone together for a few meetings about complacency. We hadn't run into any major problems, but we were in the stretch of cruise where we felt confident. Things were good.

Upon waking for my noon to 8 pm alert shift, I was informed that we would be launching to search for what might be a self-propelled semi-submersible (SPSS) in the area. Crown jewel or unicorn, it was a high value target that everyone was getting spooled up (including me, my co-pilot, our aircrewman and Coast Guard observer). We briefed, conducted a preflight check on our trusty SH-60B, spun up and requested green deck. "Gauges green, cautions clean," I said when a final visual check of the cockpit looked exactly the same as the previous 96 days at sea. After the landing safety officer (LSO) released the beams of the rapid securing device (RSD) and gave us a green deck, I repeated, "Gauges green, cautions clean."

As my copilot picked us up into a hover, our turbine gas temperature and gas generator turbine speed (TGT and Ng) both seemed higher than normal. They were still in the green range within the Vertical Instrument Display System (VIDS). Everything else looked good. As we came up and aft, away from the flight deck and out of ground effect, both TGT and Ng momentarily fluctuated into amber and then back to green several times.

I thought, "This is a bit high, but we're in limits. It's been over a week since I've flown Red Stinger 107, maybe she just burns hotter." We pedal turned into the wind and completed our takeoff. Climbing to 500 feet, I took the controls while my helicopter second pilot (H2P) completed the post-takeoff checklist, including crunching the numbers for the engine health indicator test (HIT) checks.

A few moments later and heading in the direction that Gary wanted us to search, my H2P said the HIT checks were calculated within limits. "Good," I thought, "she's just burning hotter."

Twenty minutes into the flight and with no luck yet finding the SPSS (Self-Propelled Semi-Submersible), I glanced at the gauges to ensure things were going well. Everything was green and clean, but something was out of place. The No.1 and No.2 ENG ANTI-ICE ON advisory lights were both illuminated. I remember thinking how weird that was. I could not ever remember seeing them during this phase of flight. I looked up to the overhead console and confirmed that both ENG ANTI-ICE switches were off and the DE-ICE MASTER switch was in manual.

I knew what NATOPS said about determining if there was a malfunctioning anti-ice/start bleed valve, so I figured I could simply pull power to above 94 percent Ng to see if the lights extinguished. However, both 94 percent and 95 percent were still on. There was no change to 96 percent. Puzzled, I reduced collective.

I asked my copilot if he had noticed anything I was missing, but he was just as puzzled. Then I told him to pull out the big NATOPS.

He read aloud the section in Chapter 2 on how the valves operate and how to determine if they were malfunctioning. As our troubleshooting progressed, we ensured circuit breakers were in and looked for a rise in TGT after manually selecting engine anti-ice ON for both engines. There was no rise in either engine.

The gauges were all green and well within limits. The HIT check numbers were in. All we had were two advisory lights that should not have been illuminated. I decided that it was very unlikely that both engine anti-ice/start bleed valves were malfunctioning simultaneously. Since the HIT checks were in, it was more than likely a wiring issue. "Maybe the harnesses aren't properly seated or a cannon plug is loose," I said.

Since we were not able to fix our dilemma, we did some time-critical ORM and discussed the issue at hand. Whether or not it was a wiring or indication problem, we had to assume the worst by figuring that the valves had somehow failed.

If they had failed in the open position, they would be robbing 18 percent of available torque from each engine. If they had failed in the closed position, we could flame out an engine during low-power settings, such as during practice auto rotations or quick-stops.

Because of the possible power loss, we discussed dropping rotor speed while getting into a power-required-exceeds-power-available situation during landing. To alleviate the problem, I said, "I'll take the approach and landing." We also discussed that being lighter in fuel would help. The most dangerous part of the flight with this power-loss malfunction would have been during the takeoff, when our fuel tanks had been full.

Concerned with the possible flame out during low power settings, we agreed to be cautious with the collective and not do anything aggressive, such as a quick-stop.

We continued the flight and found no sign of the elusive SPSS. Flight quarters was sounded, numbers passed, and my one approach and one landing happened without incident.

After our maintainers inspected the aircraft, they told us we would be shutting down and not relaunching. While in the maintenance shop to log the flight and write up the discrepancy, my copilot started to log the HIT check in the aircraft discrepancy book (ADB).

A minute later, he sheepishly broke the silence and admitted that he was wrong on his earlier HIT check calculations and that both engines were "way out". In the heat of the alert launch, he subtracted the reference engine temperature from the actual temperature instead of the other way around. I was frustrated with him but more so with me at the sudden realization that engine anti-ice was on for both engines during the entire flight.

Upon further maintenance troubleshooting, we discovered that inexplicably both engine anti-ice valves had failed in the open (or ON) position, regardless of the cockpit switch setting. I had flown nearly three hours as aircraft commander in a degraded aircraft, without ever appreciating what the degradation was.

Lessons Learned:

Even though we broke out the big NATOPS to read through Chapter 2 and used ORM to back ourselves up, I never considered looking in either Chapter 12 or in the pocket checklist. Had I looked in the emergency procedures section of either, we would have been given the answer we needed: land as soon as practical.

The aircraft had been flying fine. I thought the HIT checks were good and never considered it an emergency, but because of the 18 percent power loss we very well could have drooped and lost tail-rotor authority on takeoff.

A sobering thought, but more sobering was my complacency. Ignoring what the aircraft was trying to tell me: "No.1 ENG ANTI-ICE ON" and "No. 2 ENG ANTI-ICE ON". I could not see the forest for the trees. A wake up call and a great lesson in complacency.

NOTES:

FATIGUE MANAGEMENT
CHINOOK CH-47, ROYAL AIR FORCE, UNIT WITHHELD

Name Withheld, June 2012

I was one of the Chinook pilots operating out of Camp Bastion on Operation HERRICK over the Christmas period 2011. We had all flown out at the end of November, and were looking forward to a busy, but different, detachment (det). For many this would be the first winter det, and getting used to the cold of the desert at night (regularly into minus figures) compared to the extremes of the day we had experienced previously, was going to be quite a challenge. One of our sister flights had introduced a new programming system, with a 'permanent' night wave, as well as the more usual day wave. The bonus of this was that we could support pre-dawn and first-light deliberate operations on a routine basis, as well as continuing the daily tasking. The drawback was that a couple of oh-so lucky crews would be straight into the night routine, which broadly ran from midnight to midday.

Theatre familiarisations and the required re-qualifications all occurred without incident, and we achieved our Transfer of Authority on time. The departing flight had extolled the virtues of the split-shift, and had warned that it took a little bit of getting used to, but once established, it worked well. As one of the flight senior Captains, I was lucky enough to be on the first wave of night shifts, and was going to be doing deliberate operations on a daily basis. The first Op was planned and ready to go, with a 0100 get-up in the offing. Naturally I was in bed by 1700 in order to ensure I had my "8 hours available for uninterrupted crew rest". Happily, I was fairly tired and drifted off by around 2100, but woke up on several occasions, worrying 'was my frag sheet was ok', 'did I make the right fuel calculations', what if an aircraft went u/s on start, what if one cab broke en-route, what if we got engaged at the target, what if, what if, what if... Zzz Zzz Zzz...

I was up like a scalded cat with the alarm at 0100 and did my best to get dressed in the twin room as quietly as possible. Our detachment was lucky enough to be in the 'tier 2' accommodation, the unit having moved out of tents earlier in the year. My roommate was also on the night shift, but however quiet you tried to be, noise still echoed into the corridor and bounced off the walls from one end to the other. This was a major point of friction, as off-shift engineers and day-fliers were all smack in the middle of their rest period as the night fliers were sneaking around trying to brush teeth and put on boots and not make too much noise with jacket zips and Velcro (sorry, hook and loop fastening...) as possible. All the crews assembled in the HQ to brief the sortie. The admin side of the house was well sorted by now, with a standing order in place for bacon butties from the cookhouse for all crews to try and keep the early morning hunger pangs at bay. Sadly one of the crew had to walk to the cookhouse to get them and carry a box full of butties just over a kilometre to the HQ because the vehicles that our unit had since our original arrival in Afghanistan (at its peak in 2006, 2 x land rovers and 3 x pick-ups) had been slowly 'stolen' from us to provide for other, more worthy users. Furthermore, it was around 500m from the safety equipment section (for flying helmets, night-vision goggles, body armour, 'go' kit etc) and armoury (for issue of rifles and pistols) to the aircraft ramp.

It's not that I object to the free phys, but the extra time taken walking backwards and forwards chips away at the available crew duty time. Net result, more time wasted and less time available to provide a service to the troops.

Well, I am delighted to report the Op went very well, and without incident or mishap. I was pleased. The troops were pleased. I climbed out of the aircraft around 4 hours after take-off, took my flying kit off, returned this to the safety equipment section, took my 'go' kit back and stowed it, then returned my weapons to the armoury. A short debrief, and then write up the post mission report. It was now late morning and time to start planning the next deliberate op...

And so it was, for me, for the next two weeks. To be fair, as I had been promised by the departing flight, I settled into this night routine fairly quickly. There were some odd things though, like not really appreciating what time it was. If, for example, your normal day starts at 0800 and ends at 1700 and you are in at 0630, you know 'in your water' that it is an early start. The same applies for a late finish. But when your 'day' is so out of kilter, is 1500 a late finish? And here lies one of the problems — trying to normalise yourself to a very peculiar and unfamiliar shift pattern. Once the planning had been sorted for the next day, the crews would break to get some food and get into crew rest. Again, the problems of shift work in combined accommodation became apparent, as the night crews were in bed trying to sleep as the day shift were returning from the gym, or getting washed and changed for their evening meal.

There is no doubt that flying from night into day on a regular basis is tiring, but being in a regular shift pattern goes some way to mitigate against this, particularly against the circadian low in the small hours of the morning. However, my experience of the night shift was that I felt pretty good when I woke and started work. The first few hours flying were also no problem. It was only as the day started to wear on, and 5 or 6 hours had been flown with the prospect of another long planning cycle on the horizon, did things become more trying.

The surprise to me was that I found my fatigue arrived quite suddenly and my performance dropped off fairly rapidly thereafter. The good news was that we had some redundancy in the manning plot to allow for others to plan the next day's serial, taking the pressure off the mission lead. As a detachment we also tried hard to ensure that no personnel were exposed to the night shift pattern for too long, with an open and honest fatigue log being kept on a daily basis.

Lessons Learned:

To conclude, my most recent Op HERRICK det has reminded me that we are all capable of working in some pretty adverse conditions, and at some extremely anti-social hours. Our detachment was lucky to have a strong and supportive working environment and command chain, meaning that there was never unnecessary or undue pressure to 'press on' and compromise safety.

RAF comment:

Reading this narrative brought about the most intense sense of 'déjà vu' which I have experienced in recent times. This is because I have encountered the same situation and also listened to many people describing similar experiences in Afghanistan, Iraq and other Operations.

The Aviation Psychologist on the staff of the RAF Centre of Aviation Medicine summarized her findings from several accident and incident investigations. Factors which appeared repeatedly in her investigations included: disturbances of sleep due to the noise of crews working different shifts being accommodated together; lack of dedicated transport resulting in wasted time (and sometimes additional heat stress) walking to and from aircraft, briefings, dining facilities and so on; lack of availability of quality meals outside of normal eating times and a lack of time to adjust to new sleep patterns.

In addition, there are other remediable factors associated with fatigue, which operational aircrew will be only too aware of, that are not mentioned in the narrative above. The point is that, when you can't control resources such as numbers of aircraft and available people, fatigue management becomes a matter of managing multiple small aggravating factors to mitigate the risks associated with fatigue. The issues mentioned may seem trivial on their own, but aggregated, they amount to significant increases in risk, which can all be mitigated to some degree. It takes time, resolute persistence, patience, thought and some resource expenditure, but all the situations mentioned above should be addressed: people working the same shifts should be housed together; noise dampening measures in accommodation should be installed; vehicle availability is a necessity not a luxury; quality meals should be provided to people working during the night (in part so that they do not have to interrupt daytime sleep to eat). If it is impossible to correct every shortcoming, fix as many as possible. Corrective measures in no way constitute "... pandering to wimpy personnel..." — they reduce risk and enhance performance and if they can't be mitigated, then the Duty Holder needs to be made aware because they own the operating risk.

Working night shifts continuously requires thoughtfulness. It is generally reckoned not to be a good idea, but this is because, in the civilian world, demands of family, leisure time, weekends, and so on require alternating periods of days to nights and back, making it impossible to shift the workers' circadian cycles.

If, in an operational environment, one works exclusively night shifts; has accommodation which is cool, quiet and avoids light exposure during the sleep period. It is possible to shift the circadian cycle such that your body is more efficient and comfortable working at night and sleeping during the day. However, if these measures are taken, it should be possible to improve sleep patterns. But, how long does it take for a person to adapt to a new sleeping schedule? The same time you would expect jet lag to resolve if you travelled over the same number of time zones.

I note the comment above, "The departing flight had extolled the virtues of the split-shift, and had warned that it took a little bit of getting used to..." If operationally possible, crews should be given less demanding duties for the first several nights on duty.

It is encouraging to see that people are actively thinking about minimizing fatigue: "...some redundancy in the manning plot to allow for others to plan the next day's serial, taking the pressure off the mission lead..." and "...we also tried hard to ensure that no personnel were exposed to the night shift pattern for too long..." It is heartening to observe commanders and supervisors taking on board the fact that mitigating fatigue is an effective performance enhancement and operational risk management strategy. The fact is that 'Fatigue Management is Mission Critical', just as adequately trained aircrew, serviceable aircraft, fuel, spare parts, food and water.

NOTES:

AVOID THE URGE

HH-60H, UNITED STATES NAVY, HS-11,
HELICOPTER SEA COMBAT SQUADRON 11

LCDR Brian Jamison, October 2014

Our squadron was facing an upcoming workup cycle for the next deployment, and I was pushing to get our junior pilots through their Air Combat Training Continuum (ACTC) syllabus while we still had time for unit-level training at our home airfield. As the squadron operations officer, I was acutely aware of how the loss of even one ACTC event affected the long-range plan.

The brief was thorough: it covered all the risks involved and the control measures for making sure our dual-ship, night, tactical-formation (TACFORM) and terrain-flight (TERF) event would be successful. Particular emphasis was placed on the need to take it slow, as this was the first such event for the two copilots and two of the aircrew.

The original plan called for moving to a working area and 30 minutes of TACFORM maneuvers. This would be followed by a low-level route to the NOLF (Naval outlying landing field), where the rest of the flight would be spent completing various TERF maneuvers and landings.

Like all good plans, ours did not survive first contact with the "enemy" (a combination of weather and unannounced field closures). Our initial transit to our first working area had gone smoothly, but the gusty wind conditions made it difficult to keep the flight within the confines of the area during our TACFORM sequence.

As the event lead, I stopped and reset the flight several times to keep us in the working area. The resets added up and kept us working through the formation maneuvers for an hour. I adjusted our low-level route to get us to the NOLF more quickly and give us enough time to focus on landings.

I briefed the updated route over the radio and assumed navigation responsibilities for the section. The area was unfamiliar to me, and I found it challenging to navigate the flight and continue to provide TERF flying instruction to my copilot. I felt behind the flight after having to reset several times due to the wind, and I was digging deep into my adaptability/flexibility reserves. However, I had a very competent crew, and we managed to make it to the NOLF.

Unfortunately, the NOLF was not available to us. As I checked-in our flight with the tower, I received a broken transmission that sounded like my request had been disapproved. Not wanting to penetrate the NOLF's airspace without permission, I put the flight into a holding pattern. I tried again to communicate with the tower and gain entry to the field. Again, the transmission was broken, but clear enough for me to understand that my requests were denied.

The initial frustration I felt after having to adjust the formation sequence and then the low-level route now began to magnify as I realized I'd have to come up with another change to the plan to complete the TERF landings. I thought I had covered my bases by reserving an exclusive-use period at the NOLF, but we'd ended up wasting 15 minutes. I quickly decided to take the flight to a nearby civilian field to complete the event.

I had worked at the field before, but only single ship and during the day. The flight had adjusted well to all of the previous changes, so I expected we could adjust to this one.

We got our training done at the civilian field, but it turned out to be a tremendous challenge. Another helicopter that wasn't equipped with night-vision devices (NVDs) was also using the field and had the runway lights illuminated. This "bloomed" us out every time we turned toward our landing area. I struggled to keep up with providing effective training as the bulk of my attention was directed at just trying to keep the flight safe. The same frustration I felt earlier in the flight began to gnaw at me again, making the task of providing high-quality training even more difficult.

After completing our required maneuvers, I quickly briefed our route home. It was late, and the field we were operating at and our home field were now closed. I reviewed the closed-field rules for our destination and passed them on to the rest of the flight. Although this is a minor process, the fact that we had not planned on coming home after the field closed irritated me. I felt enormous frustration that I again had to come up with a brief for the section to get the flight done. I felt like I had just spent the last three hours spinning plates, a feeling that was exacerbated because this should have been a relatively straightforward syllabus event.

I put the accumulated frustration aside and led the section back to home field. Our landing was uneventful and my co-pilot taxied us back to our line. As we approached the turnoff from the taxiway to our line, I had removed my goggles and was heads-down, working through the post-landing and shutdown checklists. My copilot kept his goggles on as we taxied away from the landing pad toward our line.

As we approached our turnoff from the taxiway, the combination of the copilot sitting cross cockpit to the turn and his lack of familiarity with the field at night created some confusion. We missed the turn and continued straight down the taxiway. As Dash 2 turned behind us, my copilot announced that he thought he had missed the turn and hit the brakes. I looked up and noticed that we had stopped on the taxiway at a point where we were immediately adjacent to our parking spot. I looked over at our line and saw the plane captain looking at us, no doubt wondering what we were doing.

I now had several options. I could continue another 200 yards down the taxiway to the next turn and back taxi into our line, I could lift and complete a 180-degree hover turn and go back to the original turnoff, or I could turn off the taxiway and drive directly into the line.

The cumulative effect of all the flexing and changing of plans during the flight had taken a toll on me, and, as I was about to find out, had affected my decision-making. I just wanted to park the helo and wrap this event up. I was frustrated and tired, and couldn't wait to put this experience behind me. I decided to pursue the course that would get me to the line the quickest.

I looked at the line and decided to turn off the taxiway and pull into my spot. I didn't notice what lay between my line and the taxiway: 50 feet of rough surface with a low point in the middle, like a shallow ditch. I took the controls from the co-pilot. As I turned off the taxiway, I felt the aircraft drop slightly, like it had come down off a street side curb. The aircraft accelerated on its own; it was travelling downhill. The acceleration slowed, and I heard an unpleasant scraping sound as the helo began to move up the opposite slope of the ditch. I pulled into the line and realized that I had probably scraped some antennas on the bottom of the helo.

As soon as we shut down, I jumped out and looked at the underside to assess the expected damage. Sure enough, two of the antennas that are located directly beneath the cockpit were scraped up and bent slightly aft. I pointed the damage out to a nearby airframer, and headed into maintenance control to confess and debrief.

Lessons Learned:

Once all the work had been done, the total damage came out to about $2,000. A figure far short of what I feared, but still an expensive lesson for me.

I managed to complicate a decision that under normal circumstances would have been easy to make. I allowed my frustration and impatience to influence me. The flight had effectively sapped my adaptability and flexibility. This led to a loss of situational awareness and ultimately a breakdown in decision-making when it came time for what should have been the easiest part of the flight.

We've all discussed compartmentalizing and avoiding the urge to rush during a flight or mission. This incident has become a painful reminder for me about how important that is.

NOTES:

TIME TRAVELLING

MH-60R, UNITED STATES NAVY, HSM-70, HELICOPTER MARITIME STRIKE SQUADRON 70

AWR3 Cornelius Donnelly, August 2014

Our crew was on final to our cruiser's flight deck, but I didn't know what kind of landing we were doing, why we were landing early or why the pilot seemed concerned about me when I asked those questions. I didn't know because I had slept through the previous 15 minutes of our MH-60R flight. I woke up during our emergency landing. The landing was uneventful.

The debrief was not.

Our detachment was tasked with daily surface search and control (SSC) missions from midnight to noon during our pre deployment exercise. We found ourselves adjusting our sleep cycles to match the rhythm of the exercise, while doing our best to get rest during the high winds and seas typically found off the Virginia coast during early winter. The seas tossed our cruiser like a toy in a washing machine, making sleep difficult and fatigue management a constant battle.

While I discussed my sleep episode with the ship's medical team, the details of our morning routine came rushing back. Let's rewind the tape to that morning.

When we conducted our NATOPS and operational risk management (ORM) briefs, I felt nauseated from exhaustion and the constant rocking of the ship. The crew had a total of 12 hours of sleep between the three of us, and I'd gotten only three hours of broken sleep during our transit. The H2P and I were in no shape to fly. To his credit, the H2P discussed his fatigue with the aircraft commander and was pulled from the flight. I knew that the only replacement possible to take my place was my buddy who had flown the lion's share of hours over the last couple of days. I couldn't let him get hammered with another hard day's flying, could I? I pressed on.

Fatigue is a devious adversary, taking hold of you during routine tasks. You might not even know until it's too late. It seems that the harder you fight it, the harder it fights back. During the flight, work kept my mind busy. We had systems to troubleshoot, and I did the work quickly and effectively, returning the aircraft to full mission capability. Once I was done, we settled into the rest of a routine surface-surveillance flight. That's when the real fight with fatigue began.

I worked our forward looking infrared (FLIR) systems, but there wasn't much to see that morning. I had passed out without warning and slept so soundly that movement of the aircraft and constant yelling over ICS couldn't shake me out of the slumber.

I looked at my watch — 0830. I checked it again on final for our emergency landing — 0845. I had passed out without warning and slept so soundly that movement of the aircraft and constant yelling over ICS couldn't shake me out of the slumber. I had been effectively traveling through time without any knowledge of the trip. I hadn't even felt tired while we were airborne.

Two days later I was flown over to the aircraft carrier for interviews with the flight surgeon and a safety board. After detailing my previous week's schedule to the flight surgeon, it was determined my fatigue level was equivalent to that of 0.08 blood-alcohol content.

I was operating at about 70 percent, with the same motor skills and information-processing ability as if I had been legally drunk during the flight. My brain decided that it was time to go to sleep and it just switched off in mid flight.

Lessons Learned:

This incident opened my eyes to the importance of crew rest. OPNAV 3710 has very strict crew-rest guidelines in place to ensure that aircrew are flying at their peak level of performance.

Naval aviators tend to have type A personalities that prompt a "can do" attitude and pressure teams to disregard those guidelines. However, getting the proper amount of sleep is extremely important and directly impacts flight performance.

If you find yourself in a situation where you are encountering sleep deprivation and questioning your ability to fly, be assertive and make it known to your crew. If you don't, you'll find yourself "time traveling" too.

USN Analyst Note:

The Fatigue Avoidance Scheduling Tool (FAST) has been approved for installation on NMCI machines.

NOTES:

FIGHTING COMPLACENCY. ONE AUTOROTATION AT A TIME

TH-57 SEARANGER, UNITED STATES NAVY, HELICOPTER TRAINING SQUADRON 28

LT Chris Krueger , August 2014

The Set Up:

During the first flight of the day, I took off with my new onwing on a fam 4 via course rules to work the channel and practice emergency procedures at altitude before heading to Navy Outlying Field (NOLF) Spencer.

It was the middle of the summer: hot and humid, with high density altitude (DA). Ambient air temperature was 32 degrees Celsius, DA was +1,700 feet, and winds were calm.

We transitioned outside the NAS Whiting Class C airspace and set up for our first simulated engine failure at altitude. When students are learning how to auto rotate after a simulated engine failure, set-up is critical because the margin for error is low when maneuvering the helicopter to make the intended field.

I was on the controls and demonstrated the first simulated engine failure of the day.

Rainbow Field is an unprepared piece of farmland that we use when teaching students how to set up and conduct emergency procedures. The first simulated engine failure was a 180-degree autorotation. The maneuver, waveoff, and engine response were all on the numbers and per the book. Confident in the aircraft's performance, I let the student conduct the next four simulated engine failures. He understood the basic mechanics of the maneuver and the field geometry involved.

Because this was the student's first time doing these intense maneuvers, I was riding the controls with him and making inputs to keep the aircraft in a recoverable profile the entire time. My student progressed with each pass, maintaining Nr, airspeed, and sight picture more precisely and confidently as the flight went on.

With each attempt, I took controls before 400 feet per Wing SOP and initiated the wave off by bringing the twist grip to full-open with the collective full-down. After all five passes, the engine spooled up correctly within one or two seconds when the twist grip was brought full open, and the wave offs were benign.

The Outlier:

I decided to test my student's ability with a straight in, simulated engine failure to a different unprepared field, known as Texas Field. The student handled the entry well and the maneuver was going as planned with the helicopter descending at a controllable 65 knots. At about 450 feet AGL, I took controls from my student and initiated the wave off by ensuring the collective was full-down and bringing the twist grip full-open. This time I heard no engine spool and got zero response from my gauges. My scan first stopped on my torque gauge — it read 5-7 percent (where it remained).

This by itself wouldn't indicate a slow spool, especially if Nr was above 100 percent, but it prompted my scan to continue to diagnose.

I observed no trend or change in Ng or turbine outlet temperature (TOT), indicating no engine response. I then shifted my scan to my Nf/Nr gauge. Nr was reading about 95 percent. I gave the collective a slight pull, and observed Nr decrease slightly, and I momentarily caught the rotor-low RPM light on the caution panel.

Fearing an unresponsive engine at this point, I immediately brought the collective full-down, took the twist grip back to flight idle and then back to full-open in the hope that something would reset and the engine would spool up. No dice.

Deciding:

While this was happening, we were passing through 400 feet. I tried to keep my composure as I scanned my cockpit and continued to fly into the field. Because we had a little extra altitude to lose before making the field, I widened the entry into the field slightly for a soft 45-to-60 degree approach to guarantee our entry. As we passed through 200 feet, I noticed my reattempt at getting our engine spooled up had no effect.

I remember thinking to myself, "This is actually happening, I'm committed to this field."

I left the twist grip full-open, still hoping the engine would spool up. I quickly called, "Mayday" over Spencer traffic radio frequency. My student had the presence of mind to squawk 7700 on the transponder. I then focused on my full autorotation: 200 feet, on course line; 150 feet, collective full-down; 100 feet, flare.

Between 50 and 75 feet, I heard the familiar sound of an engine surging to life and saw movement on my gauges in my peripheral vision while continuing my flare. As I hit 10 to 15 feet and began my pull pause — level, I noticed some power and completed what I compare to an "under speed" landing profile, a sliding landing with limited power. The entire ordeal had lasted only seconds.

After landing, I radioed some of the aircraft at Spencer to let them know we were OK and to notify our duty office at Whiting of our situation. I would need to answer a lot of questions back at home, so I passed controls and started writing down everything I could think of, including times, gauge readings and ambient air temperature.

We then shut down, got out, and took stock.

After making sure we still had our composure, we assessed the aircraft and environment. The aircraft looked fine with no damage. We put all the plugs and covers on the aircraft, because the grass was 1-to-2 feet high and lots of insects were beginning to swarm the aircraft, attracted by the heat. After calling our squadron and arranging for a maintenance recovery, we looked at the field around us. We noticed we had landed in a largely dry area, but we were surrounded by a shallow marshy area on three sides. A dense tree line was to the east. There was a dirt road with gated access from a paved road, which was the obvious entry point for the truck to recover the aircraft, but the shallow marsh was a concern.

When the maintenance-recovery team arrived, they confirmed they were unable to bring their heavy truck through the 100 feet of mud. One option was to spin the aircraft up and hover-taxi it to where the truck could get to it. The other option was to have the aircraft wait several days, possibly a week, for the ground to dry enough to drive on.

I considered that there was no damage to the aircraft and that I had a slow spool issue, not a power issue. If I lost power for some reason, I could do a taxi cut gun to the deck easily and safely, even in the marsh. I called back to my squadron and my CO approved it, so we spun up, hover-taxied the 100 feet and shut down. The aircraft was loaded onto the truck, and we went back to Whiting for debrief.

Lessons Learned:

Always be prepared for the worst, just in case.

With my onwings, I emphasize that an aircraft will kill you if you let it. Training, following procedures, sound judgment and good CRM is what will keep you alive. That being said, little prepared me for this situation.

I sat down with my onwings and used the event as a teaching point. I didn't want them to be scared by this situation, of the aircraft or aviation in general, but I did want to engender a healthy respect of the aircraft and of flying. I wanted them to appreciate that wrong procedures, erroneous control inputs, or poor judgment can have consequences. I think they got it — so did I.

This event highlighted the importance of making sure the aircraft is in a safe condition prior to initiating any simulated emergency. If we hadn't been in a proper autorotational profile, or if we didn't have the field made before I took the engine to idle, my student and I would not be here today, and you would be reading a Class A mishap report rather than this lesson.

NOTES:

A SIMPLE, DAY FAMILIAR

MH-60R SEAHAWK, UNITED STATES NAVY, HELICOPTER MARITIME STRIKE SQUADRON 40

LTJG Michael Watson, February 2014

Having recently earned my wings at Whiting Field, I was ready for the real thing: transitioning to a new aircraft and flying in the Jacksonville area. The weather around Naval Station Mayport was clear with light winds. This would be a perfect spring day for an initial fam flight for a MH-60R Cat I fleet replacement pilot.

My instructor was a fleet-experienced MH-60R pilot who recently had checked into the command from one of the local fleet squadrons. The two aircrew in the cabin were senior AWRs. Everything was set up to be a great learning experience for me and a basic, day fam (familiar) for everyone else.

During our NATOPS brief, we had discussed operational risk management (ORM), especially because of the large volume of air traffic in the local area. It seems that everyone was taking advantage of the good weather. All our crew members needed to maintain a solid, proactive scan throughout the flight.

After reading the book, our crew met in the hangar to wait for a hot-seat. After launching, we left the local pattern for an area near

Jacksonville. We then stopped at Cecil Field to briefly conduct pattern-work before returning to Mayport to pick up the next student.

We entered Mayport course rules from the west and requested a full-stop landing on runway 23, intending to air-taxi to taxiway C for the fuel pits. I was flying from the right seat and landed on runway 23 at taxiway B. I requested to air-taxi to the fuel pits. Tower cleared me direct to taxiway C from present position. Not fully understanding what ATC wanted me to do (which was fly point-to-point), I picked up into a hover, pedal-turned onto taxiway B and then proceeded to air-taxi toward taxiway G (a taxiway that runs parallel to the runway).

For those of you not familiar with the Mayport airfield layout, taxiway B connects the runway to the parallel taxiway and taxiway C connects the parallel taxiway to the line area. Spaced along taxiway G are 13 designated helicopter-landing spots. Our direction of air-taxi was going to take us past helo spot 12 en route to taxiway C.

While air-taxiing across the B and G intersection, I silently scanned left and right while remaining on the go. About 10 feet out into taxiway G, I felt the HAC pull the cyclic into his lap. The aircraft immediately pitched up, and we started moving backwards. I scanned the radalt and noticed we had climbed to 40 feet, and then I quickly looked outside the aircraft. All I could see was the radome of another MH-60R heading inbound along taxiway G. No more than 20 feet separated us. I heard over the radio an advisory call from ATC, telling the inbound aircraft to hold position. The other aircraft proceeded to land full-stop in an adjacent spot.

After holding the hover for what felt like an eternity, we finally crossed taxiway G, made our full stop at taxiway C, and continued our taxi on the ground. We were bewildered at how this dangerous situation developed so quickly. None of us had seen the other aircraft, nor had we heard ATC's clearance for them to land. We completed the hot seat and the HAC went back out into the pattern with the next FRP.

Lessons Learned:

The aircrewman and I talked with the aviation safety officer about what had happened. We later learned that tower had instructed the other aircraft to land on the helo spot 12, while we were taxiing over it. Something had clearly gone wrong or had not been communicated; however, tower isn't the only source of situational awareness (SA). That comes from your senses and is strengthened and amplified by good internal crew resource management (CRM).

During the simple air-taxi to the fuel pits, I had not heard ATC's instructions to the other aircraft. I was focused on debriefing the flight with the HAC. I had been in the habit of only holding short when instructed while taxiing. From now on, I will be taking the extra two or three seconds to come to a stop before vocally clearing myself left and right; I'll use the other set of eyes in the cockpit to increase my SA. Waiting to discuss the flight until safe in the chocks will spare some distraction among the crew. I had wanted to learn something on my first flight — mission accomplished.

NOTES:

FLAT LIGHT DEGRADED VISUAL ENVIRONMENT
UH-60L, UNITED STATES ARMY, ARMY AIRCRAFT ACCIDENT PREVENTION

Name withheld by request, August 2019

The mishap crew just completed a VIP mission when the state army aviation officer notified the pilot in command (PC) that the rescue coordination center for the area requested CIVSAR assistance for a small aircraft crash and personnel rescue from a glacier area. The mission was approved as medium risk and two aircraft were utilized for the mission. Mishap crew members obtained a weather briefing and determined the weather was acceptable. Crew members of the two aircraft departed their home base and, while en route, encountered marginal visual flight rules (VFR) weather. Crew members continued the mission, maintaining VFR to their refuel stop. They departed the refuel site and continued the mission to the location of the downed aircraft personnel.

Pilot reports from the area stated the weather was deteriorating. While Chalk 2 personnel initiated contact with the crash personnel, mishap aircraft crew members (Chalk 1) maintained communications on the common traffic frequency for the area of the crash. Chalk 1 continued to the crash site while Chalk 2 remained in orbit about 3 miles away to monitor the operation. By the time the aircraft arrived on-site, the visual conditions were reduced to a degraded visual environment (DVE) induced by flat light conditions from ice and snow on the ground. During the execution of a low recon and while in a left turn to evaluate the crash site for a usable landing zone; the aircraft entered a descent and contacted the terrain. The aircraft rolled approximately 210 degrees to the right onto its roof and came to rest inverted. No injuries were sustained by crew members.

The PC had 2,182 hours in mission, type, design, and series (MTDS), and 2,850 hours total time. The pilot (PI) had 74 hours in MTDS and 3,259 hours total time.

Lessons Learned:

The aircraft PC had experience operating in the flat light conditions encountered during the mishap.

While conducting the reconnaissance to determine the condition and location to land near the crash site, the PC failed to maintain orientation of the aircraft due to the DVE created by the flat light environmental conditions. The aircraft was allowed to begin an uncommanded descent while decreasing airspeed to below effective translational lift (ETL).

Accompanying the PC's loss of orientation and situational awareness was the crew members' failure to use proper communication to assist the pilot on the controls in maintaining altitude and airspeed, both necessary to maintain flight and prevent controlled flight into terrain.

The situation these crew members found themselves in can occur anytime certain mission types are performed in like conditions for multiple hours. Aircrew members can lose that fear of the unknown while becoming overconfident in their abilities to manage the mission and the environmental conditions. In this mishap, crew members fell prey to overconfidence and lacked execution of base task crew coordination.

The flat light conditions which produce an optical illusion and cause pilots to lose their depth of field and contrast in vision produced a DVE due to light and snow/ice conditions in the CIVSAR location. Pilots and crew members must maintain their vigilance and verbally assist the pilot on the controls with input on aircraft and flight status. Simple crew member actions as stated in the aircrew training module and training support packages, e.g., PI calling out airspeed and altitude, acknowledging DVE conditions, and verbally identifying current threats to flight, make the difference between accomplishing the mission or a mishap.

NOTES:

CHAPTER 2
TORQUE & POWER

"I had to make a decision very, very quickly before we hit the trees — was I going to roll off the throttle and settle into the trees as directed by the flight manual?"

RAAF Pilot, name withheld

SETTLING WITH POWER
BELL UH-1N, UNITED STATES AIR FORCE, UNIT UNKNOWN

1st Lt. Clell Knight, August 2008

It was an uneventful August afternoon. I was sitting at the flight operations desk performing post flight duties. The squadron that I was assigned to flies the UH-1N Huey helicopter, an old helicopter from the Vietnam era that makes the famous "Whoop, Whoop" sound. Though it may not be the fanciest aircraft in the Air Force's inventory or have the latest avionics technology, it's a dependable helicopter that reliably brings crews home safely. Having been on station for 10 months as a co-pilot, I hadn't yet flown on any search-and-rescue missions.

The telephone rang; it was the Air Force Rescue Coordination Center calling to request our unit's support on a SAR. The scenario: one injured male hiker with a broken ankle who had been in a wilderness for two days. Along with GPS coordinates, the AFRCC provided a frequency to establish communication with the rescue ground party. The tasking was to extract the injured hiker and fly to the nearest hospital for medical assistance. Due to the broken trails and high rugged terrain, ground crew members were having difficulty extracting the injured hiker on pack mules.

As available crew members began mission planning, the weather shop forecasted rain showers en route to the extraction area. Due to limited manning, the commander decided which crew was going, and I was going to be co-pilot on the flight. Our crew experience level: 1,100-hour AC, 600-hour co-pilot, 1700-hour FE, and a 50-hour flight surgeon.

Mission planning was transferred to us and the AC immediately started delegating duties. Time was critical. The crew didn't want to increase the risk of the mission by running out of daylight. Crew members began performing their tasks, and it was clearly evident that because of the high elevation near the extraction area, this wasn't going to be like an everyday training sortie. The injured hiker was located in an area not far from the highest mountain peak in the state (12,800 feet MSL).

Like an airplane's wing, a helicopter's rotor blade is the surface that provides lift. The surface area of a rotor blade is significantly smaller than that of an airplane's wing. The decrease in surface area, along with a tail rotor, which consumes some engine torque used for yaw control, combine to make tail rotor-driven helicopters difficult to operate in high density altitude environments. Through operational risk management principles, the crew analyzed the mission and pinpointed the most probable area of high risk exposure. The extraction would be the riskiest portion of the sortie. In order to control the risk while maximizing capabilities and performance, the crew had to ensure enough engine power would be available, along with an adequate gross weight to land and depart from the landing zone.

Takeoff and landing data indicated we'd have a narrow power margin while operating in the remote landing area. One hundred percent power from our Pratt & Whitney engines wasn't going to be available on this sortie near the landing zone. Also, our flight plan indicated that only 15 minutes of loiter time would be available to find the survivor, land, and then depart before reaching BINGO fuel for the last leg to the hospital. Timing and fuel were our main concerns. After completing the pre-departure briefing, flight gear was checked out and the flight surgeon arrived. It was now time to go.

Upon departure, we were one hour from the LZ. The crew focused mainly on avoiding the rain shafts spread throughout the mountain ranges and navigating with limited visibility — less than two miles in some areas, due to seasonal forest fires. The FE and flight surgeon checked and rechecked their hoist equipment while the AC and I reviewed maps for possible landing areas. We felt we had a great game plan; it was now just a matter of execution.

Five minutes out and the helicopter was flying along mountain peaks over the wilderness area. The jagged terrain, along with gusty winds, created orographic turbulence that violently threw the aircraft around. It was like a roller-coaster ride.

We initiated a power check and found the No. 2 engine was the limiting factor, allowing only 91 percent for dual-engine torque. That meant if we used more than 91 percent dual-engine torque, the main rotor would droop, resulting in a loss of lift.

We arrived at the GPS coordinates given to us by AFRCC, but didn't find any sign of the survivor. Feeling the "pinch," we initiated a search. The terrain, coupled with dense vegetation, made it difficult to sight any members of the ground rescue party. The AC was finally able to establish communication with the ground members. After searching through several valleys, the FE spotted a bright red coat from one of the ground crew. We immediately prepared for extraction with only 10 minutes to bingo.

Initially, the ground party requested the survivor be extracted via the hoist, but it wasn't an option, due to our limited power and fuel status. We asked them to move the survivor several hundred yards down the mountain to a small marshy area that provided a good approach and departure path for the helicopter. The AC briefed the remote landing to confirm any major obstacles within the LZ; none were noted.

We were now on final into an LZ at 9,000 feet MSL. The FE and I made mandatory parameter calls while clearing the aircraft into the LZ: "200 feet above landing site, airspeed 30 knots, sink 400 feet per minute, torque 45 percent, clear down right, left." The AC nailed all the approach parameters, and the Huey was skids down with seven minutes until BINGO fuel.

To help the rescue ground party move the survivor, the FE recommended repositioning the aircraft another 100 feet forward in the front one-third area of the LZ. As the AC hovered the helicopter 15 feet above the ground, the crew collectively agreed to avoid small bushes that were spread throughout the marshy area. The helicopter was repositioned in a corner with 50-foot trees off the nose and right side of the aircraft. After a deep breath and sigh of relief, my initial thought was, "This is a piece of cake." Now the only thing to worry about was BINGO fuel and getting to the hospital.

The FE and flight surgeon returned with the survivor in the stokes basket, and we prepared for departure. The AC added torque, and the helicopter lifted off the ground. After adding the survivor onboard, an additional 220lbs, the AC wanted to reconfirm if current gross weight would allow the helicopter to clear the trees on the departure path. With a light headwind off the nose and only 85 percent torque applied, the helicopter unexpectedly sprang up to 30 feet above the ground. The performance was so good, it actually caused confusion. The FE recommended taking off from present position, but the AC conservatively wanted to back-taxi in order to get a run at the takeoff, ensuring obstacle clearance. The AC cleared for the aircraft to make a 180-degree turn and began back-taxiing, when the helicopter suddenly buffeted and started moving uncontrollably. Sinking uncontrollably to the ground, the AC instinctively started adding power to arrest the descent. To ensure the pilot flying doesn't over torque the engines, crews train for the pilot not flying to guard the collective any time such a situation is imminent. With my left hand over the collective, I called out, "Torque 88, torque 90, torque 91, stop pull, stop pull!"

Having never been in this situation before and seeing the ground begin to rush up, I was at a loss for words. I had the desire, but not the ability to make any more significant inputs to the crew to help maintain situational awareness. It grew uncomfortably quiet over the intercom as we were descending towards uneven ground — 20 feet, 15 feet, 10 feet, and then the FE blurted out, "Fly it to the ground, fly it to the ground." The helicopter touched left skid first, which caused it to rock to the right and wobble for a moment or two, but it was still hovering! As we gathered our wits and shifted around in our pants, we said, "Let's try this again and get out of here." The AC pulled power, and off we went, clearing obstacles, but encountering turbulence just above the treetops, causing another moment of worry. Soon, however, we were gaining airspeed and altitude and were well on our way.

Flying direct to the hospital, we were below BINGO fuel, and a tailwind that turned crosswind didn't help matters. The flight surgeon treated the dehydrated survivor, while the FE closely monitored a combining gearbox oil temperature that was at its maximum operational limit. The hospital drop-off would not be an option due to our fuel status, so the closest FBO was Plan B.

Other than reported wind shear at the airport with winds gusting to 40 mph, the remainder of the flight went as planned. Tower controllers coordinated for medical assistance, and EMTs were waiting for us on the tarmac.

The flight was finally complete, and the crew had successfully completed the assigned mission.

Lessons Learned:

My first SAR as a co-pilot was a tremendous learning experience.

The uncontrolled descent that occurred in the LZ was due to a rotary wing phenomenon known as "settling with power." The AC's initial hover pickup with the survivor onboard was accomplished with a light headwind.

After initiating the back-taxi, the helicopter was repositioned to have a direct tailwind. The tailwind simply made the rotor disk produce less lift. The rate of descent, coupled with the high DA, put the helicopter in a position where maximum power from our engines couldn't arrest the sink towards the ground. As a crew, we allowed ourselves to get into that situation by growing complacent. Until that event, every facet of the mission had gone according to plan. Most importantly, I saw firsthand how aircrews must use CRM to successfully complete a mission when exposed to high risk. As the co-pilot, I was able to make inputs to the crew to help prevent over torquing the engines. After that, I was simply along for the ride. The experienced FE quickly realized the dire circumstances, and was able to pick up the co-pilot calls and continue to provide meaningful inputs for the crew. The AC obviously showed tremendous airmanship and a willingness to not quit by flying the helicopter throughout the impact with the uneven terrain. In the end, teamwork got the crew through the "settling-with-power" situation and onto the FBO — a great display of effective communication and group effort, resulting in success.

NOTES:

WHAT'S DIFFERENT ABOUT TODAY?

MH-60S, UNITED STATES NAVY, HSC-7
HELICOPTER SEA COMBAT SQUADRON 7

LT Aubrey Hodges, August 2014

It was just another day in the Arabian Gulf, my first deployment as a HAC. I felt confident about life as a helicopter pilot; I was approaching a year as a qualified aircraft commander. I had made all the workups and had adjusted well to life on a carrier.

As I walked to the bird that morning, I was thinking about "groundhog day". Senior personnel had warned me about it, and it had started to set in. Days were running together, and time was flying by. A day plane guard here, a night plane guard there, and a sprinkling of log runs thrown in. The safety officer led a discussion about complacency during a wardroom talk.

We faced a simple, three-aircraft log run into the Omani base at Masirah. We'd be making multiple trips back and forth to drop off cargo and personnel for the squadron's upcoming detachment. We walked early, preflighted, spun up and loaded the birds. I was flying with a senior H2P. We'd flown together a number of times, and I was comfortable with his ability. I double-checked our preflight calculations and glanced at the extra weight we'd be carrying. We were lighter than planned, but I knew the next run included transporting eight passengers.

After completing our checklists, we departed forward off of Spot 2. As we broke the deck edge, we sunk slightly. My copilot had not added in enough power, and I told him "You can pull more, we have plenty of power this run."

The log run to Masirah went smoothly, and everyone was in high spirits. As we came back in for landing on Spot 2, tower warned us that there was a jackstaff on the bow. We saw it and knew we would have no problem avoiding it. The ship was at anchor and the colors were flying. Once we were chocked and chained, I looked at the power calculations. We had calculated for a full bag of gas (3,700 pounds) and had allotted 200 pounds per passenger.

My copilot asked if we wanted to get fuel, as we currently sat at 2,300 pounds, and Masirah was only about 30 miles away. My crew chief said over the ICS, "We are getting gas, right?" I agreed and told the plane captain to fuel us. As we hooked up, I heard a discussion between the two other aircraft as to whether to take fuel. One HAC agreed that he would take fuel.

As we fuelled, I checked the temperature. It was 30 degrees Celsius, exactly what we expected. I heard calls for the other two aircraft as they landed and took off. Winds were shifting. One aircraft had landed with a tailwind. Another aircraft had landed with light and variable winds.

As we embarked our passengers, I noted that all their bags were small and looked light. I reviewed our power calculations again and decided to add 200 extra pounds for gear. We had calculated 94 percent in a HIGE (hover in ground effect), and briefed the crew that I expected to see about 95 percent in our initial hover. I told my copilot that I wanted to get a good power check over the deck. We computed that we had 128 percent torque (TQ) with contingency power on, 123 percent TQ with 878 degrees turbine gas temperature (TGT), and 116 percent TQ with the environment control system (ECS) on.

We completed our checks and gave our number of souls and splash time to tower. In our discussions later, my copilot and crew chief did not remember what the wind call was. I remembered the call was winds 17 to port, 4 knots. Tower also reminded us again of the jackstaff. We lifted, and I called torque at 96 percent, stating power was good in a HIGE. My copilot said he would slide left to avoid the jackstaff, and the crewman cleared us left. As we broke the deck edge and pulled into a HOGE (hover out of ground effect), torque was at 112 percent, exactly as calculated. The next few seconds were the fastest and the longest of my life.

My copilot nosed over to start the forward transition and pulled in power. I saw our torque and TGT rapidly climbing through the yellow and into the red. I told him to "Watch power. Take a little out." As I do for every takeoff and landing, I was loosely guarding controls, with a hand resting on the collective. I felt him push the nose over more to get airspeed, take a hint of power out and pull it right back in.

We started to sink, and he brought the nose up and pulled more power. That's when the bottom dropped out of the helicopter. Our gauges lit up, and I could see several timers starting on the screen counting down. We rapidly settled. The flight deck loomed above us and we began to droop the rotor system. I knew we couldn't arrest the descent with power for fear of drooping more than what we already had and losing control of the tail rotor system. Being this close to the ship, that action would be deadly.

I was painfully aware of the 11 people in my helicopter, most likely panicking as we kicked up salt spray over the water. I took the controls as we passed through 36 feet, instinctively tried to turn on contingency power. The helo nosed over, and I flew a profile much like if we had lost an engine in a hover and were trying to fly it away. Our descent slowed and stopped, and I told the crew I was going to keep it down in ground effect until we had airspeed on the bird. After about 45 knots, I pulled the nose up gently.

Lessons Learned:

Upon reviewing the play tapes multiple times, talking to tower and the crew, and debriefing with multiple senior HACs, we discovered several important items. The helicopter control officer (HCO) was brand new that day, giving us a few nonstandard calls that we should have clarified. Talking with others in the tower, we learned that winds had probably been off the starboard quarter. Operating on the carrier, we get used to having a nice headwind component. This was the first time I had launched with unfavorable winds.

Several members of the squadron independently ran the power calculations and came up with the same numbers that we had. Our power calculations were accurate, but we were operating with a small power margin, maybe four percent TQ. If we selected contingency power, we would have had a 12 percent TQ power margin, which is easy to exceed if you aren't careful and aren't aware of the energy state of the helicopter.

Looking at the tapes, the nose-down transition appears more aggressive than it had felt in the aircraft. Our takeoff would have been fine for a normal plane guard flight, but we needed a slower, smoother, gentler takeoff that day. I think my comments to my copilot on the first go of the day gave him a false sense of security.

I should have asked the questions that have gotten so many people out of trouble before: "What is different about today?" "What is different about this takeoff?" It would have taken only a minute to look at the variables and plan a better departure from the ship.

<u>NOTES:</u>

WHEN THE PEDAL HITS THE STOP
UH-1H, ROYAL AUSTRALIAN AIR FORCE VIA CASA, 35 SQUADRON

Name withheld, reported March 2015

My first posting as a brand new RAAF helicopter pilot was to 35 Squadron in Townsville, north Queensland, to fly the Bell UH-1H Iroquois. Day-to-day work was largely army support in the High Range military training area northwest of Townsville. At an average 1500–800 ft AMSL and with summer temperatures of 35 degrees and 100 percent humidity, the Iroquois often came very close to its performance limit for approach and departure from pads when carrying loads. Towering take-offs or out-of-ground-effect (OGE) hovering with anything but the lightest load were rarely possible unless they occurred early in the cool of a morning.

This particular day I was required to do an 'admin move' for a four-man army survey team and their equipment. It was a mid-morning start and the task would be over quickly—a perfect opportunity for me as a junior pilot to get some command experience.

My co-pilot was an older fellow with previous Caribou experience, but with very little time as an Iroquois pilot. As we approached the designated landing zone (LZ) it became apparent that it was an OGE pad in a very small circular opening in the forest. The trees were perhaps 30m tall on the crest of a flattish ridge, and the approach would require coming to a complete stop in an OGE hover at tree-top height and then descending vertically down. The prospect of this required a few important checks before committing to the approach.

Approaching an OGE hover without the requisite power margin would be disastrous, as there would not be enough power to hover nor to go-around; a crash into the trees would be inevitable. We circled around the pad as we calculated the power margin, outside air temperature and spoke with the survey team by radio regarding the weight of their equipment. The prevailing wind conditions would also be critical so we asked the survey team to throw a smoke grenade to allow us to judge the wind direction and strength. The brightly coloured smoke lifted slowly above the trees and then gently dissipated to the southwest.

Once all these details were settled and we were confident we could get in and out of the pad, I made the first approach towards the north east into the very light wind. The first approach went smoothly and we descended vertically into the hole amongst the trees to lift three soldiers out with a small margin of excess power. As was the custom, I then swapped over flying with the co-pilot who took a turn to fly the approach and shift the next load. He copied everything I had done the first time, and the move was uneventful.

For the third and final approach, I had control once again and flew to the LZ exactly as we had done previously. As I approached the hover point above the opening to the pad, the crewman was leaning out of the rear door calling the clearance from the trees, and my co-pilot was calling the amount of torque I was using so that I had an idea of the power margin available to me. As I pulled in the collective and flared slightly to stop in the hover, something didn't quite feel the same as before; I felt uneasy and couldn't work out why. The co-pilot was calling torque readings slightly higher than we had used before, but something else was worrying me. Then I realised what it was—my left leg was extended much more than my right—I was using a lot of left pedal to stay aligned with the landing direction.

Just as I figured that out, the crewman called a small 'tail right' adjustment to keep my tail rotor away from a tree top below us. I applied the tiniest pressure on the left yaw pedal and felt something under my left boot that made my blood run cold—the pedal stop.

The events that followed took place so fast that they stand as a testament to the fine balance of forces that allow a helicopter to fly and what happens when one of those forces is no longer controlled. The turbine engine on an Iroquois drives the rotor blades to the left, but at the same time tries to rotate the fuselage to the right; the application of left yaw or anti-torque pedal prevents this—to a point.

Running out of left pedal means the aircraft will immediately start rotating uncontrollably to the right, and this is exactly what happened in my case. In the split second after my left foot hit the pedal stop, the aircraft started to rotate right; very fast. I don't remember how many turns we did, as the spin was so fast I lost any reference point to the trees and I just struggled to keep wings level with the horizon.

As the pilots sit about two metres forward of the aircraft centre of gravity, centrifugal forces were pushing me outwards or towards the instrument panel. My mind raced in that clichéd way—time seemed to slow and I recalled the loss of tail rotor authority emergency procedure; roll off the engine throttle and settle down onto the ground. Removing the engine torque would stop the fuselage rotation and allow directional control to be regained, however, the one major downside of this procedure was that you were now without engine power and so a quick autorotation to the impact point would be the inevitable outcome.

So here I was above tall trees, left foot to the stop, spinning right, and to make matters worse, I was now beginning to lose height. Instinct made me pull up more on the collective, but this just increased the spin rate. I had to make a decision very, very quickly before we hit the trees—was I going to roll off the throttle and settle into the trees as directed by the flight manual? Yes or no? I am not sure where my next action came from, but the option of deliberately crashing was too much to bear.

I eased in some forward cyclic and unloaded the collective a little. It was a gamble, but I wondered if I could regain some control by getting the chopper into forward flight—like a weathervane effect. The trees were very close beneath me, but they did fall away slightly from the shallow ridge line—I might just have enough height.

Moving the cyclic forward meant the aircraft started to do forward spirals rather than spinning on the spot and I managed to get some airflow over the fuselage. Unbelievably, it worked. Just prior to the skids hitting the trees, I regained forward flight, the left pedal came off the stops and there was that wonderful shudder of translational lift. We flew away from the trees. There was complete silence over the intercom. The crewman was the first to speak, 'what the [bleep] was that?'

Lessons Learned:

I felt physically sick. I had just escaped what almost certainly would have been a catastrophic accident with fatalities, and it would have been my fault. We did a wide level circuit to talk about things, check the aircraft configuration and settle my heart rate down. We noted the OAT had increased at least 10 degrees since we had started this morning and the wind was now quite a strong easterly. This accounted for using more left pedal on the NE approach to avoid weathercocking and using more power than before. The touch of left pedal to avoid the tree was the last straw, and we had exited the controlled flight environment. Luckily, it wasn't a permanent exit.

NOTES:

INTEGRATION OF THE VUICHARD RECOVERY

MH-60 SEA HAWK, UNITED STATES NAVY, HSC-25 HELICOPTER SEA COMBAT SQUADRON 25

LCDR John Edwards, Nov 2019

Vortex Ring State (VRS) is a serious hazard to helicopters operating at high descent rates and low forward air speeds. The MH-60R Naval Aviation Training and Operating Procedures Standardization (NATOPS) describes VRS as "an aerodynamic condition where a helicopter may be in a vertical descent with maximum power applied and little or no cyclic authority." This loss of lift and reduction in cyclic authority is caused by the vortices producing large areas of turbulent flow over the blades. The turbulent air disrupts the flow over the blades resulting in a serious reduction of usable lift.

The H-60 is susceptible to these effects at descent rates greater than 700 feet per minute (fpm) and airspeeds 0 - 20 knots indicated airspeed (KIAS). The condition is worse when approaching descents in excess of 1,500 fpm with 5 - 10 KIAS. The crew begins to experience oscillations and aircraft vibrations as the rotor disk is buffeted with its own vortices. The corrective action provided by NATOPS is:

• Decrease collective pitch.
• Increase forward airspeed.
• Enter autorotation if altitude permits.

VRS occurs when the rotor system begins to ingest its own vortices and thus settles down within its own wake. The result is a rapid descent without adequate thrust to counter the descent. If left uncorrected, helicopters can develop descent rates of more than 6,000 fpm with little to no cyclic authority despite maintaining 100 percent rotor rpm (Nr). The result of this condition can lead to a total loss of aircraft and crew.

The MH-60R community utilizes NATOPS, standard operating procedures (SOP) and maneuver description guides (MDG) to avoid flight profiles that can lead to VRS. Despite these controls, there is still a very real threat posed by this treacherous condition given the nature of our shipboard operating procedures, landing profiles and dipping operations. The current corrective procedures in use by the Navy, while effective when there is altitude to enter an autorotation, are not ideal for the profiles in which MH-60R helicopters are most likely to experience VRS. Therefore, there is a critical need to adopt a procedure more suited to low altitude recovery from VRS.

NATOPS also states "a considerable loss of altitude may occur before the condition is recognized and recovery is complete. During approach for landing, conditions causing vortex ring state should be avoided." Unfortunately, MH-60R crews are more likely to be in a steep and slow profile near the ground rather than at an altitude sufficient to execute the published procedure.

The key to recovering from VRS is to escape from the recirculating airflow. We can look to other communities and industries to see what other viable methods exist for VRS recovery. Claude Vuichard, a Swiss flight inspector and flight examiner, developed an alternate recovery procedure while flying high altitude helicopter operations in the Swiss Alps. The Vuichard recovery utilizes tail rotor thrust and the upward flow of the vortex to slide the helicopter out of VRS. For counter-clockwise rotating helicopters (MH-60R included) the procedure is based on two relatively simple steps:

- Increase collective to climb power while simultaneously applying left pedal to keep the nose straight.
- Displace cyclic right (10-20 degrees bank angle).

The maneuver is completed when the advancing rotor blade reaches clean up-flow. According to the United States Helicopter Safety Team, the average loss of altitude when executing the Vuichard recovery is 20-50 feet.

Lessons Learned:

The MH-60R and MH-60S are expected to operate in low altitude environments that require rapid decelerations and descents into confined landing sites or dip points. Crew in both airframes are trained to and well versed in preventative procedures to avoid VRS. However, when operating under adverse or chaotic operational environments it is easy for crews to place the aircraft into dangerous profiles. This procedure allows crews to have an out when they are most vulnerable to entering VRS – near the ground while executing dynamic operational maneuvers. The H-60 has a large and powerful tail rotor that is capable of providing a significant amount of sideward thrust to slide out of VRS. Commercial operators already have adopted the Vuichard Recovery -- the military will benefit from this procedure given the nature of our flight profiles and the relevance of low altitude recovery.

Videos online — https://vrasf.org/techniques

NOTES:

CHAPTER 3

WIRES

"If God had wanted man to fly, He would have given him olive drab fire-resistant skin and pockets with zippers."

Unknown US Army Helicopter Pilot

LONGBOW WIRE STRIKE

AH-64D , UNITED STATES ARMY, ARMY AIRCRAFT ACCIDENT PREVENTION

Name withheld by request, July 2019

Mishap crew members were conducting training operations in support of an armored division. The mishap crew was part of a four-aircraft mission supporting the ground commander while providing attack by fire (ABF) support for a breach force.

Crew members conducted mission planning and a risk assessment and the mission was approved. While conducting the mission, aircrew members were utilizing their pilot night vision systems, night vision goggles, and the target acquisition and designation system.

The PC was seated in the back seat utilizing flight symbology during the mishap phase. A system failure in the laser system required the mishap aircraft, Gun 1, to move forward of the ABF ridge line and manually pass target information to Gun 2.

As the battle developed, Gun 1 maneuvered to seek cover and concealment from enemy forces. While doing so, the Gun 1 PC maneuvered the aircraft while instructing the pilot (PI) to stay inside and maintain situational awareness on the enemy targets. The PC was concerned with Gun 2's location, so he remained outside, looking over his shoulder even though Gun 2 had called clear of Gun 1.

After Gun 1 rolled out of consecutive turns, the PI of the aircraft announced wires just prior to impacting extra-high-voltage transmission lines. The aircraft made a forced landing, impacting the ground. There were no injuries to crew members.

Crew

The PC had 2,733 hours in mission, type, design, and series (MTDS), and 2,813 hours total time. The PI had 411 hours in MTDS and 495 hours total time.

Lessons Learned:

The aircraft struck wires due to the PC being fixated on "gaining visual contact" with Gun 2 while Gun 2 had called clear and no factor. The PC failed to maintain airspace surveillance as directed in the aircrew training module (ATM). Additionally, crew members hadn't properly managed their crew endurance and did not have hazard data information in the aircraft.

A culmination of deviations from standard operating procedures and the ATM led to the transmission line mishap.

Even with the state-of-the-art information systems available on Army aircraft and the systems available for operational planning, errors can still lead to mishaps. It is important for commanders and leaders to maintain situational awareness of what is occurring in their units in relation to how accurately aircrew members are managing their crew endurance, application of base ATM standards (airspace surveillance), and the basics of pre-mission flight planning.

In our high operational tempo decisive action training environments, the culmination of deviations from standard is an easy indicator of the lead-up to a mishap.

While leaders have oversight, the crews are at the sharp end and responsible for keeping leaders informed so they can make risk decisions based on the most accurate information. Studies demonstrate that personnel exhibiting fatigue tend to fixate on cognitive tasks and their ability to address multiple tasks is reduced. Additionally, crew member monitoring may help personnel effectively spot the first signs of fatigue.

Crews are eager to execute the mission and it is paramount they don't let this desire to execute dampen their actual endurance and flight time tracking which results in leaders not having the correct information to use in risk assessing the crew for the mission.

NOTES:

CHAPTER 4

PROCEDURE

"A helicopter is piloted with precision and not by chance."

Unknown.

THE LAST OF THE HUNG MADS

MH-60B, UNITED STATES NAVY, HSM-49, HELICOPTER MARITIME STRIKE SQUADRON 49

LTJG Stephen Bauchman, February 2016

On a beautiful day in sunny San Diego our crew planned to launch on a CASEX event to track a friendly submarine. We were to work with a MH-60R squadron to localize and track our fictitious foe.

As one of the oldest rotary wing platforms still in the fleet, the venerable SH-60B Seahawk still had numerous anti-submarine warfare capabilities — one of those being technology first developed during WWI, the Magnetic Anomaly Detector (MAD). Essentially this system, when fully deployed, trails behind and below our aircraft by approximately 200 feet. It assists in tracking submarines by detecting any abnormal magnetic anomalies in relation to the Earth's magnetic field (it detects giant metal objects in the water if we fly over them).

Our event was progressing as normal, starting the aircraft, departing from home field, Naval Air Station North Island (NASNI), transiting and gaining communications with con-trolling agencies. As soon as we arrived on station and checked in, we conducted our combat checklist to include streaming the MAD.

After the MAD reeling machine finished running through its cycle, we noticed a flickering MAD LIMIT advisory light on our caution/advisory panel indicating that the MAD had stopped at an intermediate position. At no time during this cycle did we get any indications in the cockpit that the reeling machine was not operating and streaming normally. As we waited for the 15 minute time limit between MAD reeling machine cycles, as required per NATOPS, we re-checked our checklists to ensure we had not botched this operation. During this sanity check we continued to prosecute the ASW problem at hand, notified the other aircraft involved, and the range controller of our disabled state.Unfortunately, due to other system degradations aside from the MAD, we quickly became limited to only delivering buoys in this problem. We decided to deconflict and pull ourselves out of the ASW problem while we continued to troubleshoot. We executed the MAD REEL MACHINE FAILURE WITH TOWED BODY emergency procedure. After taking the appropriate actions with no success, we tried to see if we could reel the MAD back in one last time before we returned to base. As we reeled the MAD in, one of our aircrew monitored from the cabin door to see if he could tell whether or not there was any movement. When our troubleshooting proved to be unsuccessful with the MAD still deployed approximately 40 feet, we began our coordination with the range controller to return to base. Using plain language, we explained what was going on with our aircraft (that we did not have a 'dipper') and to get into contact with our squadron duty officer to relay the status of the aircraft.

Although we never officially declared an emergency, we were fortunate to be given priority handling. Each controlling agency was extremely helpful in providing us with whatever as required. FACSFAC (Fleet Area Control and Surveillance Facility) was already aware of our situation before we checked in due to our previous coordination with the range.

Upon contacting NASNI Tower, we found them ready for our recovery. Tower assigned us the 'lost communications' pad at the approach end of Runway 36 where our Safety Team and Maintenance Personnel were awaiting for our arrival. NASNI personnel were very helpful in coordinating with our squadron to sit in a high hover over the beach line away from other runway and pad traffic until we were conned in to recover. We gained radio communications with our squadron personnel on deck and waited for them to signal us that they were ready. During the transit, we discussed how we would recover and what possible scenarios and conditions awaited us.

As we waited in a high hover, we went over our plan once more. The HAC was going to take the approach in the right seat (the side the MAD and our door was on) while I backed him up on instruments and aircraft parameters. Meanwhile one of our aircrew would be monitoring outside of the aircraft, similar to a VERTREP mission, and keep an eye on the MAD as our LSE signalled us. Once the ground team was ready and Tower cleared us to land, we slowly descended over the appropriate spot. Ground personnel did a great job in hooking the MAD cable and maintaining positive control of the MAD as we sidestepped and continued down into a low hover, eventually landed with the MAD towed array body just outside of our aircraft. We shut down on deck and maintenance personnel safely removed the MAD bird and cable.

Lessons Learned:

During the post flight maintenance inspection, we deter-mined that our hung MAD was caused by a pinched cable at the reeling machine. When the MAD was streaming out, the wires in the cable could not read how far the MAD was away from the aircraft. Unfortunately, this wasn't anything that could have been fixed in flight. Our emergency was rather benign, yet it had the potential to manifest into something more serious. Crew Resource Management was hands down the driving factor behind our success in keeping the emergency benign.

We used the resources available to us, both external and internal to our aircraft. It was unusual to have two aircrew on this type of flight, but it was advantageous to have one monitoring the external towed body of the MAD and communicate what he was seeing to the crewman and pilots in the aircraft. We were able to flex easily to the plan tower created with our squadron personnel for recovery.

One of the most helpful things was to have a pilot coordinating with maintenance personnel on the ground as well as with us in the aircraft. As pilots, especially helicopter second pilots and prospective aircraft commanders, we are constantly practicing scenarios in mock-HAC boards and it was a real opportunity to actually fly through an emergency with a crew instead of just drawing it up on a whiteboard or talk through it in a simulator. It is also rare that plane captains ever get to experience this kind of aircraft emergency. Overall solid CRM and real time risk management kept the last hung MAD in the history of the SH-60B Seahawk from becoming anything more than a delayed hot seat.

NOTES:

NO FAST HANDS

UH-1Y VENOM, UNITED STATES MARINE CORPS, MARINE LIGHT ATTACK HELICOPTER SQUADRON 269

CAPT Jason Cullen, February 2014

We practice emergency procedures (EPs) in the simulator, and sometimes we even know when they'll be inserted into the scenario. Afterward, we usually discuss how relatively routine emergencies can become a big deal under complicating circumstances, such as flying at night or over water. What happened to us on a nice night in August was exactly what we had discussed following one of our EP practice sessions: a heavy aircraft, flying as wingman, using night vision goggles and over water.

The night had started out well.

We briefed a night, terrain-navigation flight followed by section confined area landings (CALs). We reviewed the weight and power numbers and had a nice power margin in our UH-1Y Yankee. There was a short delay on launch as we waited for the AH-1W Cobra crew to troubleshoot a faulty starter in their aircraft.

While they worked on the Cobra, we took the Yankee out for a few laps in the local pattern.

After taxiing back to the line, we assumed the wingman position with the Cobra as the lead. We followed them out for power checks on the midfield taxiway. Everything checked out, and we even had a little more power during our hover checks than we had calculated.

With a warm and fuzzy feeling about our aircraft's performance margin, the lead aircraft called for a present-position takeoff, and we departed the airfield.

Our route took us over the New River to North East Creek Bridge, which is a VFR course-rules reporting point. Passing the bridge at 1,000 feet MSL, the aircraft commander passed controls to me in the left seat. I began to slide our Yankee out to the cruise position on the left side of lead's aircraft. Just as we stabilized in position, I heard the unmistakable sound of a turbine engine increasing speed. This drew my attention inside the cockpit just as the aircraft computer figured out what was going on.

A litany of caution alerts began to pop up on the video display, and the aural alerting system began barking "Rotor rpm" in my ears. It took me a moment to sort through all the information and figure out what was going on.

In the Yankee, the initial indications of over speeds, under speeds and engine flameouts are remarkably similar (the one exception is main rotor speed or "Nr").

These three situations look similar because of the digital electronic control unit (DECU), whose main function is torque-matching between the two engines. Under normal conditions, the DECU matches the torque loads on the two engines. When there is a mismatch in power output between the two engines (overspeed, under speed, or engine flameout), the DECU system signals the engine still under DECU control to increase or decrease power in an effort to maintain a constant supply of power to the transmission and main rotor.

Because these issues look so similar on the engine performance gauges, the best indicator to use when deciphering between them is Nr.

In an overspeed situation, which is what we had, the over

speeding engine redlines and the controlled engine reduces power, causing the performance gauges to look like the controlled engine has dropped to idle (easily mistaken for an under speed situation on the controlled engine).

Identifying abnormal Nr (high or low) is the best way to differentiate between overspeed and under speed.

In an overspeed situation, Nr will be high, but during an under speed it will remain constant or begin to droop (depending on single-engine power available). Because of this, we are taught to always reference Nr before taking immediate-action steps, because we could possibly shut down a good engine if we execute the wrong EP.

In our cockpit that night, crew resource management (CRM) instantly kicked in. We task-shed external communication responsibilities to lead (who declared an emergency with ATC and got us an immediate clearance to land) and began to diagnose the issue. We completed our immediate-action steps and got the over speeding engine rolled back to idle. We were relieved to see the DECU work as advertised, with the good engine assuming the torque load.

We had tried to use the over speeding engine in manual fuel-control mode, but it would not stabilize. We decided to keep it at idle instead of flying all the way back to the field with over speeding Nr. Once we knew we could maintain stable, powered flight, we began to figure out our landing plan.

Although we took off with sufficient power to land dual-engine, we had more than 2,000 pounds of fuel remaining, which put us nearly 700 pounds over our single-engine hover weight. I reminded the aircraft commander of this, and we agreed that a slide-on landing would be the safest profile.

We set up the helicopter for a long, shallow straight in approach and touched down on the runway at just under 30 knots ground speed. Other than some sparks flying from the skid shoes during the slide, the landing was uneventful.

Lessons Learned:

Adhering to our training saved us a lot of heartache that night. I distinctly remember hearing the voice of Col. Spencer (one of our civilian simulator instructors, and a former AH-1W pilot and HMLA squadron and MAG commanding officer) in my head calmly telling me to look at Nr before I did anything else. Had I not first pulled that crucial bit of information, we may have wasted precious time fighting a nonexistent EP, instead of quickly resolving our issue and getting the helicopter back on deck.

NOTES:

BRIEFING BETWEEN THE LINES
MH-60S SEAHAWK, UNITED STATES NAVY, HSC-8, HELICOPTER SEA COMBAT SQUADRON 8

LT Jacob Kyzer, August 2015

If hindsight is 20/20, I would surmise that the visual acuity achieved following the completion of my flight brief was in the neighborhood of 20/400. Unfortunately, the corrective lenses that were my brief left both aircrews feeling much clearer and more comfortable than our experience, knowledge or proficiency would dictate. We were flying blind, but no one would realize this until we were able to sink comfortably into our Monday morning quarterback armchair and actually examine the breakdown between the plan and execution. Needless to say, there was much left to be desired.

For this particular flight, our mission was to link up with the CAST/HRST master schoolhouse to obtain numerous qualifications for their students going through the syllabus (CAST/HRST is Navy Helicopter Rope Suspension Training including rappelling with descending devices and fast-roping and special patrol insertion/extraction). As was usual for these types of flights, the coordination and mission specifics were left to the copilots, in this case I, another JO (Junior Officer) and a point of contact provided through operations. With less than six months into our fleet tour, we were experienced enough to know that no special operations plan ever survives first contact with the HRST master or the "good idea fairy."

Our initial plan was to draw as much information as we could from our point of contact, utilize that information to formulate our plan and brief, then any gaps would be filled in with our anticipated most likely course of action. This would cover us for the aircrew side of the house, and any discrepancies could later be identified and dealt with during our round table HRST Brief, with all parties involved.

From square one, this was shaping up to be a challenging flight. The information obtained from our POC gave us the following game plan: the HRST/CAST master students would arrive at the hangar two hours early to brief, and upon completion, walk onto the flight line to begin rigging both aircraft for the evolutions. Both aircraft were to be loaded for combat rubber raiding craft (CRRC) deployments: one aircraft would have a CRRC strapped to the underbelly via the cargo net restraint (known as a K-duck deployment); the other would have a rolled up CRRC in the cabin (known as a rolled duck). Both aircraft would transit to an area located south of Coronado Bridge, deploy their respective CRRCs and then CAST five students each from a 10 foot, 10 knot creep. The helicopters would then depart, return, and recover the students via the 20 foot special operations ladder or rescue hoist. In the case of aircraft, the intent was to have two students rig the CRRC for a cargo net recovery and then transport the CRRC and students to Turner Field located at the nearby naval amphibious base for offload. After offload, the aircraft would be configured for three evolutions of wet SPIE (special patrol insertion/extraction) rig extraction, which would require the aircraft to CAST five students into a body of water, and then extract them from the water with a 120-foot SPIE rope over to Turner Field.

From the purview of my armchair, this is the point where planning and preparation began to deteriorate. The initial questions that arose from our conversation with the POC (Point Of Contact) were threefold: what the heck is a rolled duck deployment, what the heck is a cargo net recovery of a CRRC and how the heck are we going to knock out all these requirements in a three-hour evolution? Eager to learn, we immediately set off into the pubs to find the answers to the first and second questions. With the help of a three-step procedure from NTRP (Navy tactical reference publications) and the knowledge of our local special weapons and tactics instructor (SWTI) pilot, we were able to determine what common sense had already suggested to us. A Rolled Duck was a deflated, folded CRRC that would be rolled out of the left cabin door from a 10 foot, 10 knot creep; easy enough. For the K-Duck, the SEAWOLF supplied a full set of procedures, complete with crew assignments, actions, and Intercommunications System (ICS) calls.

Reading through the procedures, the evolution seemed easy enough. The aircraft would be positioned above the CRRC in a coupled hover. Once stable, the cargo net would be secured around the CRRC. While two team members work on securing the CRRC, the three others would be hoisted into the helicopter. With the CRRC ready for recovery, the crew chief would connect a 60 foot pendant rope to the cargo hook, lower it through the aircraft's hell hole, and the pilot would then position the aircraft over the CRRC for hookup. Once the personnel in the water attached the pendant, they would be hoisted into the aircraft. The aircraft would then lift the CRRC out of the water, and transport it to Turner Field.

Since the consensus was that this procedure was foreign to all members of the crew, we briefed our helicopter aircraft commanders (HACs) and the aircrew on the procedures. All parties felt that we would be able to accomplish the tasking. To make sure all members of both crews were on the same page, we also included the step by step cargo net recovery procedures as a slide in our flight brief. During the brief, I made a point to note these procedures, but only opted to have everyone read over their responsibilities. I also delivered a minimal summary of how I envisioned the recovery evolution taking place, and was met with no questions or amplifying remarks from any members of the crew.

Since there were members of the crew who were unfamiliar with Turner Field (myself included), I also included an overhead satellite image of the helo pad, so everyone was oriented to our drop off location, and potential obstacles in the area (mainly a few palm trees and a chain link fence on approach). The information I presented was gleaned almost in full from the satellite imagery. With all questions answered, we then shifted to the HRST/cast master's briefing. We were able to iron out some details with a few minor changes, but nothing that we felt was unmanageable. Toward the end of the brief, my HAC commented that no one here had done a cargo net recovery, but noted that the procedures seemed simple enough. The HRST/Cast Master mentioned that he had numerous challenges in the past with this type of recovery due to the rotor wash pushing the CRRC through the water, as well as difficulties positioning the CRRC while it was attached to the pendant and simultaneously hoisting personnel. Though we noted these comments, at no point did this spur any further discussion on how we planned to approach and execute the CRRC recovery.

The rigging and aircraft start was met with minor hitches but eventually we were able to depart from Naval Air Station North Island and transit quickly over to the operating area. We immediately went into our K-Duck and cast evolution, inserting the CRRC and five personnel from our low creep. Once all personnel and equipment were inserted in the water, we established an overhead orbit to allow time for the personnel to rig the cargo net around the CRRC. With the go-ahead given from the safety boat personnel we established ourselves in a 70 foot hover into the wind.

The procedures called for engaging hover mode at this time, but unfortunately, when I called for it, the aircraft would not establish a coupled hover. We troubleshooted for a few seconds before the HAC (Helicopter Aircraft Commander) opted to engage the BARALT (Barometric Altitude) hold and let me hold the hover. We were so focused on the personnel and boat in the water, that at no time did anyone suggest we troubleshoot further prior to proceeding. I would spend the rest of this evolution task saturated and focused on which severely degraded my SA. Strike one. Now hovering over our personnel, we hoisted the first three swimmers into the aircraft. Once this was complete, our crew chief lowered the pendant through the hell hole and it was time to position the aircraft for the CRRC recovery. This is where the fun really began.

Not wanting to overshoot the CRRC, I slowly worked to position the aircraft overhead with the two personnel standing onboard waiting to receive the pendant. Shockingly, the boat did exactly what the HRST master and Seawolf Manual said it would: it got blown away by the rotor downwash. I steadily worked toward the boat, and it steadily worked away. This went on for a good 30 seconds before our crew chief finally called me out, telling me that if I didn't get more airspeed we would never get over the CRRC. Thank goodness for that call, otherwise I would have eventually blown the CRRC enough to beach it on the nearby strand. In hindsight that probably would have been the quicker and safer method of CRRC recovery.

Determined to make sure I got the aircraft over the CRRC without pushing it on the next attempt, I flew over the boat at 15 knots. The crew chief then notified me that I had almost yanked one of the hook-up men off the CRRC as he grabbed the pendant attached to our rapidly overshooting helicopter. The third attempt was the charm, as we found a happy medium speed of approximately 10 knots, which allowed us to safely position the aircraft and get the cargo net hooked up. During an after action review, it was noted that the aircraft should drag the sling/pendant over the CRRC at 10 knots. Though we read through these procedures prior to the flight, this number was apparently never internalized during study or the brief. Ultimately, this could have led to the injury of the hook up men trying to connect the boat. Strike two.

With the CRRC now attached to the aircraft's cargo hook, it was time to hoist the two hook-up personnel out of the water. In the mass brief, the HRST master told us that the best way he had seen to position the aircraft was to put the CRRC in front of the aircraft, or out to the 9-10 o'clock position so the boat would be visible, but out of the way of the hoist. Our first challenge was that we were looking into the sunset and could not see the personnel. Eventually, we found one out at our 3 o'clock position. Between listening to North Island tower, the HRST Teams safety boat frequency, my HAC, and both aircrew on ICS, I was completely overloaded on comms. Couple that with holding a hover and the completely new and less than fluid evolution I found myself completely task saturated.

At this point, I started receiving positioning calls from literally every member of the crew, and many of them were conflicting: Crew Chief, "Left five!", second Aircrewman "Right ten!".

Maintaining what little composure I had left, I told them I was getting conflicting calls. We were able to position ourselves to make the recovery of the swimmer we had in sight, but there was still mass confusion as to where the second swimmer was, and a log jam of position calls being made. At this point, the HAC attempted to take control by angrily stating that we did not have the swimmer in sight and that we needed better calls from the back. The second aircrewman then notified us that he had the swimmer in sight off the nose and that he needed the nose to come left. Voice activated at this point, I immediately complied and was through approximately 45 degrees of pedal turn to the left when my HAC's shouting voice emerged over the ICS unleashing a profanity laced barrage of commands and critiques that I will simply sum up as "Stop! That will turn us out of the winds. Position the CRRC on the left, and then we will move forward and hoist the swimmer on the right." Unfortunately, instead of taking a time out and calmly telling that to everyone, the HAC managed to take an extremely volatile situation and escalate it further. The recovery portion of this evolution to this day represents the worst CRM breakdown that I have seen in my aviation career. After the flight, the Crew Chief mentioned during debrief that the plan he had discussed with the second aircrewman was that he would make all the calls relating to the CRRC, and that the second aircrewman would make all calls relating to the hoisting. At no point were the pilots notified of this plan. This contributed directly to the conflicting calls that were made to the flying pilot. Also, the Seawolf procedure states, "The aircraft should be positioned quickly to recover remaining swimmers to prevent the CRRC from being blown off position". It does not say how or where to position the aircraft in relation to the CRRC, and we never discussed how we would do it in the brief. This again could have easily led to injury to personnel, damage to the aircraft, or even a mishap. Big strike three.

With all personnel recovered and the CRRC hooked up, it was time to extract the boat from the water and transport it to Turner Field. At this point, the evolution transitioned from Cast and Recovery, to Vertical Replenishment (VERTREP) procedures and techniques. Per our Standard Operating Procedure (SOP), the requirement for the first pick of the day is to note the height at which the load cleared the deck (in this case the water). This altitude is then used to establish the desired crossing altitude for dropping of the load. Unfortunately, neither pilot noted when the CRRC left the water. No problem though, I knew from the pubs that the pendant was 60 feet long and that our standard was to clear the highest obstacle by 20 feet.

Happy to find a math problem I could complete in my head, I verbalized the pendant and crossing height to the crew and stated that I would level off at 80 feet AGL for the drop. No dissension was noted from any member of the crew, and the HAC even stated that sounded right. I rolled on final for my approach at the briefed 80 feet and as I approached the water's edge, and the start of the landing pad, I received a very pointed "Up!" call from the Crew Chief. Not wanting to yank in a ton of power with the boat attached to the aircraft, I made a small collective input to increase our altitude. That input was immediately met with a second and much more urgent "UP!" call from the Crew Chief. Again I made a second collective increase and felt an aft cyclic input from my HAC. The Crew Chief then called the load clear, and we placed it in the grass field adjacent to the helo pad. At this point, I had no idea how close we had come to a very bad situation.

Being the 21st Century, I was able to get video footage of the drop evolution at Turner Field from the vantage point of the helo pad. I was shocked to note that as we made our final approach, the CRRC completely disappeared below the fence line. I was also able to note that the CRRC was not riding flat (as I had pictured it in my head). The CRRC was almost standing straight up and down in the cargo net, easily adding 10 feet to the length. Couple that with the fact that the helo pad at Turner field is approximately 20 feet above the waterline, and it does not take rocket science to figure out why the aircraft was in such a bad position.

What happened that day ended up being the *best* case scenario. The *worst* case scenario would have been snagging the CRRC and cargo net in the fence, at minimum damaging equipment and facilities, and at the max resulting in a mishap. With this information in mind, the appropriate altitude calculation would have gone something like this: 70 feet for when the CRRC cleared the water, 20 feet for the elevation at Turner Field, and 20 feet for the desired obstacle clearance for a 110 foot approach altitude. That thirty foot discrepancy was the result of not following our VERTREP procedures, and an insufficient brief and in flight recon of the drop area. Strikes 4 and 5.

For you baseball fans out there, we should have been out a long time ago.

Lessons Learned:

The flight continued on, and ultimately terminated in the middle of the Special Patrol Insertion/Extraction evolution (which was not a cake walk in and of itself) due to weather. We returned home and took to debriefing, going over all the points I have presented here.

As I took time to reflect on the flight in the days and weeks after, I could not help being upset at myself for the mistakes that I made. All of them seemed so careless, obvious, and simple to fix if we as a crew had briefed more efficiently, and then just slowed down and communicated better in flight. Though nothing catastrophic occurred, the opportunities for damage to equipment, injury to personnel, and even a mishap were abundantly present. The biggest problems I saw were that there were numerous deviations from procedures and flying without a plan. No mission is ever perfect, but if you have solid procedures and a solid plan, you have the base foundation to fall back on when the impending meltdown occurs. My challenge to you is to identify what is important when you brief a mission. Don't just check the boxes that comprise a standard whiteboard brief. Know when something is foreign, be willing to admit that it is foreign, and then be willing to break out the paper and crayons to draw out a step by step picture of what you expect to happen. If you are the person listening, do not be afraid to tell the drawer that their crayon picture is confusing or does not make sense, because as you can see from above, the aircraft is not the place to hash it out.

NOTES:

GIVE IT ANOTHER LOOK

AH-1W SUPER COBRA, UNITED STATES MARINE CORPS, MARINE LIGHT ATTACK HELICOPTER SQUADRON 269

CAPT Benjamin Carlton, June 2014

Procedures are in place for a reason, usually because aviators learned lessons the hard way and adopted procedures to ensure mistakes are not repeated. The little things most aircrew do typically have either a safety or performance component to them, even if it's just a way to mentally prepare for a flight. Habits you learned during flight school and the FRS shouldn't disappear after you become the person in charge of an aircraft.

It was a nice January day in North Carolina, and I was testing an AH-1W after it had come out of phase maintenance. This helicopter had been in a test status for a few weeks, and had given maintenance a fair amount of trouble. Just when you thought the aircraft was going to be in good working condition, something unrelated would break. Progress had been made over the previous couple weeks and there were only a couple flight regimes left to verify before that bird was back on the flight schedule.

If you hear it from them, a maintainer's job is to fix the aircraft that the reckless pilots break. So naturally, as a pilot, you relish every opportunity to sign off a downing gripe and create another up aircraft. There was no rush to get the bird back on the flight schedule. We still had plenty of aircraft available to meet the flight schedule and have backups. We also were at home in coastal Carolina and not in a place where the squadron was supporting troops in contact with the enemy.

The morning went well, and after two runs the main rotor was in track and balance. The only thing left to do was to verify that all the vibrations were within limits and check that the rotor would build turns in an autorotation. I took off with a crew chief in the front seat and flew the relatively benign maneuvers necessary to complete the tests: straight and level at 120 knots followed by a constant speed autorotation where I recovered by 700 feet.

After completion, I headed back to home field believing I would sign off the completed test card. The flight seemed normal, and the crew chief and I were confident we would be done testing as soon as we landed. Neither of us noticed any abnormal control feedback or heard anything out of the ordinary.

When landing, the crew chief loaded the disk used to record the vibrations to verify everything was within limits before the bird was secured for the evening. I talked with Quality Assurance to let them know how things were progressing. Looking at the flight data, they discovered one of the regimes didn't record any information, and we would have to fly again to ensure the test had passed. The crew chief grabbed a couple of new floppy disks, and we headed back out on the flight line to give it another run.

I told the plane captain what we needed to do and started climbing into the cockpit to take off. I realized I hadn't done a walk-around and paused momentarily to debate if it was necessary. No adjustments had been made to the main rotor head, and no maintenance had been done on the plane. I had landed only 15 to 20 minutes earlier, and I was sure everything was exactly as I had left it. But having heard stories of mishaps that happened because people failed to do a proper walk-around and because like most, I'm a creature of habit, I climbed down to inspect the bird one last time.

The plane captain saw what I was doing and ran ahead to help speed up the process. He was a few panels ahead of me when he said, "Sir, you should probably come look at this."

I walked over and looked at the cowling between the engines. There was a screw embedded in the cowling above the tail-rotor drive shaft, flush with the carbon-fibre panel. It was obvious that it had lodged itself with a great deal of force. We looked down the drive shaft for signs of a missing fastener or damage to the drive shaft, but we couldn't find any evidence indicating where the screw had come from. Expanding our search to the rest of the aircraft led us to discover a missing screw from the left side of the aircraft above the engine cowling. We couldn't figure out how it could have struck where it did.

After more examination, we found two small holes in the tail rotor. Somehow the screw had done its best magic-bullet impression, crossing in flight from the left side of the aircraft to the right, where it struck the tail rotor. Then it must have propelled forward before embedding into the carbon-fibre splitter cowling that lies between the engine exhausts.

Lessons Learned:

Things happen in aviation even when everyone does their job correctly. The forces put on the airframe itself and the natural vibration caused by rotating parts put stress on the aircraft's components, which may eventually cause them to break. This is why we have inspections — formal and informal.

Most people in the military want to do their jobs well and finish in a timely manner to make sure readiness remains high. However, when people rush to finish a job or change habit patterns to save a little time, the potential exists for vital steps to be missed or for people to see what they expect or want to see.

If I hadn't conducted the walk-around, the screw could have dislodged and been flung across the flight line, possibly injuring a Marine or worse. The damage to the aircraft could have become more severe and caused a mishap.

Nothing we do in training is worth putting the safety of anyone in jeopardy. Take the time to verify things have been done properly and the necessary inspections have been completed.

NOTES:

THE SWIMMER JUST FELL

MH-60S SEAHAWK, UNITED STATES NAVY, HSC-8, HELICOPTER SEA COMBAT SQUADRON 8

LT Rebekah Cranor, October 2014

That's what I heard over ICS, along with shouts and swear words from the back, then a radio call from the other aircraft a few seconds later; "I think someone fell from your aircraft."

The flight was a dual-ship SAR jump in the Gulf of Oman. The skipper was in the lead aircraft, and the squadron safety officer and I was Dash 2. Part of our deliberate ORM for the event was putting the skipper and the safety Officer as the HACs.

The other copilot and I spoke with the HACs and formulated a simple plan. We would rotate through swimmers and hoist operators while conducting simultaneous jumps with the two aircraft a safe distance away from each other.

On the day of the jumps, we completed a NATOPS and ORM brief, which included discussing the order of events and known hazards. We headed out dual-ship to our assigned area, cleared the area, and set up to start the jumps. I sat right seat, the safety officer sat left seat, and we had six crewmen in the cabin.

The first few evolutions went smoothly. Both aircraft were

jumping at the same time; we were within sight of each other, but a safe distance away. The dedicated swimmers and hoist operators were rotating as assigned.

We had just jumped our five swimmers and elevated to a 70-foot hover. The hoist operator lowered the rescue hoist. The swimmer hooked up the first survivor, who happened to be our HM1 (a SAR medical technician). The hoist operator raised him, brought him into the cabin, and then lowered the hook for the second survivor. I didn't think anything of it at the time, but it took a long time for the swimmer to hook up the second survivor. After they were hooked up, we saw a thumbs-up from the swimmer. Everything looked normal from above.

The other aircraft had its FLIR on our swimmer and survivor. Later analysis of this video would reveal that the swimmer appeared to be in the wrong position coming up from the water, but we didn't notice anything. The swimmer and survivor were at the door when I heard shouts coming from the back of the aircraft. The hoist operator quickly said over ICS that the swimmer had fallen. The radio call from the other aircraft echoed the same. The left seat pilot moved our FLIR to the swimmer in the water and confirmed that he was face down in the water and wasn't moving.

I focused on keeping a steady hover and communicating with the hoist operator. The two swimmers still in the water swam towards our injured swimmer. Our hoist operator was an AWS3, so he traded spots with the HM1, who got ready to go down the hoist as the dedicated SAR swimmer. He threw on the hoist operator's helmet so he could get ready to lower the swimmer. However, he had just gotten out of the water, so water from his wet head intruded into the helmet microphone and shorted out the ICS; we had now lost ICS with our hoist operator.

He yelled, got our attention. He lowered our new dedicated swimmer down. The left seat pilot had been steadily providing updates on the swimmer who fell. The swimmers in the water moved him to his back and were holding him steady. We eventually could tell that he had regained consciousness.

The two HACs were communicating between both aircraft and back to the ship. After what seemed like an eternity, the swimmer gave us the signal for the rescue basket, which was lowered. As they situated the injured swimmer into the rescue basket, the HAC coordinated with the other aircraft to have them pick up our remaining swimmers. We wanted to depart as soon as the injured swimmer was in our aircraft and secured.

We saw the pickup signal. The hoist operator brought the injured swimmer into the basket, gave me back control up front, and secured the cabin. After the cabin was secured and ready for flight, we departed and bustered back to the carrier. The tower cleared us to land and we charlie'd on the spot. Between lost ICS and HM1 taking care of the survivor, the normal flow of communication from the back calling us into the spot wasn't there. That break in routine definitely threw me; I misjudged the height above deck and planted the aircraft a bit too firmly on the deck. Medical personnel moved the injured swimmer onto a stretcher and took him to medical.

The rest of the day was a blur. The carrier was in the middle of cyclic ops, so we had minimal time on deck. The HM1 went to medical with the injured swimmer, a new crew chief joined our flight crew, and we went back out to finish our plane guard line. Eventually, we made our way down to medical to fill out our own paperwork and have labs taken, as the situation was a possible mishap. The senior medical officer did the best he could to keep us updated on the injured swimmer as we waited in medical. After several hours, we were able to see our swimmer before he was transported to Bahrain for further evaluation and treatment. He was back on the ship a few days later with only minor injuries.

The flight had started out as one of the coolest flights I had done to date, yet it turned into the most nerve-racking flight I've ever experienced. As I was walking to medical after dropping off my gear,

I overheard the skipper telling CAG that this was exactly why we needed to keep practicing the basics.

Lessons Learned:

I took away several important lessons from this event. The first was an affirmation of how important it is to brief the flight and then fly that brief. For example, our "lost ICS" procedure worked flawlessly despite the stress of a dynamic emergency.

Many of our junior pilots had previously conducted "hangar flying" discussions with our aircrew about scenarios involving problems with the swimmer. In this case, there were other swimmers who could take care of our injured swimmer, but what would have happened if he was face down in the water after falling and the only other aircrew member was the hoist operator?

In the end, the AMB concluded that our swimmer failed to attach the rescue hook to his Tri-SAR harness; he just held onto the simulated survivor as they were being hoisted from the water. Although the swimmer had performed the hoisting procedure many times throughout his career, he didn't hook up. Why? Because he didn't want to be seen as a weak link, he violated a published procedure because he felt a perceived pressure to execute at a faster pace than the pace at which he was comfortable and proficient.

Aviators and aircrew have to be cautious about an over-reliance on past experience. Currency does not equal proficiency, and a training event is not valuable at the expense of a life.

NOTES:

A HOT UH-60M

UH-60M, UNITED STATES ARMY, ARMY AIRCRAFT ACCIDENT PREVENTION

Name Withheld, October 2018

The aircrew members began their duty day at 0730 upon arrival to the airfield. The mission support they would conduct was fast rope insertion / extraction system (FRIES) training with Army personnel. The crews conducted aircraft preflight and briefings in accordance with the unit SOP (standing operating procedure). While conducting the mission of supporting a ground unit FRIES training, the mishap aircraft was Chalk 2. During the first iteration of executing the FRIES insertion, the crew chief (CE) failed to follow the correct procedure in releasing the FRIES rope as detailed in the unit standing operating procedure (SOP). The CE released the FRIES rope but did not release the safety rope first. Subsequently, the CE failed to maintain surveillance. Because of this, he failed to see the FRIES master on the ground, signalling the FRIES rope was not free of the aircraft. As the aircraft departed the FRIES insertion location, the ropes rebounded from terrain contact into the aircraft main rotor system. The aircraft crashed into a wooded area with injuries to all onboard. A post crash fire destroyed the aircraft.

Crew

The pilot in command (PC) had 3,123 hours in mission design series (MDS) and 3,271 hours total time. The pilot had 73 hours in MDS and 159 hours total time. CE 1 had 146 hours in MTDS and as total time. CE 2 had 585 hours in MDS and as total time.

Lessons Learned:

When supporting missions which require systems that present flight hazards (external loads, ropes out the doors, static-line parachute operations, water bucket, etc.), crews must thoroughly brief the mission and cover critical points. In this instance, a critical point for conducting FRIES is the proper sequence of events once coming to stabilize at the insertion/extraction point (ropes out the door) through departure from the point.

As the crew members were completing the release post-insertion, the CE failed to follow established procedures, which resulted in damage to the main rotor system and the subsequent mishap because he didn't release the safety rope.

It is important for CEs to be trained to standard on the applicable mission sets the unit conducts. Human error failures result easily when the aircrew member fails to retain technical or procedural knowledge after training.

The crawl-walk-run method of Army training has served us well and mission rehearsals. But within the run phase, unit trainers must still reinforce the skills learned and spot check to verify aircrew members still understand and have the latest information on the task, are current for the task and conduct refresher training when necessary. Within this scope, unit and higher headquarters commanders are responsible to ensure they implement the Army approved methods for executing aviation METL tasks and these procedures are incorporated into their SOPs or they have an approved waiver providing for an alternate method.

A simple human error of not following established procedures (release safety then release FRIES rope) caused the loss of one aircraft and four seriously injured aircrew members. Commanders and aviation trainers are the first line of defense. Make sure your run-trained Soldiers are maintaining their proficiency in METL tasks and conduct refresher training regularly on those tasks which are conducted sporadically.

NOTES:

CHAPTER 5

WEATHER

"No sight is more welcome to a storm-damaged area than the fleet of rescue helicopters that magically appears immediately afterward."

Francis G. McGuire

COMBAT SEARCH AND RESCUE
PAVEHAWK HH-60G, UNITED STATES AIR FORCE, COMBAT SEARCH AND RESCUE (CSAR)

Capt Chad L. Summitt, April 2008

Before I get into my story, I need to give some background for those who don't know much about Air Force Combat Search and Rescue. The basic premise is that each service rescues its own people. However, if there are circumstances where one service turns down a mission, such as the Army when the moon illumination goes below 20 percent, then other services get tasked. That is when Air Force Combat Search and Rescue (CSAR) generally gets missions assigned, when it is very dark, the weather is very bad, or both. The CSAR motto is "These Things We Do ... That Others May Live." Very similarly, the Air Force Special Operations Command motto is "Anytime, Anyplace." Now, on to the story.

We had been in Iraq for about a week and were finishing the swap out between units. We were taking over the CSAR mission from a unit from another base. For this round of deployments, it was the initial one, which meant we had to bring in all our equipment, unpack, and set up everything. Because of this, we brought experienced crews. Most of us had not only previously deployed, but we deployed to this very location the year prior. Therefore, we had a solid experience base to establish our operating standards.

We had just finished our local-area familiarity flights and took over the alert schedule from the outgoing unit. It was our first night on alert, and the weather was degrading rapidly. Lightning was starting to flash all around, the winds were picking up, the tents were whipping around violently, and the dust was getting worse, resulting in degraded visibility. Walking around the compound, we joked with each other, saying, "Well, we have mission weather tonight." Sure enough, those words rang true.

Not too long after that, we got the call to heighten our alert posture. This means we send part of the crews to the helicopters to allow us to respond quicker. Usually when our units first take over the alert schedule, there is a practice scramble or alert scenario. This was in the back of our minds, but with the weather deteriorating the way it was, we were pretty sure something was going on. Soon after, we got the tasking from the Joint Search and Rescue Center to launch our crews to search for two Marine fighter pilots who'd had a midair collision. Due to the weather, we took a little longer than usual to take off, because we were making sure we had our game plan together. The weather then had winds exceeding 40 knots, low visibility due to a sandstorm, a thunderstorm in the area moving from west to east, and lightning striking all around. The field was IFR, but the visibility was acceptable, with the close cultural lighting around the base.

We caught the tower controller by surprise when we requested our "Special VFR" takeoff, but we were eventually cleared and off we went. We were a Pavehawk (HH-60G) two-ship, of which I was on the lead aircraft. We fly low-level, below 500 feet AGL most of the time, especially in combat. At night on NVGs, we typically fly around 125-150 feet, and this night was no different. The visibility worsened once we got away from the lights of the base and surrounding towns. Not five minutes after takeoff, I remember looking up from following our position on the map and not being able to see in front of the aircraft because of the blowing sand. However, when I looked down at the forward-looking infrared radar picture, I was still able to see the ground along our flight path. That gave me some relief, but just two minutes later, I couldn't see outside or on the FLIR picture. That was the first real uneasy feeling I experienced on the mission, and we were only seven minutes into the flight. I asked the engineer if he could still see the ground. At times he could, and at times he couldn't. Flying at 150 feet AGL with little to no visual references is not a comfortable feeling. It would be like flying less than 200 feet above the ground in clouds.

On top of a low-level, low-visibility formation flight, we also couldn't identify hazards until we were right on top of them. For anyone not familiar, Iraq has many power lines taller than 300 feet. I remember following along on the map and informing the crew of "wires" at several points along our route. Once we were within a half mile of the wires, I directed a climb to a sufficient altitude to clear them, and we wouldn't see the wires until we passed directly over them. After two or three sequences of climbing and descending to avoid power lines, we finally decided to fly at 500-700 feet to keep us clear of most obstacles. Plus, altitude really was not a factor in terms of being shot at, because there was little chance of any hostile forces seeing us in those weather conditions. Even at 500-700 feet, sometimes I could see the ground and sometimes I couldn't. Needless to say, it took the entire crew on both aircraft to safely execute and fly the mission.

The next significant event occurred when we had our first major turn on our course routing. It was not flown aggressively at all, but the course line turned left somewhere between 60 and 90 degrees. After we made the turn, our wingman, No. 2, asked us to slow down because they were having trouble keeping up. We slowed down 10 knots. A couple of minutes later, they said that they were still not catching us, and we slowed down another 10 knots. A few more minutes passed with the distance between us continuing to increase, and then the co-pilot on No. 2 said, "Hey Lead, I think we're in front of you."

Silence came over the radio at this point. How could our situational awareness have allowed this to happen? We have four crew members in the back of our helicopter, plus all the crew members on No. 2 who should continually have the other aircraft in sight. At this point, we decided to stay in the trail position at about 0.7 to one mile and continue to give position calls between each aircraft. We have the capability with our air-to-air TACAN to display the distance between aircraft, but it doesn't tell us where each aircraft is in relation to one another. That was the reason for the position calls.

Then we were over a fairly large lake and able to keep No. 2 in sight at 0.7 to one mile spacing. Once we crossed the lake and were back over land, we closed our spacing to maintain sight of one another as we approached the objective area to search. Unfortunately, the farther we went, the more desolate the area became. Flying across this featureless desert terrain, environmental conditions worsened, if you can believe that, and were such that there was near-zero effective illumination. We tried several different things, such as trolling at slower airspeeds and lower to the ground in an effort to do a better search. But we were having a hard enough time just seeing the ground directly below us, so we weren't able to effectively search the area. We could have easily flown within 25-50 feet of the wreckage and would not have been able to see it. It was around this time that we heard an MH-53 formation on the radio, but they were having no more luck than we were. We had been flying for a couple of hours by then and had all we could stand, so we decided to knock it off. We finally made the smart decision to divert to Baghdad, get a weather update, and wait until dawn if need be.

Once on the ground, we refuelled both aircraft and collected ourselves. We talked to No. 2 and found out that earlier they were doing all they could just to stay on our wing and keep us in sight. When we made that 60-90 degree left turn, they were on the left side and broke over the top of us. To compound their situation, the co-pilot's door flew open during this maneuver. They barely missed hitting us, but that put them in a nose-down right bank, heading toward the ground, with few visual references outside the aircraft. They managed to get it back under control, levelling out around 150 feet, and somehow overtook us shortly after that. We had no idea that we nearly had a midair collision.

The rest of the mission was uneventful. We mission-planned on our portable flight-planning equipment and launched again just before dawn. Visibility was still bad, but by the time we were away from the cultural lighting around Baghdad, the sun was rising, which improved the visibility. We searched multiple sets of possible coordinates and finally found some wreckage later scattered for miles across the desert. The pilots unfortunately did not survive the incident, and they were later found several miles from the wreckage. All in all, we refuelled multiple times that day and logged 10.8 hours per aircraft before returning after a long duty day. We did multiple brownout approaches in the desert to verify wreckage parts, and returned with minor problems, such as cracked windshields from the brownouts. We gave up the aircraft to two fresh crews that went back out to continue the search, logging more than 11 hours of flight time per aircraft before returning to base.

Lessons Learned:

Here are some lessons I learned and recommendations I have on how we can do our jobs safer:

1. Seriously analyze the importance of the mission. Is it a military asset, or is it a local civilian? Although not in this case, too often we've crashed and killed entire rescue crews going after foreign civilians who were driven out to safety the next day and survived whatever injuries they had.

2. With weather conditions as bad as those, delay until daylight if possible. I realize this may not be an option, but it would help mitigate some of the risk.

3. When launching in bad weather, have the formation take both lateral and vertical separation from the beginning, to avoid potential midair collisions and to reduce the overall workload. Instead of getting closer to maintain visual contact with each other, take a mile separation and stack 500 feet in altitude from each other. Then, either pick a point to rejoin, or set hard boundaries, search on either side, and rejoin after the search.

4. Consider setting a limit and sticking to it, like the Army's not less than 20 percent moon illumination, instead of allowing aircrews to fly into "o/o" weather conditions on life-and-death missions.

To my knowledge, our HH-60Gs (CSAR) and MH-53s (AFSOC) were the only helicopters flying that night. Both communities were flying in horrendous weather conditions. Many times it is necessary to execute missions in such conditions when the reward is worth the risk; however, I think we can do a better job of mitigating the risks to protect our valuable assets. Ask nearly any rescue aircrew member who has been deployed, and I bet you'll get a similar story. Some of us have been lucky, but unfortunately, far too many have made the ultimate sacrifice. To make a difference, it's going to take some fundamental changes in the way we think, operate and execute our missions. I think the time has come, before we lose another aircrew member, helicopter, or both.

NOTES:

I DIDN'T SEE THAT COMING!
SEA KING WS-61, ROYAL AIR FORCE, SEA KING RESCUE, C FLIGHT, 22 SQUADRON

Flt Lt Iain Smith, November 2010

One cold and snowy winter afternoon, Rescue 122 was called into action to evacuate a housebound casualty in Shropshire to the local hospital; his predicament had been caused by several inches of fresh snow blocking access for an NHS ambulance. Our problems started with 10 miles to go when all 3 of our Attitude Indicators (AI) began to indicate slightly differing information; notwithstanding this, we managed to complete the rescue and recovered the casualty to Shrewsbury Hospital. It was now dark and following a crew discussion on how to get home if the AI were still malfunctioning, we realised that we couldn't due to worsening weather over Wales and the lack of reliable attitude instrumentation. We decided to get ourselves to RAF Shawbury - a mere 5 minutes away — but as we transited fuel began to leak into the aircraft cabin. Fortunately, we were able to land safely at Shawbury and shut down without further incident. Overnight, the temperature was forecast to reach minus 15 degrees, but the aircraft would have to spend the night outside.

The next morning our engineers arrived and carried out

rectification on the 'snags' — the main rotor head and tail rotors were re-greased as the cold soaking had frozen it off, but other than that the aircraft was serviceable. We said our goodbyes to Shawbury and started the journey home. A phrase you will sometimes hear in a Sea King is: "This cab feels a bit rough," an inherent characteristic of flying an aircraft in which all the moving parts are headed in different directions. Not overly alarmed we continued for home. The vibration very quickly became uncharacteristically severe just as I began to feel a rattling through the yaw pedals. A 'PAN' was transmitted and we landed in a field 1½ mile from the North Wales Police HLS. On the ground, still with rotors running, everything seemed normal but any application of power produced marked vibrations so for the second time we shut down somewhere unexpected.

On a beautiful crisp winter's day in a field in Conwy you wouldn't expect to be faced by a survival situation, but that is what it quickly turned into. The aircraft temperature gauge read minus 6. Standing in flying suits and thermals that you had been sweating in 5 minutes before, we quickly became chilled. Fortunately we all had hats, gloves and extra layers to put on, but even this wasn't enough and the cold quickly penetrated the soles of our flying boots. My co-pilot (ex-SERE School instructor) became concerned about frost-nip on exposed extremities and so we were soon wrapping ourselves up with anything we could find. Not long after, we sat on our 'go-bags' having a good old sing-song in the emergency survival shelter. One foray into the aircraft to get a Mars bar revealed that the drugs had frozen in the first response bag! Worse still, so had the Mars bar.

It is not often that a set of circumstances will conspire so effectively against you to culminate in the strangest of survival situations, but in a field in Conwy that is exactly what happened to us. The phrase "dress to survive" is glibly overlooked by some in our world — and probably in yours. It certainly had been by me, but when packing for winter think about what you'd do and how well protected you are outside of your aircraft; if you're cold and shivering walking across dispersal I'd suggest it's not a good start!

Lessons Learned:

When we consider the risks to aviation that extremes of weather bring we often focus on the more obvious conditions like driving snow or thick ice. However, what these articles have so ably demonstrated is that 'simple' high winds, cold or heavy rain can all have second order effects on flight safety. In the examples above, cold and rain can drive personnel deep into the Error Zone, increasing fatigue, reducing physical and mental abilities and ultimately, affecting their judgment and decision making skills. For flying and engineering, there is little margin for this type of error to creep in and it is worth all of us being aware of the effects even more benign conditions can cause during prolonged exposure.

In addition, it is very easy for personnel not directly working on the airfield to forget how easily loose items, temporary structures and rubbish around the station can rapidly become a significant hazard when the wind picks up. Objects like these have the tenacity of a pit bull when it comes to finding innovative ways to end up on the airfield on a windy day. So as the nights draw in please remember that even autumn and spring weather bring with them their own particular flight safety hazards; and it takes all personnel on station to make sure they don't contribute to the next accident.

NOTES:

NOT DESIGNED TO BE FLOWN IN THE CLOUDS

AH-1W COBRA, UNITED STATES MARINE CORPS, UNIT UNKNOWN

CAPT Adam Scholl, March 2016

When I arrived to the ready room on an overcast March day at Marine Corps Air Station (MCAS) New River, there was no reason to think that this night would be any different from most. As one of our squadron's senior night systems instructors (NSI), I was the section leader for a flight of two AH-1W Cobras. We are tasked with conducting a low light level (LLL) specific weapons delivery (SWD) training mission at BT-11 (bombing range), our primary aerial gunnery range located 50 miles to the northeast along the North Carolina coast. My co-pilot was the incoming squadron commanding officer, and the training and readiness manual dictated that he would fly this refresher event in the Cobra's rear seat. My wingman was the squadron's current commanding officer, who was also giving an LLL SWD training flight to a junior pilot.

At brief time, the operations duty officer (ODO) gave us our standard brief. We received the current and forecast weather, NOTAMs, and information regarding active ranges in the local area. The weather was forecast to degrade steadily throughout the night, but was expected to stay above VFR minimums of 1000-3. After the ODO finished, I briefed my section on the conduct of the flight, which would involve flying from MCAS New River to MCAS Cherry Point. There we would conduct forward arming and refuelling point (FARP) operations in order to load ordnance and take on additional fuel before entering the range. After the section brief, I briefed my co-pilot on our inter-cockpit procedures. We then walked to the helicopters, conducted thorough pre-flight inspections, and launched as a section into the night.

Our SWD training on the range was uneventful, and took us approximately an hour to complete. After our training objectives were met, we egressed as a section back to Cherry Point to de-arm our aircraft, download our remaining ordnance, and take on more fuel. While on deck at Cherry Point, ATIS at New River called 800 foot ceilings and two miles of visibility. Although below VFR minimums, I opted to continue with the plan we had briefed and return to New River. We were all familiar with the area, and I was confident I could lead the section back using Special VFR (SVFR) procedures for the short 25-minute flight home.

Shortly after takeoff from Cherry Point, the weather degraded rapidly. New River ATIS now called ceilings at 500 feet and one mile visibility. This was still acceptable weather for a SVFR arrival, so we continued. The further we pushed, however, the worse the weather became, until we were flying at 200 feet AGL to avoid the clouds. Once we could no longer maintain 200 feet, I decided to split the section using our NATOPs inadvertent IMC procedures. I began my climb up to our briefed minimum safe altitude of 3000 feet MSL, flipped my goggles up to help transition to an instrument scan, and positively switched the section to approach control. Approach quickly established radar contact with both aircraft, assigned us separate transponder codes, and began giving us radar vectors for PAR (Precision approach radar) approaches into New River.

En route to New River, we were vectored at 4500 feet MSL. I transferred the controls to my copilot, the incoming CO, because the

AH-1W is better suited to be flown from the rear seat in instrument conditions. Before beginning his refresher syllabus, he had been away from the cockpit for two years while stationed in Washington D.C., so I felt that this was a perfect training opportunity. As expected, his procedures and airwork were solid. We were in thick clouds 90 percent of the time, only occasionally breaking out for a short periods of VFR-on-top conditions. Approach informed us that New River was now calling 200-foot ceilings and one fourth-mile of visibility. This is the absolute minimum weather an AH-1W crew can accept based on published approach procedures and the fact that the AH-1W is designated as a single-piloted platform for instrument purposes.

For those unfamiliar with the Cobra cockpit, the front seat is designed around the aircraft's weapons and targeting systems. The center portion of the dash consists of the targeting optics, the multi-function display (MFD) for the targeting sensor, and a joystick to control sensor movement. A hand controller similar to a video game controller is located on the left side of the MFD and is used to operate weapons systems, control the FLIR and optics, optimize images, and perform a number of other functions.

The flight controls are small joystick-like controls located on the left and right sides of the cockpit in order to minimize interference with the weapons and sensor controls. Additionally, the flying instruments in the front seat are located to the right and behind the sensor optics, requiring the front-seat pilot to tilt his head slightly in order to see them. In short, the aircraft is only designed to be flown from the front seat when absolutely necessary, and is not optimal for flight in IMC conditions. The rear seat is the primary seat for flying and for ballistic rocket delivery, and has a more conventional cockpit setup, with the cyclic between the pilot's legs and the instruments directly in front of the pilot.

Due to my wingman's position, ATC vectored him for the first PAR to Runway 23. The order did not matter to me, because both aircraft had taken on a full fuel load at Cherry Point. Maintaining the inter-flight frequency in our back radios, we were able to update each other on conditions at the terminal phase of the approach. My wingman, the squadron CO, shot the first approach and informed us that he was unable to see the runway environment at the decision height and was executing a missed approach.

Knowing that my wingman was unable to break out of the clouds, it was my turn to give it a shot. With my co-pilot still at the controls in the rear seat, I backed him up on altitude and airspeed and transitioned between aided and unaided flight in an attempt to break out the runway lights. Approaching the decision height, I noticed we were rapidly decelerating and instructed my co-pilot to gain airspeed.

At the decision height, I saw our airspeed bleed all the way down to 20 knots. My co-pilot informed me that his instrument scan was breaking down task saturation, but that he knew we needed to regain airspeed and altitude. He immediately began to make the appropriate control inputs. I closely monitored the instruments as he pulled in max power and began a climb-out at low airspeed. Once back to relative safety at 1,000 feet, he began to increase airspeed.

At this point, approach informed us that they were switching both aircraft from Runway 23 to Runway 5 because the latter had the approach lights on. Unsure why they didn't give us this runway in the first place, we acknowledged the switch. It was my wingman's turn for another PAR.

Once again, he did not break out the landing environment, even with the runway lights on. Upon hearing him call a second missed approach, I decided not to try another approach to New River, opting instead to return to Cherry Point where the ATIS was calling 400-1. The plan was to execute a PAR there and shut down for the night, away from home field.

We were vectored back to Cherry Point, requested the PAR approaches, and were sequenced into the instrument pattern. My co-pilot was still at the controls in the rear seat. Though he was still doing a solid job, he informed me that the high work-load of instrument flight in the Cobra was finally taking its toll. As we neared our decision height on the PAR, he stated he was beginning to experience vertigo and called for a control transfer to me in the front seat.

I took the controls and told him to let me know if he could break out the airfield. At the decision height, we finally saw the approach lights and were able to safety land. Taxiing back to the line to park the aircraft, we were both extremely relieved to be out of the clouds and safely on deck. I parked the aircraft and we shut it down for the night.

Lessons Learned:

Despite the collective experience of the four pilots in our section, there were many valuable lessons learned on this night.

One being pilots should never pass up extra fuel when given the option, it is often hard to tell when it will be needed.

This may seem obvious to many pilots, but it is not uncommon for East Coast H-1 aircrews to pass up extra fuel in order to save time. Often, when landing at Cherry Point to de-arm and download ordnance after shooting at the range, we only refuel if we don't already have enough fuel remaining to make it back to New River with our NATOPS minimum of 300 pounds. This saves time after long nights on the range. However, if we had chosen not to refuel on this night, the outcome might have been much different.

Even more valuable, though, was re-learning the lesson of how important it is to maintain instrument flying proficiency.

Unfortunately, this is a skill that is not often emphasized in H-1 squadrons. Our training plans are so focused on weapons delivery and mission essential tasks that pilots struggle just to achieve their yearly instrument minimums. Our lack of instrument time is also due to the well-founded fear of IMC flight in the H-1 community. Our aircraft are not designed to be flown in the clouds. They are rated for instrument flight, but not well suited for the task.

This is a dangerous cycle.

H-1 pilots must find the time to practice instrument flight in actual instrument conditions. This is the only way to build confidence and proficiency in a skill set that is critical to safe mission execution. You never know when it will be the only skill that will get you home safely on a dark and cloudy night.

NOTES:

SAND BLOWS

MH-60R SEAHAWK, UNITED STATES NAVY, HELICOPTER MARITIME STRIKE SQUADRON 73

LT Adam Cohee, February 2016

At 6 p.m. one evening I awoke to fly another night of Persian Gulf maritime intelligence, surveillance, and reconnaissance (MISR) coverage in support of the CARL VINSON (CVN-70) Strike Group.

My crew and I performed our operational risk management (ORM) NATOPS briefs and then headed down to the Combat Information Center to build our situational aware-ness about the operating area. This flight was a little different because our parent ship, USS GRIDLEY, was the escort for the carrier into port, but we all viewed it as just another MISR bag. The brief from the tactical action officer and anti-submarine/anti-surface tactical air controller revealed no contacts of interest or critical contacts of interest in the area. The weather report showed the typical Persian Gulf haze with no ceiling and seven to nine miles of visibility.

The plan was to launch at 0330 and recover at 0630, a night time launch, and land after sunrise. It was nice to finally get some daylight flying since our typical coverage periods had all been at night.

The first flight of the evening landed on time and we strapped in to take the aircraft for the second go. During our helicopter aircraft commander (HAC) to HAC turnover, I received the report: "Aircraft is flying great, no gripes. Not many contacts out there, and the weather is a bit hazy around the ship but it clears up down to the south."

We launched on time and began our transit 40 miles to the southeast where the carrier was headed towards port.

As we flew toward our operating area, we noticed the weather was not clearing as expected. We heard a MH-60S crew from HSC-15 (helicopter sea combat squadron) on our helicopter common frequency debating whether or not to take off from the carrier. Ultimately they decided to take off, so the weather couldn't be as bad as we thought.

Around that same time, we received a call from our controller with an updated weather report from the carrier, which called for a sandstorm. Most people call it their "spidey sense" or "hair on the back of their neck". All I know is that I started to feel some sensation that made me uncomfortable. I called back to our controller in an attempt to get more information on the sandstorm: when was it forecasted to occur, where, altitudes, expected visibility ... anything. We also began asking for frequent updates from GRIDLEY's bridge watch team on observed visibility around the ship since we were now 50 miles to the south.

The ship reported better than two miles visibility so we didn't get too worked up about it, but decided to head back north anyway to get a look for ourselves. The aircraft carrier has aerographer's mates to observe and forecast aviation weather around the carrier. The CD ships do not have that luxury and rely heavily on predictions pushed by the carrier. Once the weather begins to deteriorate, aircrews often have a better vantage point than the shipboard watch standers in terms of "real-time" conditions.

For the transit north, we decided to climb to 5,000 feet to get above the haze and minimize our time flying in the sand. I'd never flown in a sandstorm before, and really was not sure how the aircraft would respond.

The engines' inlet particle separators seemed to perform as advertised as we never noticed any rise in engine temperature due to airflow interruption or any other signs of performance degradation.

Once within 10 miles of the GRIDLEY and with the sun rising, we began to descend to see what the conditions were really like in the vicinity of the landing pattern. The visibility grew a little worse as we descended, but we could still see the sky above us.

Passing through 1,000 feet, the conditions turned into full brownout. My plan was to level off at 500 feet and evaluate but at that altitude all we could see was brown. We decided to continue to descend to 200 feet, which was our pattern altitude; however, we could still see nothing. So we continued down to 150 feet. Unfortunately at that altitude, we could only make out the tops of the whitecaps on the water below nothing else. It was surprisingly uncomfortable flying around that low with a complete lack of visual acuity.

Time for a quick rundown of my options: I could try to land on my ship with weather below minimums for a normal approach, set up for an emergency low visibility approach (EVLA) or even a smoke light approach (both considered last resorts with no divert available), or head back to the carrier approximately 50 miles south.

I elected to have the ship turn all their lights and try a normal approach, and if that didn't work I would still have enough fuel to make it to the carrier for a carrier controlled approach (CCA). On the approach, we reached 0.2 nautical miles astern of the ship at 100 feet and gained no sign of the flight deck. Any closer and I didn't feel confident I could safely wave off. As we headed back outbound, we decided we had time for one more approach before being forced to choose another option. We shot the second approach with the same results which solidified my decision to fly south to the carrier where I knew the weather was at least a little better.

They also have a precision approach option where I felt I had a better chance of breaking out and safely get a lot closer to the ship. I am sure I could not have landed safely on the GRIDLEY. I could have shot an automatic approach to 50 feet over the water and then slowly closed the ship until I acquired it visually. This scenario is sometimes discussed on HAC boards (something I had completed just two weeks prior). However, such a procedure would be reserved for an extreme emergency situation where there was no other option short of ditching the aircraft in the water. For this reason, such a procedure is not written in any publication.

I could have tried an ELVA or a smoke light approach, but both of these procedures take a while to set up and would have burned significantly more fuel. Furthermore, this would have taken away my option to get to the carrier, a much larger landing environment with experienced controllers and equipment designed for handling aircraft in degraded weather conditions. The choice seemed obvious.

As we headed south back toward the carrier, we had the help of a 30-knot tailwind while the USS GRIDLEY watch team and combat element officer in charge coordinated our deck hit. The carrier was not at flight quarters and was prepared to enter territorial waters to pull into port. However, by the time I reached communication range with the ship, they already knew I was en route and had a plan in place for our recovery.

As we continued our transit, we realized the sandstorm had rapidly engulfed the entire area. We checked in with approach controllers about 10 miles out, and immediately received vectors for the CCA. I elected to have the co pilot fly the approach, while the aircrewman slewed the forward looking infrared (FLIR), in search of the carrier.

I was responsible for the outside scan to gain visual con-tact of the ship and landing environment once close enough. On the approach, one mile from the tactical air navigation (TACAN) system, the controller asked us to "confirm visual."

Our response was, "Negative".

The controller replied, "Roger, continue."

At a half mile our aircrewman started to get a silhouette of the ship on FLIR, but I still could not see the ship visually. At least this gave me a little "warm and fuzzy" feeling that the ship was actually where we thought and we were looking good on lineup with a chance to break out.

The controller once again asked us to "confirm visual"... " negative,"..."roger, continue." At approximately 50 yards from the back of the ship I started to make out the aft edge of the flight deck. Without taking my eyes off the deck, I took controls to slide the helicopter over the landing spot.

Lessons Learned:

It turns out the swap of controls versus swap of scans procedure that was taught during instrument training in-flight school actually works. When I took controls, my co-pilot stated that he didn't gain visual of the ship until we were hovering alongside. After landing, we noticed that we were unable to see the bow of the ship from the spot.

We knew there was no way we were re-launching in these conditions and Air Boss confirmed by saying, "Just so we are all on the same page, you are shutting down." Happy to be out of the sandstorm and done with the flight, we replied "Roger, concur". Certainly this was not just another MISR bag.

NOTES:

JUST ANOTHER CROSS-COUNTRY WEEKEND

TH-57 SEARANGER (BELL 206), UNITED STATES NAVY, HELICOPTER TRAINING SQUADRON 8

LT Becca Smith, October 2015

Jet-setting is one of the highlights of advanced helicopter training, and one cross-country weekend, we found ourselves in Atlanta, Georgia. It was Sunday morning and we were fat, dumb and happy. It had been a successful, albeit rainy, weekend and we were three short flights from home. A large storm was west of Atlanta and north of South Whiting Field (KNDZ), so we planned to head south to avoid it and then west to KNDZ.

Everything looked good on preflight and start-up. I was smug because the other two crews we were with had to service their hydraulic and transmission systems. That's when the holes started lining up in the proverbial block of Swiss cheese.

After receiving ATIS and calling for clearance, we switched to ground to inform them we would be requesting a present-position takeoff. They switched us to Tower and I requested takeoff. Crickets.

I requested again. Crickets. I switched back to Ground. Crickets. By this time, my comrades had finished their servicing and had started up. I switched to UHF and contacted them on the discrete frequency we had discussed.

After a series of attempts, we determined that we could transmit on VHF, but not receive. I asked another pilot to inform Tower that our aircraft would be shutting down to troubleshoot and to cancel our clearance. I also told them not to wait on us and that we would see them back at KNDZ.

After shutting down, I called maintenance and the CDO. Since I had a working UHF, they both recommended I plan a route that would accommodate UHF only communications. My students and I pulled out the charts and approach plates. The only route we could find was to head west to Montgomery (KMGM) and then south to KNDZ.

I was apprehensive because ceilings were forecasted to remain low for the duration of the flight as a result of the storm. To get to KMGM, we had to fly IFR for the entire route, and the last thing I wanted to do was go lost comm while IMC. We discussed the possibility but decided that we had no reason to believe that the UHF would stop working. After all, they were two completely separate systems. We filed IFR, started up, got clearance and took off using the UHF radio.

Shortly after takeoff, we found ourselves squarely in the clouds with heavy rain. No big deal. The mighty TH-57 is an all-weather aircraft. As we continued west, we started having issues communicating with approach on UHF. I asked one of my students to look up a VHF frequency for approach on the off chance our VHF fixed itself. We plugged in the frequency and it worked. There was no avenue of fame, yet.

I explained to the controller the nature of our radio issues. He gave us a handful of UHF and VHF frequencies to try. The only one that worked was the VHF frequency we had initially used to contact him. My students and I began discussing what we would do if we lost contact with him and whether we should turn back to Atlanta (KPDK) or continue on to KMGM.

As I was about to inform approach that we wanted to return to KPDK, approach asked us if we were in a turn. I looked at my RMI and my copilot's RMI: they were steady. My observer was following along in the back with fore flight and informed us it looked like we had completed a 270 degree turn. He instructed us to look at our magnetic compasses and sure enough, our magnetic compasses were showing a 120 degree difference in heading. We manually slaved the RMIs and made several attempts at troubleshooting. The RMIs began spinning.

We were still IMC, had unreliable radios and appeared to have lost our directional gyro. I thought we should declare an emergency, and my students agreed. My copilot pressed the magic button, and I declared an emergency with approach. I told him the nature of the emergency and requested vectors back to KPDK. We had only been airborne for about 30 minutes, and I assumed KPDK was our closest and best option.

The weather had been fine when we took off and had been forecasted to stay the same. Approach said there was an airport that was 10 miles away with an ILS (West Georgia Regional, KCTJ). My copilot looked it up in the approach plates to see if we could do it. The ceilings were low, but we had the approach plate and the weather, so we accepted.

As approach vectored us, we divvied up responsibilities. My copilot was responsible for figuring out our rollout headings on the magnetic compass and calling them. She also briefed the approach and kept me honest with heading. My observer, who was eagerly sticking his head between the seats and white-knuckling the crossbars, helped by calling out my altitude and airspeed deviations.

I had done plenty of no-gyro PAR and TACAN approaches with students in VMC, and I naively thought that a failed card ILS in the clouds would be as easy as a VMC no-gyro PAR. I could not have been more wrong. I also assumed that my students had already completed their failed-card training hops. Strike two. Upon reaching final, I turned to intercept and went full deflection almost immediately. I held my altitude and informed approach that I was executing a missed approach and requested vectors for another attempt.

My observer, still white-knuckled, mentioned that we should request "no-gyro" vectors. I relayed the request to approach, they obliged and our workload was instantly cut in half. As we snaked and slithered through the pattern and turned onto the final approach course, confidence built in the cockpit. With the help of my students, I was able to maintain something that resembled the course and glideslope of the approach we were attempting.

As we got closer and the ILS became more sensitive, the CDI began to walk out. We were about 200 feet above decision height, right at the base of the clouds, and the rain on the windscreen was nearly blinding. Our focus had subconsciously shifted from an aggressive partial panel scan to looking outside the aircraft for the airport.

Before we knew it, I had gone full deflection again. Our confidence quickly turned to doubt. My copilot referenced the Atari-era GPS and said we were about a half mile from the airport. Holding our altitude and heading, we frantically scanned in front of the rain-distorted windscreen.

Just as we were about to admit defeat and go missed approach for a second time, I looked to the right and left of the helicopter. At 7 o'clock and no more than 50 yards, I saw the huge, white approach end numbers. There were a few choice words, followed by "runway in sight." We turned, landed and shut down without any further incident.

We climbed out of the helicopter. A wave of relief swept through us as we realized the gravity of what we had successfully battled through . When the maintenance representative arrived the following day, we discovered that our all-weather aircraft's avionic compartment was a veritable swimming pool, and the source of our faulty equipment.

Lessons Learned:

During the debrief of the events, we all agreed that our success was as a direct result of solid CRM. The student-instructor hierarchy had been left at the door during the emergency, and all three of us had equal stakes in finding a place to land.

We made a few missteps along the way, but our ability to swallow our pride, accept critique and offer guidance to each other helped us successfully navigate to a safe conclusion of a less than textbook situation.

NOTES:

INADVERTENT IMC

UH-60L, UNITED STATES ARMY, ARMY AIRCRAFT ACCIDENT PREVENTION

Name Withheld, January 2018

The crew of the accident aircraft was conducting a multi-aircraft continuation training mission with another UH-60L. Planned for a daytime departure, the training mission was from an airfield on the installation to a civilian airport. They would return under NVGs. However, due to an unscheduled maintenance delay, the first leg of the flight started as a daytime departure with an in-flight transition to NVGs, after sunset.

The aircraft departed, stopped at the civilian airport, departing at 2318 under NVGs. On the return leg of the flight, the crews of both aircraft noted deteriorating weather conditions with rain, low clouds and fog increasing in low-lying areas. The crews then discussed an inadvertent IMC plan for both aircraft to recover to their home installation under instrument flight rules (IFR), if necessary. A few minutes after discussing the IMC plan, the rain became more intense. The accident aircraft reported being in the soup and initiated the discussed recovery plan.

While executing the recovery plan, the accident aircraft levelled along the roll axis and initiated a climb straight ahead with the cyclic to allow the airspeed to decelerate to climb airspeed. The airspeed slowed to 50 KIAS, and the pilot brought the steep pitch and 50-knot airspeed to the attention of the pilot-in-command (PC). The (PI) lowered the nose briefly and then raised it back again to approximately 20 degrees up before the airspeed had a chance to build. The accident aircraft then entered a 20-degree, nose-high decelerating attitude. The PI then issued a second challenge by calling out that the airspeed was 0 KIAS and they were descending. The PC did not take corrective action. The aircraft rapidly descended at 2,000-foot-per minute, a near-vertical descent. The PI said, "I have the controls," grabbed the flight controls, and pulled up fully on the collective as the aircraft descended into the trees.

Crew

The PC had 969 total hours with 597 in the UH-60. The PI had 356 total hours and 170 hours in the UH-60.

Lessons Learned:

When crews plan missions, it is important to make sure that they have the most current information. As aircrews conduct briefings and flight planning for training missions, they should brief how changes to the plan will be handled and further addressed in terms of mission aborts or modifications. Maintenance and weather changes occur consistently in the aviation realm and it is important to brief how to handle those changes. Following regulations and briefed parameters help make sure crews are able to conduct operations safely. The briefing process is such that it positively impacts safety and the ability to execute missions in a manner which allows crew and aircraft to live to fight again.

NOTES:

CHAPTER 6

COMMUNICATE & AIR CREW

"This is why being a helicopter pilot is so different from being an airplane pilot, and why, in generality, airplane pilots are open, clear-eyed buoyant extroverts and helicopter pilots are brooders, introspective anticipators of trouble. They know if something bad has not happened it is about to."

Harry Reasoner

CLEAR, CONCISE, COHERENT, CONSEQUENCES

UH-1N, UNITED STATES AIR FORCE, 1ST HELICOPTER SQUADRON

Capt. Adam Ackerman, July 2008

I had recently been upgraded to aircraft commander during my first assignment. I was still the newest aircraft commander in the 1st Helicopter Squadron at Andrews Air Force Base, Md. It was a great feeling to know leadership now trusted me to maneuver a UH-1N Huey helicopter and command a crew of three (pilot, co-pilot, flight engineer) in the highly visible and security-restricted National Capital Region. This area includes a great number of America's treasured buildings and monuments, and its security is vital to the government's continued operation. Helicopter flight provides a panoramic bird's-eye view of the lively District of Columbia and more than a few unique memories; however, I can no longer recall any details from the standard 2 ½ hour helicopter flight that occurred just a couple of years ago. What I do remember are the events and lessons that followed. The sequence taught me that the responsibility of an aircraft commander extends beyond maneuvering an aircraft and managing a crew.

The flight itself was of the most popular flavor, vanilla. After shutdown, I remained strapped in and started to work on the aircraft forms while the flight engineer hopped out and began to walk around the helicopter and conduct the required post-flight inspection. The crew chief met us at the aircraft and began his standard duties. About the time I finished the forms and was ready to help finish the post-flight, the flight engineer told the crew chief and me that he had discovered some fuel on the deck of the No. 2 engine compartment. The puddle was a foot or two in diameter and definitely a concern for an aircraft the size of a Huey. We poked and prodded around looking for the source, and checked the general condition and security of everything in the compartment. After a few futile minutes, I returned to the forms to write up the leak. The crew and I then gathered our personal equipment and went inside to avoid interfering with maintenance and to finish our post-flight duties.

A few minutes later, I received a page over the intercom from the Supervisor of Flying (SOF) to report to the operations desk. I already knew what was coming (a maintenance ground run for the aircraft), so I grabbed my helmet and checklist on the way. The SOF delivered the expected news, and I went to the aircraft to meet the crew chief again. I conducted an extensive ground run with the crew chief, but there was no evidence of a fuel leak in the engine compartment during operation or post-flight. I documented that no leak was discovered during the ground operations and returned the aircraft to maintenance. The end of the day was approaching, and I expected the leak to be investigated further, so I was shocked the next day to learn the same aircraft conducted a precautionary landing in the middle of downtown DC due to the smell of fuel in the cabin. No leak was discovered in the engine compartment, but maintenance eventually found the source in the compartment just forward of the engine that isn't examined during pre- or post-flight. The fuel my crew observed the previous day was only what worked its way into the engine compartment during flight and didn't indicate the actual size of the leak.

When I heard the news, I felt a sinking feeling in my stomach, but luckily no damage or injury resulted from the leak during the flight. The full extent of my responsibility and mistakes became painfully clear. After the ground run on the previous day, I didn't intend for the aircraft to be returned to flight before fixing the hidden leak. I assumed this was implied to the crew chief in our conversation and wouldn't be passed to other maintainers as a problem that couldn't be replicated. Regardless, a large chunk of responsibility still rested on my shoulders since I filled out the events in the forms. First, maintainers, just like pilots, always prefer the opportunity to have face-to-face conversations about an aircraft with one another. It's important to realise the chance doesn't always exist, due to workloads and other external factors. It's also important to recognise human factor topics, such as "the strength of an idea" and "hidden agenda" don't only apply to people operating aircraft. While the tiny box in a 781 may be the only method of communication a maintainer or aircrew member receives, we hope it will be the most valuable one. I used to look at the forms as simply a place to write down problems for maintenance. However, now with each official write-up, I try to think about the "Four Cs:" Clear, Concise, Coherent and Consequences.

Lessons Learned:

When I land, I'll be the first to admit I'm generally focused on either quickly emptying my bladder or filling my stomach, thus the readability of my penmanship often suffers like my organs. I have to force myself to focus on making a clear, legible write-up that won't be lost in translation.

The write-up itself is important, but I think the biggest culprit is the name block. You never know when someone is going to have additional questions about a write-up for you. Making write-ups concise saves the writer's ink and the reader's time.

When I find myself with a relatively complex problem, I find two questions helpful in determining whether a write-up is concise.

1. Does maintenance need all this information to fix the problem?
2. Should this go as two separate write-ups?

Next, bullets and fragments can be coherent, but good grammar is a more dependable way to produce something understandable and easy to read. It is also crucial to use only the most commonly accepted abbreviations (e.g., ACFT, ENG, etc.), in order to correctly grasp the whole message.

Finally, I ask myself the consequences of my writeup, and whether it'll be helpful to others. While it's important to provide helpful information to fix the problem, maintenance should not be told how to fix the problem in the write-up. If a part is broken or missing, just put that, don't direct a repair or replacement. While repairs and replacements are expected outcomes, write-ups will also have the consequence of additional paperwork for the crew. If it's an unusual event or occurrence, see your neighbourhood flight safety office for appropriate actions.

NOTES:

MILITARY EXERCISE CAUSES JET TO DEVIATE

HH-65 DOLPHIN, COAST GUARD NATIONAL CAPITAL REGION AIR DEFENSE FACILITY

Name Withheld, October 2010

I was pilot in command of a US military helicopter engaged in a NORTH COMM/NORAD sponsored mission to deter and prevent incursions into the Washington D.C. SFRA and FRZ (Flight Restricted Zone). For this mission, the aircraft was crewed by two pilots and a flight mechanic.

We were conducting a routine training mission within the FRZ. The co-pilot assisting me was an experienced MH-65C pilot, but he was assigned to a distant Coast Guard command, and had never flown in the FRZ or SFRA around Washington, D.C. The primary purpose of our mission was area familiarization for this new pilot.

We were conducting pattern work at DAA when the Eastern Air Defense Sector (EADS) contacted us on their dedicated frequency to inform us that they had spotted a target-of-interest (TOI) on their RADARs (and other sensors), and they immediately directed us to "investigate." EADS passed vectors for the suspect air-track (initially bearing 050 from us, reported at 5,000 ft, heading southeast).

Under tasking from EADS, our protocol is to immediately

suspend training and conduct our Rotary Wing Air Intercept (RWAI) procedures. RWAI procedures are an extremely challenging, and checklist intensive, evolution for Coast Guard pilots, and we are specially trained for this mission. Part of the protocol requires one pilot to work ATC frequencies while the other pilot works EADS tasking on a separate frequency. Because of the intensive workload, neither pilot is able to monitor the external communications of the other.

Hence, I was communicating on the EADS radio, gathering and confirming a steady stream of EADS tasking, while the other pilot was working the ATC radios, in this case Potomac Approach. Neither of us was privy to the external communications of the other.

As a result, we climbed into Class B airspace without securing proper clearance from Potomac Approach. Potomac Approach informed us (post flight, via phone call) that the event triggered a TCAS "RA" advisory in a nearby Air Carrier aircraft.

In retrospect, as the pilot with better area familiarity, I should have been working the Potomac Approach radio. My Co-pilot should have been working the radio with EADS (which would not have required any local area knowledge). I knew for certain that the Co-pilot had established communication with Potomac Approach, and assumed (erroneously) that he had been able to communicate our intent and secure the required clearances to operate in Class B airspace. This was my error, and I should have been more assertive in confirming with him that we had coordinated proper clearances into the airspace above us.

Another contributing factor was that EADS use of the Domestic Events Network (DEN) and other multi-agency notification tools was either slow, or non-existent. Normally, EADS quickly announces (via the DEN) that they are tasking helicopter intercept of a TOI (Target of Interest). As a military pilot, my paradigm is to assume that the FAA Controller is already aware of our general tasking from EADS the moment we check in. The Controllers in this case had no knowledge of EADS tasking and furthermore that the tasking EADS gave us ("investigate") is non-standard. We are normally either tasked to intercept, or orbit a certain location to stand guard against distant TOI's that may come closer to the FRZ. There is no "investigate" procedure.

Lessons Learned:

I have mentally replayed this event hundreds of times, assessing the chain of events that lead to it. The following corrective measures come to mind:

1. Never assume that the pilot communicating with ATC has secured clearances. Be proactive about getting confirmation from the Co-pilot that he/she has secured proper clearances.
2. To the maximum extent possible, a military pilot with no flight experience in the SFRA should be afforded a familiarization flight where the flight is not divertible. This IS our practice, but weather/maintenance sometimes precludes that orientation flight. This was the case in this instance as well (previous day's orientation flight with a non-divert aircraft was canceled due to maintenance).
3. Challenge EADS if tasking is vague or non-standard.
4. Encourage EADS to be more proactive about communicating TOI concerns and tasking to the FAA via DEN and other instantaneous reporting methods.
5. Slow down the pace of the intercept if the prior four items have not been accomplished.

NOTES:

THE RISKS OF NOT COMMUNICATING YOUR LIMITS

MH-60S SEAHAWK, UNITED STATES NAVY, HSC-9, HELICOPTER SEA COMBAT SQUADRON 9

LT Andrew Galvin, June 2015

It was an early 3 a.m. brief for a five-hour vertical replenishment (VERTREP) flight about seven months into a nine-month deployment. All the members of the crew had been on at least a couple of these flights and were excited to get started on the fastest way to pass time in a helicopter.

Due to operational requirements, the aircraft was configured with a single internal auxiliary fuel tank and external wings. In order to lower the starting gross weight of the aircraft, the fuel load was reduced to 2,800 pounds. In the brief, we discussed ORM aspects of the long flight and early start. Preflight calculations were reviewed by the entire crew and responsibilities for each crew station delineated.

Because of our fuel load and the high DA, the max external cargo load would be approximately 1,500 pounds. After a few minor maintenance issues on deck, we took off and completed the appropriate max power check and HIT check to ensure engine performance matched our calculations.

We achieved a max continuous torque of 120 percent. According to our squadron SOP, a no-go torque of 114 percent was established for our external cargo operations. There was another aircraft in the VERTREP pattern organic to the supply ship that did not have external wings or an internal aux tank installed and therefore could lift heavier loads.

Our aircraft was brought in for the first pick from the aft-port corner of the flight deck on the supply ship. Tower called the winds off the bow of the ship, but the actual winds seemed to be more to the starboard side, about 20 degrees off the bow.

Based on this relative wind direction and the supply ship being to the port of the carrier, we made a port-to-starboard approach with the left-seat pilot flying. The pilot placed the nose of the aircraft just forward of the starboard beam and pointed at the aft section of the carrier.

When the load was hooked up, the crewman calling the pick directed the left-seat pilot to come straight up. When he called, "Load off deck, check power," the pilot glanced down to check the torque, saw 112 to 114 percent, and called, "Good power". The pilot kept the controls for the departure and began to climb straight up to get clearance from the flight deck.

A few seconds later, the flying pilot noticed the flashing low rotor light and saw torque above 120 percent and Nr going below 94 percent. The pilot realized there was no way to use the left pedal (which requires more power than a right pedal application) to get the nose fully into the wind in the power-limited situation. So the flying pilot initiated a gradual right pedal turn and small descent off the back of the ship. This maneuver lowered the power required and swung the helicopter around approximately 270 degrees, getting into the wind with some forward airspeed.

The pilot verbalized the plan to the crew chief, who stood by to release the load if the descent continued past his comfort zone. The pilot monitored the gauges and maintained a level VSI at about 90 feet with 90 percent Nr and slightly over 120 percent torque.

Once the aircraft was into the wind with some forward airspeed, the collective was lowered and Nr regained. The pilot then initiated a climb back to 150 feet, responded to tower and reported the aircraft status as OK.

The drop was executed without incident on the flight deck of the carrier, although it was clear the load was heavier than expected. Once the load was on deck, we debriefed the incident and decided to continue with the mission after asking the supply ship tower to choose lighter loads for our aircraft. The delivery ship directed us to hold-off while the crew re-stacked the loads to conform to our power requirements.

Lessons Learned:

In retrospect, the combination of a loss of wind effect behind the superstructure and HIGE to HOGE transition contributed to a sudden increase in power required. Also, the power check over the deck was non-standard. It was called by the flying pilot instead of the non-flying pilot, who could have seen the full progression of torque increase as well as any torque fluctuations and directed the crew to set the load back down if the 114 percent limit was not the actual max torque pulled.

Before the flight, we should have informed the supply ship of the max loads desired by our helicopter, and the deck could have been stacked appropriately from the start. Good crew coordination, once the aircraft was in extremis, enabled each crew member to positively contribute to keeping the aircraft airborne and ready to jettison the load if it became necessary. This division of tasks allowed the successful execution of a difficult maneuver. We were confident that the mission could still be executed after this incident occurred early in the flight.

<u>NOTES:</u>

MH-65C DAUPHIN VS CESSNA 172 SKYHAWK

MH-65C DAUPHIN, UNITED STATES COAST GUARD, UNIT WITHHELD

Name Withheld, Dec 2013

MH-65C operating in VMC conditions on an IFR flight plan accepted a best speed approach at 120 KIAS from ATC due to converging fixed wing traffic in trail on VOR/DME Runway 15 approach.

At approximately 8 NM north of the field, ATC cleared MH-65C to switch to CTAF and canceled radar services. In error, pilot not flying tuned incorrect CTAF in COMM 1 and announced position and intentions to perform a go-around at the approach end of Runway 15 followed by a departure to the south.

At an estimated 2 NM north of the field at 880 FT MSL, the Flight Mechanic noticed and announced a shadow of an aircraft projected on the ground in the vicinity of the departure end of Runway 33.

As the pilot not flying and pilot flying began searching for traffic, the Flight Mechanic announced "break left." The pilot flying immediately performed a descending left turn at an estimated 30 degrees angle of bank to avoid the oncoming traffic.

The single engine, general aviation aircraft passed left to right at an estimated distance of 400 FT. The pilot not flying immediately realized the wrong frequency had been entered into COMM 1, tuned the correct CTAF, and announced intentions.

The MH-65 continued flight on its original IFR flight plan without further incident.

The pilot not flying reported developing a habit pattern of not utilizing the Preset frequency when in the left seat since that practice requires reaching across the cockpit and putting the flight helmet in close proximity to the FADEC control switches.

Prior to tuning the CTAF, the pilot not flying verified that the pilot flying had tuned the proper frequency in the Preset position. When instructed by ATC, and in an attempt to quickly change to the CTAF frequency, the pilot not flying reverted back to an old habit pattern and selected the COMM1 right line select key (instead of the Preset button) which made the CDU "buried" frequency the new COMM1 active frequency.

The pilot not flying admittedly felt rushed due to accepting the best speed approach at 120 KIAS and failed to verify the correct frequency had been entered into COMM 1 after depressing the right line select on the CDU. No aural TCAS alert was heard by the crew prior to the mishap.

The TCAS tested properly on deck and exhibited normal operation throughout the flight.

It is suspected that the general aviation aircraft was either not equipped or not operating with a transponder. The crew was unable to establish good communications with the general aviation aircraft due to a heavy workload immediately following the mishap.

After the flight, it was noted that the field is utilized heavily by a local flight school.

It is unusual for [our] unit aircraft to operate in and out of this area.

This was the first time the crew had been to [this field].

Lessons Learned:

There are two valuable lessons we can learn from this mishap.

- The first is the utmost importance of the Flight Mechanic maintaining a good outside visual scan during IFR training flights. Had the Flight Mechanic not seen the oncoming aircraft and had the Flight Mechanic not been accurate, bold, and concise while commanding the pilot flying to "break left", we could have lost an aircraft and crew.
- The second lesson is that we had a crew experience a loss of situational awareness because they were rushing an instrument approach.

Oftentimes, you'll find yourself slowing down the pattern as a helicopter while operating in the IFR environment. This is a situation that can be stressful if you unnecessarily impose pressure on yourself to comply with optional ATC requests. Don't accept more risk than you should for the convenience of ATC or the aircraft behind you. If you are uncomfortable with the request, simply state that you are "unable". ATC is not always fully aware of your capabilities and it's your responsibility as an aviator to prevent ATC from getting you in a bad situation behind the aircraft.

<u>NOTES:</u>

GROUND TAXI MISHAP
CH-47, UNITED STATES ARMY, ARMY AIRCRAFT ACCIDENT PREVENTION

Name withheld by request, June 2018

A CH-47 was on a redeployment ferry mission from a port to a regional airport for staging to redeploy to its home station. The aircrew was conducting a limited maintenance test flight during the ferry mission. Once the aircraft had landed at the regional airport, the crew was given taxi instructions to transient parking. The pilot in command (PC) taxied the aircraft to the transient area where there were no ground guides.

As the aircraft taxied between a parked CH-47 and a hangar, the PC stated he would be making a 180 degree turn near the hangar. The crew chief stationed at the cabin door addressed concern about the proximity to the hangar to the crew. The PC continued the turn and the crew members stated the aircraft was clear to make the 180 degree turn.

While conducting the turn, the aircraft's aft three rotors struck the hangar. Three aft rotor blades, the corner of the hangar and two aircraft inside were damaged.

<u>Crew</u>

The PC had 1,647 hours in series and 1,806 hours total time. The PI had 49 hours in series and 133 total time.

Lessons Learned:

Aircraft operations are just as hazardous when taxiing as when in flight.

The crew's ability to successfully negotiate aircraft ground operations in confined/congested areas requires accurate aircrew visual surveillance and appropriate crew communication.

While aircraft are being ferried, post and pre deployment, commanders, aviation safety officers (ASO) and leaders must be involved in the planning.

The operations cell should ensure the locations in which aircraft will be refuelling and/or overnighting have been surveyed and a pre-accident plan has been integrated for the flight ground staging area.

When Army aircraft are operating at non-military sites, it becomes even more important for unit ASOs to actually conduct onsite safety surveys of the transient parking and refuel locations and provide a detailed pre-accident plan and what operational issues must be addressed for safe operations.

The aircrews involved in post-deployment ferry operations back to home station must make sure they don't become complacent.

For aircrews, they must maintain vigilance in performing their crew duties and aviation decision-making. When something doesn't look right it probably isn't, so crew members should communicate this and the PC should halt operations of the aircraft until they can assess the danger and either mitigate it or choose an alternate course of action.

After high OPTEMPO deployments, leaders must make sure they place the appropriate controls in place to reduce the risk of a mishap.

Leaders can assist in reducing complacency errors by:

- Minimizing multiple flights by the same crews
- Ensuring Army personnel (properly trained) are on ground at the staging airfield parking area/refuel area to ground guide aircraft.
- Ensuring the ASO has completed an onsite safety survey of the planned staging airfields.
- And develop pre-accident plans for each location.

NOTES:

OUT FOR A DIP. LIFE, LIBERTY, AND THE PURSUIT OF SUBMARINES

MH-60R, UNITED STATES NAVY, HSM-70, HELICOPTER MARITIME STRIKE SQUADRON 70

LT Robert Crosby & AWR2 Matthew Ballard, October 2014

It was the second launch of the night. Our crew of three had already shut down once after a frustrating three-hour flight without gaining contact on the OPFOR submarine participating in Carrier Strike Group Two's COMPTUEX.

When the USS Theodore Roosevelt (CVN 71), part of our strike group, received possible contacts, we got the call to launch the alert anti-submarine-warfare (ASW) helicopter and give it another go. It was now 2:30 am and our NVGs strained to provide us a picture. The only illumination was from the position lights of passing ships.

When we got to the position of last known contact on the sub, we fired off sonobuoys into a search pattern. After finding what could be our target, we unleashed the MH-60 Romeo's dipping sonar. With the help of one of our squadron's other helicopters, we began to carry out a simulated attack.

We made an automatic approach to a 70-foot hover into the wind to a position we believed would give us an excellent chance of detecting the target once we lowered our sonar transducer.

We were in "the dip," which can be challenging at night without visual cues for positioning and drift.

Five minutes into our dip, we received strong contact that correlated to the area where we believed the submarine was operating. This hit immediately grabbed the attention of all of us; including the pilot at the controls, our helicopter aircraft commander (HAC).

The HAC lost focus on flying as she watched over my shoulder while we refined the track. This drop of scan led to an undetected aft drift and yaw out of the wind line.

AWR2 Ballard was the first to notice our situation. The system protested with multiple advisories as we were no longer hovering directly over the transducer. He asked from the back, "Is everything all right up there?"

I turned my attention to the instruments and saw we were rapidly departing from the proper parameters of a normal dip. The aircraft was about 20 degrees out of the wind line and had developed an aft drift of five knots. The HAC assured us that she had control of the situation, and tried to eliminate the drift and turn the nose back into the wind, but her inputs were insufficient to stop the developing disaster.

Our automatic flight control system (AFCS) kicked off, which disabled our altitude hold. We began to rapidly descend toward the water. As my low-altitude warning system began to chime along with AWR2 Ballard's calls for power, I pulled up on the collective with the HAC. We arrested our descent at 8 feet over the water.

We rapidly climbed to 300 feet, well above our prescribed dipping altitude of 70 feet. I had to push down on the collective to keep the aircraft from exceeding engine and transmission limits. We momentarily stabilized with our transducer barely in the water. I wasn't even sure if it was still attached to the cable. I quickly reset our AFCS and enabled altitude hold during our momentary respite. However, the HAC began another aft drift, probably from unrecognized vertigo.

With the insistence of AWR2 Ballard, I took controls and stabilized the aircraft. We coordinated to raise our transducer, depart our hover, and return to the carrier.

Lessons Learned:

The first lesson is that during night operations, you should always heed your instruments. In a multi-piloted aircraft like the MH-60R, one of the pilots should always be focused on flying. There is a huge temptation to focus on the tactical scenario at the expense of maintaining proper control of the aircraft. This temptation needs to be recognized and addressed thoroughly in the mission brief.

The next lesson was in the critical CRM skill of assertiveness. I should have demanded control of the aircraft at the first signs of the HAC's vertigo, even if she was not willing to give up control right away. Our AWR2 demonstrated excellent CRM when he alerted us to the problem and added his voice in calling for a swap in controls. If our drift had been caught earlier, we never would have lost our AFCS and would have avoided our close call 8 feet over the water.

CRM is preached during all phases of training and is permanently burned into our memory. On nights like that of our incident, we look back and realize the importance of these proven techniques. Despite our initial CRM breakdowns, our AWR's assertiveness allowed us to recognize our descent and bring the aircraft back safely.

NOTES:

STICK TO THE PLAN

MH-60S, UNITED STATES NAVY, HSC-7, HELICOPTER SEA COMBAT SQUADRON 7

LTJG Ivan Chernov AND LT Jason Sutton, April 2014

It was the first week of a nine-month deployment onboard USS Harry S. Truman (CVN 75). Our crew was scheduled for an early morning log run, followed by a standard plane-guard flight to support carrier qualifications. The plan was to drop off a passenger and his baggage on a cruiser, then return to the carrier for a SAR training flight while also standing plane guard.

The scheduled timeline for the event was tight. We had to launch at 1130 for an 1145 overhead at the cruiser and make it back to support the carrier at 1205. This meant minimal time on the cruiser deck before we had to be within 20 miles of the carrier.

During the brief we verified the position of the cruiser with strike ops and briefed the timing aspect of our schedule. The cruiser was 19 miles away, and if we got off the deck early we could make it there and back with plenty of time to spare.

Because this was my first flight in the squadron, we walked to the aircraft early to make sure we'd be ahead of schedule. We were airborne by 1115, 15 minutes early, leaving us with what we thought would be plenty of time to complete the evolution. However, the passenger arrived with more baggage than we had planned. It took at least five minutes after getting chocked and chained on the cruiser to move him and the cargo out of the helicopter.

Shortly after takeoff, we completed communications checks and switched to the cruiser's TACAN. To our surprise, the DME read 45 miles, which was 26 miles farther away than briefed. Our crew reassessed the situation, and we decided that we could buster to the cruiser and still get back in plenty of time.

By 1130 we spotted the ship and tried to establish comms. We were in the cruiser's port delta a few minutes later. We tried to contact the ship on every available frequency, with no luck. We contacted the carrier and asked them to verify the frequencies we had on hand. The carrier replied that our frequencies were correct and that they had good communications with the cruiser. At exactly 1145, our original overhead time, the ship finally responded.

We were farther away from the carrier than anticipated, and we were quickly running out of time. The crew discussed the possibility of not returning to the carrier on time to assume our plane-guard duties. We decided to set a hard limit on when we would return to mom. Our crew decided to give the cruiser five minutes before cancelling the passenger transfer.

Five minutes later, the ship was not ready for us, so we told them that we were departing and would return later in the day. At the same time, the helicopter control officer (HCO) came back and asked us to wait one more minute for the green deck.

This is when our crew resource management (CRM) began to break down. Because we were so close to delivering the passenger, we decided to extend our time. This was our first mistake. It was now 1151, and we were still 30 miles from the carrier, with plane guard starting at 1205. In retrospect, we should have stuck to our original timeline to arrive at the carrier on time. Instead, we let ourselves become indecisive, tempted by at least getting the passenger dropped off. We continued to circle the cruiser.

Five minutes later, we still didn't have a green deck. We announced our intentions to depart, and again the HCO requested that we stay for one more minute. The crew decided to set up for an approach, and if the deck went green we would land. Otherwise, we would leave to get back within 20 miles of the carrier. Finally, on short final the cruiser called green deck, while at virtually the same time the carrier called to find out when we would be on station, because our absence was delaying flight operations for the rest of the air wing. We waved off and turned back to the carrier.

We set max torque and busted back to the carrier, arriving at 1209, four minutes late, still with the passenger onboard. And we ended up burning too much fuel while bustering back and had to set a max-endurance profile to stay SAR capable until our land time, preventing us from completing the SAR training we had scheduled.

Being the most junior pilot in the squadron, I didn't feel I had the experience to establish an effective timeline for the flight and deferred to the HAC. By being indecisive as a crew, we ended up having the cruiser needlessly set flight quarters, delayed CQs by four minutes, and did not complete the grade card for the SAR flight.

Our indecisiveness resulted in an incomplete mission and affected the carrier air wing's plan for that day. Had the distance between the ships been farther, we could have put ourselves in a critical fuel state, inducing our own emergency.

Lessons Learned:

This situation could have been avoided had we stuck to our original departure time from the cruiser. No single CRM principle is more important than any other. They are all critical and must be continually used to ensure a safe and successful flight. No matter what rank you wear or how many hours you have flown, always use CRM and be assertive.

NOTES:

NVG LIMITATIONS
BELL UH-1N TWIN HUEY, UNITED STATES AIR FORCE, UNIT WITHHELD

Name Withheld, October 2008

The mission seemed easy enough. The plan was to transport several passengers to a nearby National Guard base to participate in an exercise. Due to the early morning start of the exercise, the crew arrived at the squadron and quickly began mission planning. Since the flight would commence in the dark, we checked out and preflighted NVGs from life support. The weather forecast looked good and spoke well for the coming flight — good visibility and high ceilings. I noted that the temperature/dew point spread was only one degree, but I assumed that the spread would increase as the morning progressed.

The preflight brief was quick and to the point. There seemed little need to go into excessive detail on how we would handle various contingencies since the flight seemed relatively benign. Since we flew the majority of the flights routing to the exercise site daily and planned to stay above 500 feet AGL, little time was spent discussing the route or various low-level obstacles along the route.

We were a young and inexperienced crew. I had just recently

returned from my aircraft commander upgrade while the co-pilot and flight engineer had been in the Huey for less than a year. Our NVG flight time was low, and our NVG experience was limited to mostly fair weather flights. As I completed a quick walk around, it seemed to me that the ceilings were lower than forecast, but nothing that made me or anyone in the crew overly concerned. After an uneventful start and takeoff, we began the 40-minute flight to the exercise location. As the flight progressed, it was becoming obvious that the actual weather was much less ideal than the picture presented by the forecast. Since we were wearing NVGs and the illumination was very low, it was very difficult to determine the exact ceiling and visibility. After discussion with the crew, we decided that we would continue pressing on with the flight and would turn around and return to base if the conditions continued to deteriorate.

Looking forward through our goggles, the visibility appeared to be three to four miles, but there were hints that things weren't exactly what they seemed. Scintillation in the NVGs was starting to become more prevalent the further we progressed, an indication that the weather was probably worse than what we were seeing. I knew from my various NVG classes that it was relatively easy to get suckered into an inadvertent IMC situation on NVGs, since goggle users often could see farther though less dense clouds than unaided vision. Looking under our goggles and using the landing light as a measuring tool, we confirmed that the visibility was actually closer to one mile and getting worse by the minute. Looking behind us, the FE gave us the unwelcome news that the visibility behind us was worse than that ahead of us.

It was now obvious to the crew that our original mission was over, and our new priority was to get the helicopter and our passengers safely on the ground before we went completely IMC. The nearest helicopter pad was about two miles ahead. We used this pad frequently and knew it well, so I decided that we would press forward and land at the pad.

We started to descend in anticipation of the approach and in search of better visibility. As we were just starting to make out the outline of the helipad and brief up the approach, our luck ran out and visibility went to zero. I had practiced inadvertent IMC in the simulator many times, but I was truly unprepared for the reality of it. It was as if someone had thrown a switch and instantly we were in the dark.

Two undeniable facts came quickly to my mind. First, we were about 80 feet above the ground and descending, and secondly, I really didn't know exactly where the numerous towers were that I knew were in close proximity to the nearby helipad.

As the words "climb" came out of both my and the FE lips, the CP was already applying power and transitioning to instruments. I quickly flipped up my goggles and began turning on our cockpit lights. We were climbing slowly but surely away from the ground. When we climbed past the highest altitude of the nearby towers, I dialled up approach and let them know that we had gone inadvertently and requested vectors for the ILS.

After turning to our assigned heading and after what seemed like hours, we broke out of the clouds into one of the most beautiful skies I had ever seen. We were completely in clear blue sky, a solid deck of white clouds beneath us, and the sun was just starting to peak out above the horizon.

As the sun climbed higher in the sky and we flew on our downwind vector to the ILS, the clouds began to slowly break up. The ILS approach went smoothly and we broke out with enough ceiling to make it back to our helipad.

Lessons Learned:

After we returned to base and confessed our sins to our squadron leadership and fellow aircrew members, we finally had time to think about what had just happened to us.

I had made numerous mistakes, and things could have turned out much worse than they did.

First, I had blindly put my faith in our weather forecast and ignored the many signs that things weren't as predicted. The fact that temperature/dew point spread was a mere one degree should have set off some cautionary sirens in our heads. A forecast can sometimes be completely wrong, and there's no replacement for carefully monitoring local conditions before flight, coupled with a healthy dose of skepticism.

Secondly, there's no such thing as a "benign" flight, and preflight briefs should reflect this way of thinking. The time to wonder about where towers are is during the safety of pre-mission planning and the brief, not during a frantic climb out.

Lastly, never forget the golden rule of helicopters — you can land them almost anywhere. If it's safe to do so, land and think about what you're going to do next — from the safety of the ground.

NOTES:

CHAPTER 7

NEAR MISS & SEPARATION

"For those who love flying, the ability of the helicopter to hover and move in any direction from the hover with complete control gives a thrill and fascination that is not found in any other form of powered flight."

John Fay

HELICOPTER HAD TO TAKE EVASIVE ACTION
H-60 BLACKHAWK, UNIT UNIDENTIFIED

Name Withheld, July 2016

I was returning to [the] Heliport after a training flight with Night Vision Goggles (NVG).

We had flown the East Corridor route into the Class D and were in communication with Tower 5 miles prior to entering Class D. Prior to entering Class D airspace we were already at traffic pattern airspeed (100 KIAS) and had our landing light on.

About 1 km before reaching the highway interchange that sits on the approach path of Runway 23, Tower gave us clearance to proceed for [the heliport]. We turned to about a 090 heading toward [the heliport] to comply and began descending from corridor altitude (1300 MSL) to traffic pattern altitude (900 MSL). As we were crossing the Rwy 23 centerline, Tower cleared us to land on the approach end. He then amended the clearance to land departure half of [the runway]. We read back the clearances both times.

At this point I observed another H-60 Black Hawk that appeared to [be] outbound (I did not hear the takeoff clearance, but in retrospect Tower must have cleared them to takeoff from the departure end of [the runway], and then amended our clearance). I announced the traffic to my crew, and we saw the H-60 turn downwind in traffic pattern. Since we were cleared to land on the departure half of the runway, we figured this other H-60 would extend their downwind slightly and be cleared to land number 2 behind us.

As we were about 1.5 km final from the approach end of [the heliport], we were still at 100 KIAS to avoid delaying the traffic we were expecting to land behind us. At this point the H-60 in the traffic pattern turned base and called tower. Tower cleared them to land number one to the departure end and instructed them to keep their pattern inside of us.

As he was issuing the landing clearance to them, I could see we were converging. The opposing H-60 was at our 2 o'clock, so I executed an evasive 45 degree bank decelerating right turn to keep them in sight while allowing them to land first. I instructed my co-pilot to tell tower we were turning and confirm we were cleared to land. She called tower as we were turning and tower asked if we had the opposing H-60 in sight (we did obviously), and cleared us to land number 2 approach end of [the heliport]. We came within about 600 feet of the opposing H-60. I then turned left behind the opposing H-60 and executed a landing and taxi to parking.

Neither aircraft was informed by tower of traffic until the opposing H-60 called their base turn. It is difficult to judge distances at night under NVGs, so the opposing H-60 crew, if they saw us before turning base, may have thought we were over Rwy 23 because they had not been told to expect traffic and land number 2. Tower should not have cleared them to land in front of us since we had already been cleared to land to the departure end of [the heliport].

When Tower realized the conflict as the opposing H-60 turned base, he should have told them to standby and called us to cancel our landing clearance and turn us out of the way. Instead he gave a clearance to the opposing H-60 while we were converging, and forced me to take evasive action before he was done giving clearance.

The contributing factor may have been the fact that Tower was fairly busy with 2-3 other aircraft operating around the airport as we approached on the East Corridor.

Lessons Learned:

To prevent the issue, I could have called tower when I realized the other aircraft was remaining in the traffic pattern for [the heliport].

To avoid coming as close to the other aircraft, I could have made my evasive turn to the left and used a shallower bank angle, but I was sitting in the right seat and did not have as good a view out the left side and did not want to potentially cause a conflict with traffic on Runway 23.

NOTES:

CREW RISK MANAGEMENT DANGERS

MH-60S SEAHAWK, UNITED STATES NAVY, HELICOPTER SEA COMBAT SQUADRON 25

LT David Hicks, April 2015

We were deployed as the armed helicopter Det onboard USS Bonhomme Richard. However, that day we were tasked to support the ship and provide vertical replenishment (VERTREP) services. Because of the ship's limitations, we would not be permitted an early start, but would instead spin up at 1400 and conduct day-into-night VERTREP operations.

Having never conducted night VERTREP, I was excited to get a grade card (and finish out a syllabus) and I didn't perceive the Helicopter Aircraft Commander's (HAC) discomfort with the proposition of slinging loads throughout the evening.

I was to be on the third go in the second aircraft.

First up was a day card, followed by my HAC regaining his night VERTREP currency, and then we would finish up the evolution. Everything went smoothly.

Weather was holding about 2000/5 with favorable winds, both aircraft were performing flawlessly and I was starting to feel comfortable after a few loads.

The only hitch was getting optimal lighting between the two ships and the night vision goggles (NVG), but we were operating within expected parameters.

While our deck crew was readying the retro loads, they put my aircraft into the starboard delta and the other into a close port delta. It was a pitch black night, and this is where we made our first mistake — not using all of our resources contributed to a degradation of situational awareness.

We had a Multi-Spectral Targeting System (MTS) on the aircraft and yet we weren't monitoring the progression of the deck operations or the other aircraft.

After two laps in the pattern, Tower called in the other bird to pick up the first retro load and told us that we would be cleared in after they departed. I was sitting in the left seat and my HAC was flying from the right. I could search for our playmate visually during the close-in leg. We had heard them call inbound for the pick and wanted to be right behind them to make the evolution happen more quickly — we were already behind the airplan's landing time.

Still blind on our playmate, the HAC decided to move the pattern in much closer from the 1 and 3 mile legs and extend further aft on the ship to help us get eyes on the evolution and be more in position to move in for our pick. I started to feel uncomfortable with this.

I hadn't flown with him before, but I trusted his judgment based on his reputation and the conviction with which he was making decisions. This was my second mistake.

I had effectively eliminated a second and third pillar of CRM by not communicating the feelings of unease I was getting and sandbagging when I should have been more assertive with questioning his decisions.

We found ourselves about half a mile on the ship's 5 o'clock at 300 feet and heading up her starboard side in tight when we both almost simultaneously declared that we were uncomfortable.

It felt like minutes since playmate called inbound for the pick, we didn't have visual on them and we were significantly closer to the ship than tower had cleared us to be.

I strained at the harnesses and leaned out the window as much as I could, searching on and around the ship for other aircraft.

Conveying that I was blind to the crew, the second crewman and I began nervously scanning out as we were rapidly approaching the amidships position. I knew that the HAC couldn't see anything past me and if we needed to maneuver away from the deck, I would be the only one with a visual reference.

I saw a blur through my NVGs and some movement under the goggles. To my horror, I saw our playmate climbing directly towards us at about two rotors separation. I slapped the cyclic to the right to open the distance while yelling out the danger to the crew.

We were close enough that I could make out my friends in the other aircraft doing the same thing as they stared directly at me at about 100 feet of separation.

After the near-miss, we put the aircraft back in the starboard delta to figure out what had happened and to determine if we were safe as a crew and a flight to continue. We decided it would be best if we knocked off the dual ship operations and sent the second bird to recover after she dropped her current of retro, allowing us to finish the last six loads as a single ship.

Lessons Learned:

Looking back on the events of that night, it is still frightening to see the holes in the Swiss cheese lineup. We all learned a nearly fatal lesson that night. A simple slip and loss of situational awareness complicated with a further breakdown in CRM could have cost us dearly.

I will forever be a proponent of CRM in and out of the cockpit. I'll pass that information to everyone that I fly with in the future.

NOTES:

MH-65C DAUPHIN VS BEECHCRAFT

MH-65C DAUPHIN, UNITED STATES COAST GUARD, AIR STATION HUMBOLDT BAY

Name Withheld, Dec 2013

We were returning to ACV (Arcata–Eureka Airport) with a second MH-65C approximately 3 NM in trail. As the first aircraft approached Trinidad Head, a large rock outcropping 6 NM NW of ACV, the PM (Pilot Monitoring) transmitted their current position and altitude of 600 AGL and intentions to land on CTAF. Shortly thereafter, the PF (Pilot Flying) made a slight left turn around Trinidad Head and noticed a small, low wing, single engine aircraft less than a quarter of a mile off the MH-65C's 12 o'clock position. The PF called out the traffic to the crew, announced intent to make a descending right turn, reduced power, and made a smooth 10-20 AOB (Angle of Bank) turn to avoid the oncoming aircraft. Simultaneously, the PM warned the second MH-65C (still in trail) of the oncoming traffic to avoid a second incident. The general aviation aircraft passed to the left and above the MH65C within an estimated separation of 225 FT. The general aviation aircraft was not observed taking any evasive maneuvers.

Lessons Learned:

Additional Findings and Corrective Actions Taken:

1. TCAS did not display the target, nor did it provide a traffic alert. During preflight checks, the TCAS tested properly with no deficiencies. It is suspected that the general aviation aircraft was not equipped with an operating transponder.

2. No radio calls were heard over the ACV (Arcata–Eureka Airport) CTAF from the general aviation aircraft. The MH-65C was monitoring the ACV CTAF within 10 NM of the field in accordance with section 4-1-9 of the AIM. Additionally, the ARC210 was tested and found to be fully operational and configured properly. It is suspected that the general aviation aircraft was not utilizing or monitoring the ACV CTAF.

3. A transmission was heard on ACV CTAF just prior to the mishap of an aircraft on short final to Runway 32. It was confirmed later that this was not the aircraft involved in the mishap. There were two separate general aviation aircraft in the terminal area at the time of the mishap.

It is unknown if the general aviation aircraft involved in this mishap is a locally based aircraft or an aircraft transiting the area. However, as members of the local Pilot's Association, we intend to discuss this mishap with the civilian pilots who operate in and around the local area to make them more aware of locations where they may likely encounter a CG (Coast Guard) aircraft.

<u>NOTES:</u>

BLOCKS, BLOCKS, BLOCKS

MH-60S SEA HAWK, UNITED STATES NAVY, HELICOPTER SEA COMBAT SQUADRON 26

LT Sarah McGuire, Winter 2019

Our squadron was three weeks into our third long work-up. I was flying a night over water Tactical Formation (TACFORM) and aerial gunnery sortie in the lead aircraft with our new Super JO and two aircrewmen. We were planning to shoot a few hundred rounds for currency. The other helicopter had a junior helicopter aircraft commander (HAC), a budding Helicopter Second Pilot (H2P) getting a TACFORM grade card and two aircrewmen who were shooting for currency.

We thoroughly briefed the TACFORM maneuvers, gun patterns, bent weapons contingencies and the sequence of events. Although both crews were current and proficient in carrier operations, it was a dark night, and the Composite Training Unit Exercise (COMPTUEX) air plan was intricate. Dash two was the plane guard asset, so we planned to drop a smoke for a target and do gun runs within 10 nautical miles (nm) of the carrier.

Both aircraft launched uneventfully and proceeded 7 nm to the west while the carrier continued to make a path of intended movement (PIM) to the south. We assessed the many surface contacts and winds to determine our heading. COMPTUEX typically yields crowded airspace, lots of surface contacts and clobbered radios. However, despite these complexities, we were confident we could conduct our training without interfering with the fixed-wing cycle and still be available in the event the plane guard bird was called upon. After declaring green range, lead called for the first gun pattern, "Knight flight, L-Attack, left side, 360, follow-on timed race track."

The Seawolf maneuver description guide states that an "L-Attack" is an initial, quick method to suppress a threat, commonly used to transition to a race track pattern. It allows the helicopter to engage enemies on both the ingress and egress legs while protecting friendly forces and setting up an easy transition to follow-on patterns. The heading in the radio call is the firing leg heading, and the side clarifies which gun will be employed, either the long-range GAU-21 or the short-range M-240D.

A common configuration is to have the GAU-21 on the starboard side and the M-240D on the port side. The configuration plays a large part in setting up gun pattern geometry, and this common configuration in a race track pattern typically calls for a clockwise flight path to employ the M-240D on the inboard leg due to its shorter range and the GAU-21 on the outboard leg because of its longer range. However, on this night we had a port GAU-21 and a starboard M-240 to support search and rescue, so our configuration dictated a counterclockwise pattern. We neglected to clarify this in our brief or in the gun pattern call.

In formation, we turned north to heading 360 and set up to enter the race track pattern on the outboard leg. There was confusion regarding the pattern setup and entry. The flight lead attempted to clarify what was happening as we began the left turn for a counter-clockwise race track pattern.

As lead continued the pattern, wing was still confused on how the pattern would ultimately be executed.

Our aircrewman called "Aft stop" on the inboard leg, and the flight lead called "Out" and began a left turn to enter the outboard leg again.

As soon as we called "Out" in the lead aircraft, we saw a low-flying, fixed wing aircraft off our nose with bright lights. The carrier had turned without an updated Base Recovery Course (BRC) call and began recovering aircraft. What we saw was a jet on short final.

As we diverted our attention to regaining situational awareness (SA) on the geometry of the jet pattern, we lost SA of our own section.

Rolling out at 300 feet on the outbound leg of our gun pattern, we immediately noticed our wing aircraft's altitude, right off our nose. Our brief loss of SA had placed us in a head-on collision course with our other aircraft.

Both crews recognized the immediate need for vertical separation and called "Blocks!"

We maneuvered as briefed and began a descent to 150 feet while wing remained at 300 feet. Each aircraft maneuvered to pass port to port, and flight lead reiterated "Blocks" to emphasize the importance of altitude separation.

The near mid-air coupled with the realization that our section was operating on the final bearing yielded a "Knock it off" call from flight lead, and each aircraft proceeded to opposite holding deltas.

Enroute to the starboard side, we switched off air-to-air tactical air navigation (TACAN) and tuned up the carrier's TACAN.

While the crew was aggravated, we discussed the perfect storm that had brewed over the course of the flight and used good Crew Resource Management (CRM) from front to back and side to side to keep our heads in the game.

While we didn't expend all the ordnance we had planned for, we decided as a section that the training could be accomplished another time.

Both aircraft recovered uneventfully.

Lessons Learned:

We should have briefed the non-standard gun pattern and sacrificed brevity for clarity on the radios to ensure both aircraft clearly understood where they needed to be.

In the dynamic environment of carrier aviation, we should have expected the ship to turn without notice. In the execution of something non-standard, we had lost SA on the bigger picture of what was happening around us. While we have tools like Link 16, no single tool can be a substitution for good situational awareness.

It is imperative that pilots and aircrew maintain an aggressive scan of what is happening within their own aircraft, their section and environment around them. When a safety of flight call is made, pilots must react instantly to protect their crew and their aircraft. Practicing contingencies like altitude blocks, inadvertent Instrument Meteorological Conditions (IMC) and join-up procedures more frequently would create the muscle memory needed to safely execute these maneuvers when called upon.

As thorough as we thought our brief was, in the actual execution of our flight that night we allowed ourselves to become distracted by something non-standard that was not clearly briefed and we neglected to constantly assess our surroundings. Thankfully, good CRM proved effective and allowed our section to recover safely.

NOTES:

AIM POINT CHELSEA BRIDGE
PUMA HC MK2, ROYAL AIR FORCE, ASST HD SAFETY, JHC

Gp Capt Pete Warmerdam, November 2019

Of the many near misses that I have had over a long flying career, this one was the closest that I have come to meeting my maker. Had events taken a subtly different twist, there would have been 2 JHC helicopters crashing onto Chelsea Bridge in the middle of the day. It still gives me shivers when I think about it. I am sure that there would have been a lot of people left wondering how did that happen and, more importantly, why? My hope in writing this article is so that you can see where we went wrong for the lessons remain as valid today as they were then. Hopefully, you will avoid the pitfalls that we fell right into.

I was a very junior Wessex pilot in Northern Ireland. I had only just completed the Conversion Flight and much of what we would now consider core Conversion Flight Training was actually carried out on the Front Line as opportunities arose — this was one of them.

I was selected to occupy the co-pilot's seat for a formation trip to the mainland. It was broadly tied with my captain's final flight on the Squadron before being posted to another aircraft type — minor alarm bells should be ringing. He was an experienced and very competent operator, as was the crew of the Puma who would be leading the formation all the way to London. As the 'new boy', I was still 'water-skiing' someway behind my platform every time I got airborne and I was working hard to learn my trade. I was also not yet completely up to speed with how some of the systems on my aircraft worked. Fundamentally, I was nervous about making myself look stupid in front of some very experienced Squadron members and did not want to let the side down. Not wanting to be a complete sandbag, I asked if I could help to plan the sortie. For reasons that I cannot remember now, this was not to be; it was completed by the Puma crew. I was told by my captain that all we had to do was follow the other aircraft so not to worry — alarm bells getting louder...

The first time that I saw the route was during the brief. Not ideal, but not disastrous. However, I do not recall a detailed talk though of our route through the London Heli-lanes – particularly where we would be landing. Or if we did, I was so far behind the conversation, that I missed it. However, I was reassured by my captain that, as we were following the Puma, we would have the capacity to flight follow. I should have spent more time looking at the maps, but I felt reassured by his calm demeanour. As you will see, this was to have serious consequences...

As we launched and flew across the Irish Sea, I was back in my familiar territory of water-skiing a couple of miles behind the aircraft and desperately trying to haul myself back into the cockpit. I was not helped when the captain asked me to change the aircraft's Squawk in response to some ATC direction. A simple task but at no point through our Wessex Conversion Training had we discussed IFF (Identification Friend or Foe transponder system). As I recall, it was not used in Northern Ireland and so was seen as surplus to requirements. After failing to locate the IFF and looking at my captain blankly, he returned my plea with a diatribe of contempt along the line of 'standards slipping' , etc.

Doing my best, we progressed towards London. In fact, I had

broadly clawed my way back into the aircraft someway across the Irish Sea and I was actually beginning to enjoy the trip and relax.

Entering London's airspace is a busy undertaking. There are multiple radio changes and you have to fly exactly on the Heli-route or you are challenged by the radar controller. Get this wrong and the chances are that you will be denied a further routing and asked to leave London. When we were looking to land at Chelsea Barracks, that would have been less than ideal. Our lead was doing a super job and we followed the route to join the Thames and fly westwards. With us sitting in echelon left at 2 rotor spans all seemed to be going nicely. I was following the route on the 50' thou map and calling the bridges as we passed them. For ease, the route had been helpfully marked with a yellow highlighter. Our route had continued along this 'yellow brick road' until the edge of the map.

As we reached this fold, I turned the map over and was 'heads in'. Confusingly, there was no yellow highlighted route on the other side of the map. Just as I turned the map back over to try and establish where we were going, a loud expletive came from my captain, and the next thing I knew was that we were pointing nose down 'banzai style' directly at Chelsea Bridge. This was rapidly followed by the aircraft's nose being dragged back up into the sky. I looked at the captain to work out what that was all for, but he looked rather deathly pale — so I dropped it. We regained the Puma in a descent into the barracks and we followed them down to the landing point.

What had occurred was that the Heli-lanes map had been folded over very close to the landing point, and the highlighter had been drawn to the edge of the map. I had followed this 'yellow brick road' a little too far and had missed the small 'x' marking the landing point. The Puma co-pilot had made the same error as me but, as the author, he had recognised his mistake much quicker. At risk of flying past Chelsea Barracks and voiding our clearance, he called for his pilot to make a hard left. As you recall, we were in echelon port and all my captain and crewman saw was a face full of Puma getting very rapidly closer. He firstly bunted the aircraft down to get under the

Puma's disc and then pulled back on the stick to avoid the Puma's rotor disc chopping our tail off.

Lessons Learned:

On the ground, we had a frank debrief, with some members using choice words to discuss my performance. Others refused to even talk about it, still suffering from the shock of our potential demise. So what could and should we have done better:

1. There are no 'freebie' sorties. Treat every one of them in a professional manner, your life may depend on it.
2. Even in this era of electronic maps, time spent route studying is seldom wasted.
3. If you are not clear about anything in the brief or something has been omitted, then you must speak up. Silence is a tacit acceptance that you understand the plan.
4. Know how to use the systems on your aircraft.
5. As the deputy in a formation, it is your responsibility to avoid the leader. We should have been on the right-hand side. If you are the lead, be aware where your subordinate is and try not to 'break' into them unless you have to.
6. If you have junior people in the crew (and this is increasingly the case) build time into the planning, briefing and the sortie to ensure that they are able to function as a member of the crew.
7. Lastly, share the experience so that others may learn from your mistakes.

NOTES:

WILDCAT AW159 V AW169
WILDCAT AW159, ROYAL AIR FORCE, UNIT WITHHELD

Name Withheld, March 2019

The Wildcat Pilot reported that he was on a Low-Level NVD NAVEX, flying at about 90kts, having climbed to a minimum safe height (MSH) of 300ft AGL in the vicinity of an unlit mast.

The handling pilot in the right-hand-seat saw an aircraft/strobe at 2 o'clock slightly low, constant bearing just emerging from behind the aircraft frame at the right-hand-side on the windscreen. The other aircraft was also masked by cultural lighting.

He turned the Wildcat to the right to increase the separation and pass behind. The other aircraft made no discernible change in direction. His TAS registered no contact or alert. He informed Yeovilton ATC and filed an Airprox.

The AW169 Pilot reported that he had been tasked to recover a medical crew from Southampton General Hospital after a previous HEMS (Helicopter Emergency Medical Service) mission.

Whilst on the ground during take-off checks it was noted that the aircraft's transponder had selected 0000 by itself instead of the usual

0020 Squawk. 0020 was therefore reselected but he believes he failed to turn on the TA/RA selection at this point.

He departed Henstridge and climbed to 1500ft. During the climb out no other aircraft was observed by either himself or the technical crewman. He believes that his aircraft's TCAS system would have potentially alerted him to the position of the other aircraft, but he was in a sustained climb throughout the incident having just departed his operating base and with high ground on track to the east.

During a telephone conversation with the Secretariat the AW169 pilot said that there is a known fault with the transponder on this aircraft type where it will occasionally reset to 0000.

It was whilst resetting the transponder to the HEMS code that he inadvertently forgot to turn the transponder back on. This was discovered later in the sortie and rectified. Unfortunately, this was after the Airprox and therefore resulted in the AW169 and Wildcat electronic warning systems not being able to function as expected.

Lessons Learned:

The Wildcat pilot spotted a single strobe against cultural lighting. The conflict turned out to be an AW169, departing on a routine transit, which was not speaking to an ATC agency, not squawking and did not have a route on CADS (centralised aviation data service).

- The Wildcat pilot in this Airprox (operating on NVD, looking at a backdrop of cultural lighting with the conflict emerging from the aircraft frame) did a good job of spotting the AW169.
- NVD seriously reduces your field of vision — keep your head moving to optimise the chance of spotting another aircraft.
- Aircraft conflictions can happen anywhere and at any time.

Other aircraft encountered at low-level in Class G airspace may well not be talking to ATC, not squawking and not have routes published on CADS. In this high work-load environment, rely solely on TAS at your peril! If you expect not to be able to contact your nearest ATC agency before getting airborne, why not call them on the landline and pass your intentions? Had the AW169 called Yeovilton on the phone beforehand, the incident might not have happened.

NOTES:

THAT WORST NIGHT
CH-47 CHINOOK, ROYAL AIR FORCE, 18 SQUADRON

Sqn Ldr Paul "Foo" Kennard RAF (Rtd), March 2003

Aviation sometimes deals us a difficult hand. How we play it depends very much on our training, our experience, our crew mates and, sometimes, simply dumb luck. I've always believed in two clear tenets of aviation; firstly 'fly the aircraft' – it's the only thing that will ultimately stop you from hitting terra firma, an obstruction or your wingman with enough momentum to hurt. Secondly, 'Maintain Situational Awareness' — keep your head, stay ahead of the aircraft and the circumstances you're in and, just maybe, one day (or night) it'll help you to fly your way out of a tight corner.

I'm still here to tell this tale as a result of all the above, including the 'dumb luck' part.

March 20th 2003 was this 'night of nights'. We'd spent the previous 3 months preparing for our small part in the opening act of Operation Iraqi Freedom. We, 18 Sqn and our 5 CH-47s embarked on HMS Ark Royal, were to help insert the Royal Marines of 40 Commando into the Al Fawr oil refinery the night before the invasion 'proper'. The Commander's Intent was to prevent the Iraqis from wrecking the facilities (which would be needed for post-war reconstruction) and minimise the potential for catastrophic environmental damage to the waters of the North Arabian Gulf if the Iraqi Regime elected to enact a 'scorched earth' policy.

The plan was for 8x USAF MH53E 'Pave Low' Special Forces helicopters to insert a number of SEAL teams to secure HLS' throughout the facility for our 5x CH47s to insert a double-company lift (200+) Marines and light weapons shortly afterwards. Elsewhere, RN Sea Kings would be inserting small groups of Marines to capture pumping stations and valve buildings. With the first wave complete, the Chinooks would start to build up combat power with vehicles, anti-tank weapons and other support equipment. As the helicopters were inserting the troops, landing craft and hovercraft would be delivering light tanks and other vehicles to nearby beaches. It was to be a classic 'all-arms' amphibious Coup de Main.

The original intent for me, as the Sqn's lead Qualified Helicopter Tactics Instructor (QHTI) and Training Officer, was to sit on the jump-seat of the lead aircraft and provide tactical advice/guidance to the flight lead. On the day we disembarked from the carrier to pre-position for the assault, one of the pilots had a welfare crisis at home and had to leave the ship immediately. As I knew the plan intimately, I slotted in as the co-pilot of "Vader 5" and flew with our Army exchange officer, Nick, who, though experienced in aviation terms, was still relatively new to the Chinook.

Like most plans, it started to fall apart almost as soon as it started. Firstly, the beaches that the Landing Craft and hovercraft planned to use were found to be mined and obstructed. The weather conditions were appalling with inflight visibility down to 500m in blowing dust/sand in places. The plan was for a 2200hrs (local) insertion to provide some protection for us against optically laid weapons, and for us to fly in at extreme low level to stay below the detection and engagement threshold height for any mobile SAM or AAA guns thought likely to be in the area. Therefore, as we launched on the first wave, we were flying at about 60ft with atrocious inflight visibility. A flight of a few minutes rapidly stretched as the MH-53Es and SEALs were struggling as well. We finally received the 'go' code at last, turned off all external lights, armed up the DAS kit and pressed from the hold point into the target area at 140kts / 50ft. Then things began to unravel...

"BREAK RIGHT! No... don't bother..." came the shout from the crewman.

"What the hell was that for?" I shouted.

"Pave Low, co-alt, opposite-direction about one or two spans" came the somewhat numbed response. What? The routes around the target were all one-directional to prevent exactly this near miss from happening. We were less than 100ft laterally separated from a head on mid-air collision — exactly the same scenario that would kill 7 fellow Ark Royal Air Group aircrew when two Sea King Mk7s collided a scant two days later.

I reflected on the dumb luck that had saved us — as the deconfliction plan had clearly failed to do so.

We entered Iraqi airspace — the Radar Warning Receiver was clear apart from the odd tag from friendly aircraft radars. We knew that, high above us, a B-52 was systematically jamming Iraqi comms frequencies and radars, and that we had flights of A10s and F/A-18s in a stack 'on call' if we needed them. There was also an AC-130 Gunship in the overhead of the target acting as a rebro facility, illumination and fire support platform. We turned onto our target run and were just starting to make out the lights of the refinery through the murk when we were told to change HLS – about 45 secs from 'wheels down'. I punched the new grid into the kit, set up a Tac Steer for Nick and yelled "quick stop when we fly past a mast" — just as we flew past it. Nick hauled the nose about 30 degrees nose-up and dumped the lever as we tried to shed 140kts of airspeed quickly and, as he eased the nose down, I saw the IR strobe that marked the new LS and steered him to it. We landed between a number of buildings with sporadic contact reports coming in over the net. As the troops cleared out of the ramp, I realised that the only person leaving who knew they were in a different place to that they'd been expecting for 3 months was the stick commander on the jump seat... who was the last man off the aircraft. The 'fog of war' exemplified.

We lifted and followed our one-directional route back to Tactical Assembly Area (TAA) Viking where Nick flew a textbook night dust landing onto the refuel spot and we took a suck of gas. Almost immediately the call for "Wave 2" came. Vader 1-4 all had a similar planned load of 1x internal and 1x external Landrover WMIK (Weapons Mount Installation Kit) – known universally as "Wimmicks" - plus crews. We, in Vader 5, were required to carry a BV206 Ambulance. The BV206 is a two-part articulated tracked vehicle, beloved by the Royal Marines due to its literal 'go anywhere' capabilities. Nick was a little nervous as the Ambulance BV, as only one of two in Theatre, had never appeared at any of the mission rehearsals as it was assessed too valuable to risk damage. He was now going to have to pick it up for the first time in Degraded Visual Environment (DVE) conditions due to both darkness and severely restricted visibility — down to 15-20m in our own downwash generated dust cloud. To help, two land rovers were parked in front of us to give Nick at least one reference. In a superb piece of flying, he got the BV attached first time and started to pull pitch to lift it off the ground. I felt the aircraft 'self-centre' as it normally did over a heavy load. The BV was 'advertised' in the fly-out manifest as being approx 5000 kg and was contained in an under-slung net rated for 5600 kg (plus 10% margin). Based on the temperature, our aircraft weight/fuel load and the estimated mass of the BV I'd briefed Nick to expect the load to come clear off the ground at between 75 and 80% matched torque. I watched, and felt Nick continue to raise the lever... 80%...85%...90% - Damn it — this BV was grotesquely overloaded. A rule of thumb in the Chinook is that 5% of torque equates to around 1000 kg so as the BV finally got airborne at 96-97% torque we knew it was about 3-3500 kg overweight. Nick settled the hover and I informed him that the BV was outside the tolerances for the rigging and that, in peacetime, we didn't have the power margin to transition

As captain he weighed my advice and reached the same decision I'd already made — "It's wartime guys, we'll take it" and transitioned gently with me watching the torque and engine instruments closely.

Initially as the speed increased all was well. I felt the Cyclic moving a lot between my knees, with commensurate 'pumping' of the Collective. I glanced across the cockpit and saw Nick's head fixated to the right window. The load was unstable under the aircraft, there was no horizon due to dust and no features on the ground as we were over the desert. The only reference Nick had was the Main Supply Route (MSR) out of his right window — he was flying the aircraft totally via reference to it. We both knew that as we turned east to follow the route to the target this reference would disappear. Normally when a load becomes unstable you attempt to stabilise it by climbing and turning. We couldn't climb as we had a number of coordination levels above us (fixed wing, cruise missile, fire support etc) and we were still very concerned re Iraqi radar-laid weapons. With the load we were flying at about 100ft agl and 75 kts and as we turned onto the route the oscillations didn't damp out.

Now Nick was struggling. He now had zero outside references. The control inputs got bigger as he 'chased' the instruments which were 'lagging' the actions of the wayward BV. He was slipping deeper into Pilot Induced Oscillation (PIO), and he knew it.

My Situational Awareness (SA) 'Spidey-sense' kicked in and a massive surge of adrenaline coursed through my body. I rationalised that we were likely to have to jettison the BV before too long. In the dark, bucking cockpit I reached up located and lifted the switch guard on the "Emer Release All" switch and placed my finger on the switch. Nick was, by now, totally task saturated and deeply mired in a PIO; he simply had no reference to null the oscillations to and the instruments, control inputs and aircraft were out of synch.

"Do you want to take it?" he asked, almost pleadingly. Every single part of me wanted to grab the sticks and try to fly us out of the situation, but my SA told me that it would be pointless and that I'd likely only delay the inevitable. Through gritted teeth I told Nick that, no, I wouldn't take control as I was prepped to hit the jettison and that he should 'stick with it' in the hope we'd get to the coast and find the reference he desperately needed.

Then it all fell apart in the blink of an eye. And time stood still. I remember the events of the next couple of seconds in detail.

First, I felt the nose pitch up rapidly. The BV had 'swung-through' underneath and caught Nick exactly at the wrong end of a PIO, with the stick fully back. I felt the Collective hit my left elbow as Nick pulled it up rapidly to the stops. I glanced at the instruments — they looked like the worst Simulated Unusual Position (UP) ever. The Artificial Horizon was indication nearly 25 degrees nose up, the Airspeed Indicator o kts, the Vertical Speed Indicator needle plummeted as I watched it and the torque gauge read a scarcely believable 130% matched, the Master Caution came on with the "Emer Pwr" caption. Then the Rad Alt noise went off. It was set to 50ft I think, due to the load, but the RadAlt sensors on the Chinook are under the nose, which was 25 degrees above the horizon...how much space did that leave under the tail and the rear rotor disc? Vanishingly little.

I felt that horrendous 'sink' that helicopter pilots get at the end of a Quick Stop when they forget to pull in enough power to hover OGE.

That settled it. My rationale for maintaining SA, locating the Jettison Switch and refusing to take control culminated at this point. Without hesitation I shouted 'JETTISON JETTISON!" and flicked the "Emer Release All", designed to trigger a canister of nitrogen to 'blow open' all 3 hooks under the aircraft. At the exact moment I was doing this, the Air LoadMaster monitoring the load through the load hatch in the floor felt the aircraft lurch nose up, begin to 'fall' out of the sky and received a face full of dust through the hatch. This combination of events passed his personal threshold and he pulled the mechanical 'Emer Release All' which used cables to achieve the same effect as nitrogen.

Subsequently we found out that he'd pulled first — probably by a fraction of a second. Regardless, the result was the same.

I remember tales from WWII bomber crew of how their aircraft would 'buck' as the bombs left — especially if dropping a large weapon such as a Tall Boy or Grand Slam. I now believe it. The Chinook was 25 degrees nose up, zero airspeed, 130% torque applied and suddenly approximately 8500 kg lighter. The result was predictable. The aircraft surged up, backwards and yawing into a sandstorm. We smashed through the fixed wing co-ordination level, the cruise missile level and the Fire Support Coordination Level. Nick shouted did I want to take over? This time I did — he was mentally shot from the efforts of the past 10 minutes.

I took control — 'Fly the aircraft' was all I would allow myself to focus on. Treat it like the worst Unusual Position recovery you've ever practiced — except this is real and there's a chance you could end up in an irrecoverable situation – or shot down by your own side. First, Ball, stamp it into the middle, wings, level... Ok, still climbing ease off the power, gently, so as not to cause any large attitude changes, airspeed, zero — in fact we're probably going backwards – so select and hold 10-15 degrees nose down and wait. After what seemed an age, the ASI flickered and we moved back into positive airspeed. I allowed myself to breathe as we passed 40kts and the aircraft started flying normally again. Okay, altitude. Damn it — we're sat at over 1500ft agl – and now the highest threat is mid-air collision or being shot down. With great reluctance, I stuffed the nose down and dived back to the comparative safety of a desert floor that I couldn't see through my NVGs.

I checked the crew in, checked the aircraft which, like the absolute Beast the CH-47 is, seemed perfectly happy with no Captions or warnings. Once established back at 100ft agl Rad Alt and broadly on track I handed control back to Nick. I suggested that we should head back to the Carrier as we couldn't tell if the hooks had been blown by nitrogen or mechanically and would need resetting, and the over-torque would require at the very least an inspection. After a somewhat emotional radio call to HQ informing them that we'd dropped the BV ("Why did you do that?" — "Because the f*cking thing tried to kill us!") we flew back to the ship with only the mild inconveniences of AWACS warning of a suspected ZSU-23/4 on our route (it wasn't, but it robbed a few more heartbeats) and the final flourish of the night, a cruise missile launch off a frigate that flashed past our nose within a couple of hundred feet.

We were numb with shock when we walked into the Ops Room. We were the first crew back and we walked in white as sheets. "How bad is it?" was all they could say.

Lessons Learned:

One is reminded of the old adage that:

"Superior pilots use their superior knowledge and superior experience to prevent situations that require their superior handling skills."

I could sense things were not going to go well, and mentally prepared myself to release the load (in itself not easy — screwing an important mission on the first night of the war railed against my sense of duty and pride). I identified the switch and flicked up the Guard. Had I needed to do that in the endgame I would not have been able to due to time and the lurching airframe.

The hardest thing to do was turning down Nick's request to take the aircraft the first time. I had the SA; I knew if I took control I would be consumed by the flying task – I had to maintain the bigger picture.

With the load gone, I knew that it was time for my considerably more hours on the Chinook to be exploited and I it was the right thing to do to take the aircraft and recover it from the UP.

'Fly the aircraft'. I knew I was going to bust all of the height restrictions during the recovery, but I also knew that to be safe, the

UP recovery needed to be methodical and unhurried to reduce the chances of a total loss of control, and to minimise exposure above our cleared height. I took one element at a time. Yaw, then bank, then pitch, then attitude, get positive airspeed and finally reset to a safe altitude.

Crew cooperation. We functioned superbly as a crew that night. Nick did all he could but realised when he'd reached his limits as aircraft commander and handling pilot — and it was superb airmanship and captaincy to realise this and ask for help. The rear crew carried out their duties faultlessly — and the independent decision to pull the Jettison speaks volumes for the trust between the 4 of us. I like to think I displayed good 'followership' that night. As soon as I could, I gave Nick the aircraft back again — his own development as a captain depended on it in my opinion.

So, there you have it, my worst night. The near mid-air with the Pave Low and the Cruise Missile were freakish dumb luck incidents, both of which another time may have resulted in a different outcome. The rogue BV was entirely of our own side's making; we were later told it was over 3000kg overweight and all of it was loaded into one of the two coupled vehicles, making it exceedingly out of balance as well, hence why it was utterly out of control underneath us.

Several months later I was a student on the Royal Marines Amphibious Ops Planning Course, learning how to plan, organise and execute missions like the assault on the Al Fawr. One of the lessons, from a RM Quartermaster, started with a picture of the BV I dropped, and he began a spiel about 'some useless Crab pilot who ran out of talent and threw away a perfectly good BV'. I raised my hand and enquired, politely, if he'd like the 'useless Crab pilot' to tell his side of the tale?

The last lesson, from the classroom — know your audience!

Safe flying!

NOTES:

LESSONS FROM AN AIRPROX

SQUIRREL HT1/2 AS-350BB, ROYAL AIR FORCE, UNIT WITHHELD

Name Withheld, December 2011

As someone who is all too familiar with the student end of the flying training system, I have often been briefed to be wary of cockpit authority gradient.

This is a difficult balancing act for a young student whose relationship with an instructor is normally characterised by dependence on the instructor's skill and knowledge. Equally, the benefits of being a meek and dutiful student are all too apparent if an instructor has his own unconventional opinions about risk and the rules (and doesn't mind scoring a tick sheet with these opinions in mind!) For these reasons, it can be easy, under some circumstances, to accept the practice of an instructor, even when it contravenes what the student knows to be the correct course of action. Nonetheless, despite inferior rank and experience, a student is repeatedly told that they should never slavishly follow the example set by their instructor.

My anecdote regarding cockpit authority gradient began in earnest on Ground School. The Air Operations instructor posed an important question to his captive audience one Friday afternoon:

"what is an Airprox?" The answer was, of course, "It is a situation in which, in the opinion of a pilot or a controller, the distance between aircraft as well as their relative positions and speed have been such that the safety of the aircraft involved was or may have been compromised," and our class chanted the answer in perfect unison, having done all the required reading the previous night.

Not only did the instructor tell us exactly what an Airprox was but he also told us exactly what to do, should we ever have one. We were told that we must report the occurrence. We were left in no doubt of our responsibility to make sure that everyone be made aware of an airprox occurrence.

After ground school, I eventually found myself in the rotary wing training pipeline; however, my memory was undimmed by the time that had passed since EFT ground school. My hard won and lightly worn learning had, if anything, been polished by my time in the air and on training squadrons.

This was fortunate, because the airspace around Shawbury can be quite congested and LFA 9 (Low Flying Area) contains a large number of students in helicopters. Keeping a clear and up to date situational awareness is paramount; it is an area of sky which offers almost unlimited opportunities for an airprox, or worse.

One fateful day I was flying a dual trip in LFA 9 with my instructor, a highly experienced pilot who commanded a great deal of respect from the students and his fellow instructors alike. The trip was towards the end of the Squirrel syllabus and this meant that the content of the sortie varied enormously as the instructor tried to prepare me for everything I might encounter in my Final Handling Test. As the exercises changed quickly, it was difficult to keep track of other aircraft and to predict how our new activity might impact other users of LFA 9.

At one point in the sortie we started conducting PFLs (Practice forced landing). We were aware of another Squirrel operating nearby, also carrying out PFLs, and a large proportion of our combined effort was devoted to maintaining a positive awareness of the location and activity of this other aircraft. Simultaneously, we were carrying out autorotations to the flare-recovery (quite capacity intensive).

During a particularly difficult autorotation, we lost track of the other aircraft but decided that we were clear of the other aircraft and elected to continue. Little did we know, the other aircraft was carrying out their PFL into an area only a few fields away. Once I had finished the handling exercise, my instructor asked me to climb away, so I carried out my checks and did exactly that.

My instructor was 'heads-in' at this point, working out the next phase of the sortie and as we climbed, the other aircraft, in autorotation, came straight through our vector from top left to bottom right with only 3 rotor spans of clearance. As I manoeuvred to avoid a collision, my instructor missed the event.

Lessons Learned:

After a brief discussion in the cockpit, my instructor informed me that it was not an airprox, and, based entirely on his judgement, I agreed. Despite ground school, I was easily convinced to misdiagnose an airprox and not report it.

RAF comment

A sharp intake of breath and a 'welcome to the club' would be a good old legacy response to this young cub's story. Perhaps the most encouraging point we should note from this article is that of the young trainee's gut reaction to his crusty instructor's entrenched attitude. From this we can conclude that at least one member of the next generation of our fine Royal Air Force has Reporting Culture embedded in his young soul. Fantastic to see! So much so that when I first read this letter, I held it aloft and shouted 'hurrah!' For too long our senior aircrew have cast a jaundiced eye over the whole business of reporting and safety. Indeed, I cannot excuse myself from this accusation.

I would be lying by omission if I didn't admit to having trimmed the VHF aerials from a Meteor travelling in the opposite direction at 250 feet and thought, 'best not mention that to the boss.' Safety reporting just seemed so lengthy and lifting your head above the parapet only seemed to draw fire from every direction. I can only imagine the number of lessons this culture prevented us from learning and, consequently, the number of aircrew who went on to make the same, potentially fatal, mistakes. However this kind of thing doesn't have to continue and shouldn't.

On a positive note, we are developing a strong Just and Reporting Culture and it's easy to get on board. It just requires old lags like myself to drop their legacy baggage before getting in the cockpit, and for all of us to prick up our ears and pay attention to what's going on in the air, and pipe up where appropriate.

NOTES:

CHAPTER 8

KNOWLEDGE, DECISION MAKING & RISK

"It would be right to say that the helicopter's role in saving lives represents one of the most glorious pages in the history of human flight."

Igor Sikorsky

MAXIMISING ALLOWABLE RISK
PAVEHAWK HH-60G, UNITED STATES AIR FORCE, UNIT WITHHELD

Capt Chris K. Cunningham, May 2008

Military aviators are acutely aware of the inherent risk involved in their missions. Whether leading the initial attacks or providing humanitarian aid to others around the world, aviators are expected to perform their jobs, often overcoming daunting challenges.

The training environment is where pilots begin their quest for a career in flying. Over the years, it has become more apparent that pilots require training that emphasizes safety and realism. Scenarios are increasingly designed to model the fight that the US Armed Forces are facing in the current War on Terrorism.

Unfortunately, simulated scenarios can never provide the complete experience. Conditions in the real world often merit higher levels of risk than are warranted during a training scenario. While weather minimums and emergency procedures are rarely challenged without consequences in the training environment, they may not be strictly adhered to in the combat environment, especially when actively engaged by enemy forces.

A dangerous downside to "combat adrenaline" is the desire by aviators to push the limits in combat situations, often leading aviators to bypass critical fundamental procedures unnecessarily.

One such example was clearly demonstrated by an HH-60G combat search and rescue crew on a mission in Afghanistan. On a moonless fall evening in the heart of Afghanistan, a Pavehawk crew received a tasking to rescue two critically wounded coalition soldiers. A convoy had come under attack, and the soldiers were bleeding from multiple bullet wounds. The area was still under attack when the mission came down to launch. Originally, leadership hesitated launching the aircraft to avoid further casualties. However, further information led them to believe that the attack would be repelled before the end of the hour-long flight to reach the wounded soldiers. Leadership approved the launch, and the HH-60G crew, with an AH-64 Apache escort, took off near their maximum gross weight. Calculations by the pilots and flight engineer showed that the Pavehawk would likely have a 2 to 3 percent power margin for an out-of-ground-effect hover after the fuel burn during the hour-long flight. In the meantime, both leadership and the rescue aircrews hoped that the convoy on the ground would fend off the attack with their A-10 and AH-64 air assets on-scene.

Upon arrival south of the landing zone, the rescue aircraft determined that the area was still "hot." Enemy combatants had largely been contained, but sporadic mortar attacks and gunfire were still factors, limiting the convoy's ability to move from behind their cover to a safer location. The rescue crews were strictly instructed to not proceed until the ground team deemed the area "cold." The consensus from the rescue crews and the coalition ground forces was to attempt the rescue due to the critical condition of the two wounded soldiers, estimated to be within two hours of fatality. Focusing largely on the sporadic enemy gunfire, the HH-60G crew overestimated the necessity to enter the landing zone with a tactical approach. Generally, tactical approaches are reserved for combat situations, because performing a remote profile in the aircraft would be overly time-consuming and expose the aircraft to enemy fire. The remote profile incorporates multiple passes in a circular pattern overhead at a high altitude and a low altitude, referred to as high and low reconnaissance, close to the landing parameters to give the aircrew a good visual confirmation on the probable landing area. The aircrew diligently determines the existing conditions in the potential zone with their instruments and by direct sight during these reconnaissance passes. In contrast, the tactical profile omits these high and low reconnaissance reviews over the landing zone. The tactical approach is implemented in lieu of the remote approach by evaluating the most critical information before arriving at the zone, such as winds, elevation, temperature, pressure and terrain (analyzed via maps that give little detail on the exact landing location often picked on short final). The unfortunate dilemma is that evaluating such information before arriving at an area gives the aircrew at best a "wag" of the actual conditions. The mountainous environment often presents drastically different conditions from one ridgeline to the next, and performing evaluations of current conditions en route before arrival can give significantly unrealistic expectations in the actual landing area. More importantly, the tactical approach gives pilots little opportunity to see intricacies that often accompany the landing zone. Too many times, helicopters come too close to unknown hazards, such as trees and ditches, when landing in unfamiliar territory.

A further problem with incorporating tactical approaches unnecessarily is that it also limits the aircrew's ability to apply thorough operational risk management. It's generally understood that ORM is a continuing process throughout the sortie and that it must be constantly updated as the mission evolves. While aircrews may still accomplish an update to ORM when using a tactical approach, they may not have enough information to adequately update the situation. Thus, an essential tool to weighing the risk versus benefit is often omitted or used in less than its full capacity.

Consumed by the urgency of the medical situation and the threat of the enemy, the Pavehawk crew expedited their approach into the zone to recover the two critical coalition soldiers. The tactical approach was initiated with a direct crosswind, due to the mountainous terrain that rose from the direction of the wind. With little information on the landing area, the crew began its approach and encountered a brownout beginning about 50 feet above the ground. Brownout is dirt or sand kicked up by the rotor wash of a helicopter, completely blinding the pilots when landing. It's common for pilots to use a combination of their instrumentation and outside visual cues in these situations; brownouts typically don't blind pilots until the last 15 feet above the ground. This brownout severely limited the crew's ability to visually navigate into the zone with the normal outside/inside crosscheck, and a go-around was called for. The pilot quickly maneuvered the aircraft around for another approach, with no evaluation of the conditions encountered on the first approach. On the second approach, the brownout began at virtually the same height above the ground, and the pilot was excessively slow, requiring a second go-around.

On the third approach, it was decided that shooting the approach directly into the wind might be a more suitable flight path, despite the lack of an escape route ahead caused by the rising terrain. The aircrew was unaware that the landing zone itself would now have a cliff off the right side with this new approach angle. The third approach culminated with a nearly catastrophic ending. The pilot, determined to not get slow as he had on the second approach, kept a higher airspeed going into the zone. As the brownout engulfed the Pavehawk, a slight right drift was induced by a minor case of spatial disorientation that is quite common with a rapid disappearance of any discernible outside visuals. The aircraft quickly drifted toward the cliff, missing the landing zone by only a few feet. The cliff had a 30-degree slope near the top and quickly increased to greater than 60 degrees further down the ridgeline. The Pavehawk was nearly double its allowable slope limit upon the left wheel at touchdown, and began a right roll to tumble down the mountainside. With a combination of training, luck and divine intervention, the Pavehawk ceased its rolling momentum, and the pilot was able to take off.

As if the mission had not already had its fair share of tests, another challenge arose during takeoff out of the zone. Unknown to the crew, the aircraft experienced significant power deterioration stemming from the ingestion of sand on the three approaches into the landing zone. The number two engine was now producing roughly 20 percent less power than it did when the mission started. As the aircraft flew away from the impending destruction of the ridgeline, the rotor rotations-per-minute slowed below acceptable flight limits once the momentum from ground effect ceased. The engines simply didn't have enough power to keep the rotor at its required speed, and the aircraft, having reached 100 feet, began to settle back toward the ground. The FLIR image showed nothing but mountain ahead, and the pilots could only hold the power in at the level required to clear the terrain, hoping that the engines would eventually catch up. Pulling in more power would only exacerbate the situation by demanding more pitch from the rotor and slowing it down further. Taking power out would clearly lead to the inevitable crash into the terrain ahead. Slowly, the engines caught up to the rotor, and the Pavehawk cleared the terrain by 10 feet. The aircrew climbed safely overhead and gathered their thoughts on how to proceed for the rest of the mission, nearly forgetting about the enemy who drove them to choose the tactical profile in the first place.

It was at this point that the Pavehawk crew identified hazards and assessed the risk. First, the crew discussed that they were ready for one final attempt to rescue the two coalition soldiers. The crew was shaken up, but determined to make things right. Next, the crew discussed the enemy and realized that the occasional muzzle flash was not really a factor in their approaches into the zone. Third, the combination of the significant brownout, coupled with a moonless night, required further planning to identify the actual landing spot that the convoy was expecting. The crew felt that the benefit of saving the two lives outweighed the risk of going in for a fourth and final attempt.

The crew used their new epiphanies to analyze risk control measures. They agreed to dismiss the enemy threat, opting to perform a high and low reconnaissance analysis of the landing spot in a right turn and a left turn, so that the entire crew would have a good view of how to make the approach. On the low approaches, the pilots each took a turn flying down to about 50 feet, maintaining good forward airspeed to attain temperature, wind, pressure and a close-up view of the landing zone. Finally, the aircrew requested that the ground team light up the edges of the area with chemlights. This gave the aircrew a clear outline of exactly where to land the helicopter. Having made the control decisions and implementing the risk control measures, it was time to make the final attempt. Nervousness pervaded the atmosphere of the aircraft as the aircrew began their descent into the dark bowl of the landing zone. The landing was picture perfect, and both coalition soldiers were loaded onboard the aircraft.

Lessons Learned:

Safely returning both soldiers to the hospital, the Pavehawk crew learned an essential lesson: there is never a situation where some form of safety awareness and risk management cannot be applied. It's tempting at times to forego the litany of regulations and guidance during real-world missions that often seem to inhibit mission execution. There are certainly situations where higher levels of risk are acceptable, perhaps even warranted, but a careful analysis of that situation should be attempted when possible. More often than not, as this Pavehawk crew experienced firsthand, there is time to make responsible and carefully considered decisions, even in the heat of battle.

NOTES:

THAT'S HOW WE ALWAYS DID IT YEARS AGO

PUMA HC MK2, ROYAL AIR FORCE, PUMA FORCE

Name Withheld, November 2010

February 2010... It's the Puma Force's first deployment to Norway for winter training in 3 years. During the European transit en-route to Bardufoss, Norway, for Exercise CLOCKWORK 10, our 3-ship Puma helicopter formation had planned a 3-day route stopping in Aalborg, Denmark and Trondheim, Norway before reaching our destination on the third day. However, in true Support Helicopter fashion, we were constantly hampered by bad weather... pretty much the norm for Europe in February.

Due to the bad weather, the formation never actually stayed or refuelled anywhere that was originally planned, instead overnighting at Groningen, Holland... Odense, Denmark and then Molde, Norway. Having lost a day-and-a-half in Denmark, there was also the perception within the crews that we had to try our utmost to get to Norway in order to commence training, as the Puma Force had very limited time to get many of its personnel qualified in arctic techniques, and a limited number of days on the Exercise. This was pretty much a self-induced pressure as the detachment commander and the training officer were both part of the transit party.

In hindsight, a call to the Duty Flight Commander (DFC) at Benson or indeed the Squadron Boss would have been the better option as they would definitely have given us advice and reassured us that these 'pressures' were not there!

Having previously refuelled with F34 fuel (with icing inhibitor) and F35 fuel (without icing inhibitor) through the low-countries we had yet to experience sub-zero temperatures on our transit. However on a clear-weather day in Norway, the decision was made for a straight-line transit between Kristiansand and Floro rather than a lower-level coastal route, as it saved approx 2-3 hrs and another refuel stop.

This route would have kept us within the Outside Air Temperature (OAT) limits laid down in the Puma Release to Service which states that flight without icing inhibitor in the fuel is not permitted below 0°C.

We refuelled the aircraft with F35 (this was our first mistake) and planned our sortie. Terrain meant that a high-level (above Flight Level 70, OAT -15 deg C) transit was needed and all 3 crews (consisting of 2 pilot instructors, 3 training captains, 1 pilot standards officer (STANO), one crewman instructor, one crewman trainer and one crewman STANO) agreed it as the best course of action.

This was our second and potentially most critical mistake. By choosing this course we were disregarding the Release-to-Service (RTS) limits with respect to the use of F35 (i.e. fuel without icing inhibitor (FSII)), which is not to be used below 0°C OAT).

Everyone was working on the 'old wives tail' that as long as there was some FSII in the tanks from the previous fill, then everything would be fine. We further compounded our earlier errors when we were ordered, under Radar Control, by ATC to climb further still into even colder air at FL100 which we complied with, without question, and continued to fly there for 15 minutes with an OAT of approx -21°c.

The formation then began a descent for the approach to Floro and during this descent the lead aircraft experienced a momentary drop of engine performance (Ng) on the No 1 engine. The drop lasted less than one-second and fortunately for us, recovered to normal readings with no further fluctuations. All the aircraft then landed at Floro approx 20 mins later without further incident, where the crew concerned heaved a sigh of relief and then refuelled with standard F34 fuel with FSII.

Although there is no way of knowing what actually happened to the engine that day, we came to the conclusion that the event may have been caused by the early signs of fuel icing.

The possibility is that the lack of FSII in the tanks caused residual water within the fuel to freeze and under the pressure change in the descent the ice formed was dislodged, travelled through the system and thus caused the engine speed to drop.

The Release to Service limits are based on the temperature exposure the fuel has prior to entering the engine and in a Puma the fuel pipe routing unintentionally ensures that the fuel is cooled to the ambient OAT, in this case well below the 0 °C specified. We disregarded clearly specified limits in our haste to arrive in good time and in doing so we could have seriously damaged our chances of arriving at all.

OC CLOCKWORK's Comments

The crews involved in this incident were well practiced, current and qualified, had flown for several hours and indeed days prior to what at first sight seems a minor event; a momentary drop in engine performance.

Where the crews have been entirely proactive, is in their recognition of the potential seriousness of their lapse of judgement taking unprotected fuel and their post-flight analysis of the events. It is seemingly minor events that can trigger a sequence which can lead to a serious incident.

In this case the minor event has led to a learning exercise for current arctic operators and a dispelling of certain 'myths and legends' about the way we used to do business.

A DFSOR was raised to ensure that the lessons that this deploying crew learned will not be lost and I'm really pleased that Air Clues is back to ensure that there is a vehicle to pass this information on to a wider audience. A double engine flame-out over mountains, in the winter, in Norway, at -15 deg C, is not the place to remember the reason for using fuel with FSII; these crews were probably lucky (although we will never really know), but most importantly are to be commended for their honesty.

Lessons Learned:

I fully concur with OC CLOCKWORK's comments, the crew of this aircraft are to be fully commended for their professional and honest analysis and subsequent reporting of what appears to be a 'non-event'.

The inculcation of a questioning culture, where we review our actions and errors is **fundamental** to ensuring that we not only report errors in the first place, but also that we are able to learn valuable lessons about preventing their reoccurrence as well.

The key to understanding error is not to glibly construct an obvious error chain, that is forged in the fires of hindsight, rather we need to put ourselves in the position of this crew as they made each decision and think, "Why did they take this particular course of action?"

As an example, when the crews decided to make a high level transit without FSII in the tanks, we can all look back and say that was a risky decision, but why did they take it? The fact that so many were involved in the decision making process and approved the final decision, points toward a high degree of 'risky shift'; where the degree of risk that the group is willing to take is significantly higher than individual members would take on their own.

So what? What factors actually convinced that group that this was a good call, despite their years of aviation experience? Pressure, overconfidence, unrealistic risk reduction? Ultimately, I leave the analysis to you, for it is fundamental that you question the decisions and glean the 'whys and wherefores' of error. From there you can consider how often you have been in a similar situation and how you would deal with it in the future without inducing unnecessary risk.

NOTES:

OH NO. WE'RE GOING OVER!

CH-146 GRIFFON, ROYAL CANADIAN AIR FORCE, 403 OPERATIONAL TRAINING SQUADRON

Captain Scott Boer, 2019

The following is an account from an instructor's perspective on how quickly a routine landing can go wrong, and how luck and muscle memory prevented a catastrophic loss of a helicopter. I have 2700 hours instructing on the Griffon over an 18 year span, and have over 5400 hours of flight time.

Our squadron was on a night surge to get our students graduated before the arrival of the next course. As part of the weekend flying routine I was scheduled for a Sunday night formation flight.

The squadron had removed the skis during a warm weather deployment so I planned to modify my landing to prevent the helicopter from burying too deeply in the snowpack.

The weather was clear with ¾ moon and moderate northerly winds, night vision goggle (NVG) illumination was very good but due to the fresh snow and a bright moon, the contrast conditions were flat light. This meant that the subtle shadows and textures that give you a sense of depth perception were being washed out.

We started at 20h30 and began with formation confined area circuits, navigation and lead changes. At the first two landing zones (LZ), we had large areas that had been in direct sunlight that day, which helped to melt down and solidify the snow pack. The snowballs were weak to moderate and we could easily see through them by turning off the NVG searchlight. Unfortunately the third LZ was a different beast altogether!

We were #2 in formation approaching the LZ from the south. The landing area was ringed by a forest and the southern half had been in the shade all day. We arrived over the tree line. I turned off the NVG searchlight to prevent washout and we began to descend into the area. The student was in the left seat and I was monitoring the controls and the student from the right seat. The descent initially was very smooth, and although the lighting was flat, we could pick out some bushes and small trees as references.

At about 5-10 feet above the ground the flight engineer (FE) noted some right hand drift, and the student was correcting. Then in a split second the upper crust of snow broke free and a snow bomb of fine powder was exposed. We were instantly engulfed in a total whiteout! Before either of us could say, "whiteout;" and before I could take control, I felt a sickening thump and an immediate lurch to the right.

We had impacted with right drift and the right skid had immediately impaled itself into the snow pack and stuck tight. We were in a dynamic rollover situation!

My eyes snapped to the attitude indicator (AI) and it felt like I was watching in slow motion from the third person as my hands and muscles began to fly faster than I could consciously think.

Impact... As I felt the lurch, time began to dilate as I grabbed the controls and my mind went into high gear.

1 second... we were at 7 degrees, left cyclic, power going down to flat pitch.

2 seconds... 14 degrees, still rolling, hard left cyclic, power is down at flat pitch.

3 seconds... 23 degrees and still rolling. I could visualize the right disk only inches above the ground now, and felt myself lean left away from the ground. Cyclic alone wouldn't stop the rollover so my body pulled collective to hover neutral in an attempt to power the aircraft up and out of the snowpack.

4 seconds... With hover power and full left cyclic the aircraft heaved out of the snowpack and immediately swung like a huge pendulum over to the left at 20 degrees of bank.

5 seconds... Now I was in a blinding snow ball, oscillating left and right, hovering somewhere around 4 feet, and with a tree line lurking about 25 feet off my right wing. Crap! I didn't trust the ground under me, couldn't see anything outside except an angry swirling green ball of snow, my only out was straight up.

6 seconds... My life now centered on the AI as I used my unusual attitude training and muscle memory to dampen the oscillations, apply climb power, and keep the disk level in the climb.

15 seconds... At about 40 feet we broke out of the snowball with ½ rotor clearance from the tree line that was on our right side.

Time returned to normal and my limbs began to shake as I felt a cold wash of adrenaline leaving my system.

Lessons Learned:

I learned the following lessons that night:

1. Having an aircraft not properly configured for the environmental conditions made things worse when the landing was non-standard. An aircraft equipped with skis would not have dug into the snow so quickly or so deeply.

2. Rushing a landing before you can assess environmental conditions can quickly put you in a whiteout. I should have ensured we were descending slower and not at a rate that was faster than our reaction times. Especially on NVG's.

3. Core training on muscle memory and scan allowed my body and subconscious to react faster than I could consciously assimilate the information from the AI. I impacted, rolled right, had full left cyclic, power on and broke free of the snowpack in less than 4 seconds. It truly felt like 30-40 very long seconds. My hands were flying faster than my brain was working.

4. LUCK is not a skill, I was lucky, very lucky that the blades did not hit the ground. Lucky that the skid was not hooked under an object; and lucky that while in the snowball I did not drift right into the tree line, or left and up into my lead aircraft.

5. The old saying, "Truly superior pilots are those who use their superior judgment to avoid those situations where they might have to use their superior skills" is still true!

NOTES:

NO MOON, NO HORIZON, NO INSTRUMENTS

MH-60R, UNITED STATES NAVY, HSM-51, HELICOPTER MARITIME STRIKE SQUADRON 51

LT Matt Petersen, LTJG Blake Smith & PO3 Ryan Morina, December 2016

The MH-60R can be described as a network of computers, with a helicopter built around them. On a midnight flight, we were going to find out what happened when those computers went haywire.

It was in the third month of an extended Forward Deployed Naval Forces (FDNF) cruise; and my second time as a helicopter aircraft commander (HAC), and LTJG Blake Smith and PO3 Ryan Morina's nugget cruise. We had flown together as a crew dozens of times, and we were well-versed and comfortable flying together. This mission was looking to be an exciting night of searching our operating area for a contact of interest.

As we got off deck, we realized it was also going to be a varsity night behind the boat. There was no moon, no horizon; a thick blanket of haze up through several thousand feet; and nothing to look at but green static through our night vision goggles.

Two hours into our event, with no joy so far, we found a radar contact that looked interesting.

We were already 70 miles from our ship, with no diverts in the area. We pushed farther out to get eyes on. As we did, the computer popped a GPS unavailable advisory. A few minutes later came drift velocity miscompare and longitude miscompare. The aircraft was flying just fine — it's possible it was just software problems.

We had a bad feeling about it. We had never seen these two new advisories before. In fact, they weren't in the Naval Air Training and Operating Procedures Standardization (NATOPS) pocket checklist, or even in the NATOPS manual. MH-60R software development outstripped NATOPS development, and it was not uncommon to see advisories in the aircraft that were not mentioned in the NATOPS manual. Thus far, they had been annoyances only; not safety-of-flight related. Although our aircraft seemed OK , we discussed our discomfort with a mysteriously degrading aircraft on a moonless night. We turned for home.

The soul of the MH-60R is the embedded GPS inertial navigation system (EGI). The two EGIs draw from onboard accelerometers as well as GPS, and feed the flight instruments and the automated flight control system, or AFCS. The AFCS keeps the aircraft spinning side up. If the EGIs lose touch with GPS, in theory, they will kick over to only the onboard gyros (INS) and continue to provide attitude instrument information to the pilots.

Because there are two EGIs, a dual-EGI failure was considered unlikely, and we had never trained on it. A glass-cockpit aircraft, the MH-60 has four analog back-up instruments, which are rarely used.

These are a steam gauge altimeter, airspeed indicator, magnetic compass, and an attitude indicator the size of a wristwatch. We called the back-up attitude indicator the "peanut gyro" due to its size. When we lost EGIs and AFCS in IMC in the simulator, we typically departed controlled flight. The last time that we knew of a crew of an H-60 series aircraft losing their primary flight instruments at night, they didn't make it home.

We were 60 miles from the ship, headed home, when our EGIs bit the dust.

Our primary attitude indicators processed, giving opposite readings on pitch and roll. Our heading indicators rotated unrealistically. Our vertical velocity indicators read substantial climbs and descents, even as the aircraft wallowed in level flight. The aircraft displayed a series of miscompare indications for almost every parameter of digital flight instrumentation. Our AFCS control panel spit out a slew of failures, and we felt the aircraft controls become squirrelly, with the nose wandering up and down in pitch and mucking about in roll. The GPS-derived groundspeed indication accelerated to 255 knots, a physical impossibility for this aircraft. Every malfunction was written across both the right and left seat flight displays.

While we wrestled with the aircraft, barely maintaining straight and level flight on the peanut gyro, we declared an emergency and attempted to troubleshoot the EGIs. Amazingly, both our EGIs were shown as fully functional. Without miscompares in NATOPS, we were drawing a blank for troubleshooting. We considered cycling our EGIs, but also saw that possibility as further degrading the aircraft, which still claimed to have good EGIs. As a crew, we quickly assessed our situation. What do we have that still works? The helicopter was still spinning side up. The engines were running. Trim seemed to work. Altitude and airspeed seemed to be valid. "Trust your instruments" had been drilled into us a million times — but tonight, there were hardly any instruments that we could trust.

It became rapidly apparent we could focus on little else beyond flying the aircraft. The back-up instruments were mounted in the center of the cockpit, between the two pilots. In order to read them accurately, one had to lean inward, away from the vertical, essentially begging for vertigo.

As we flew, the aircraft kept wandering off to the left. At first we thought this was part of the controllability problems, but we realized that as the left-seat pilot flew, leaning to the right to read the instruments, he was unconsciously rolling us back to the left, to level his vestibular plane.

We realized that we were getting close to falling down the rabbit hole of vertigo. We fought this by flying and reading instruments together, talking back and forth as we did. We weren't so much "flying pilot" and "monitoring pilot" any longer. Instead, we combined all of our inputs, corrections, and instrument readings together into one steady stream of communication. As one pilot moved the controls, the other read the instruments, calling for corrections and slight movements in a given direction. The magnetic compass tumbled every time we turned (think back to the good old T-34 sims) and we swagged rollout headings on turns. We talked to each other, continuously, for the next 45 minutes, and as we did we kept vertigo at bay.

Approaching the ship, we needed to descend to our landing pattern altitude. We stepped down, calling every 100 feet, stopping our descent in stages to ensure that we could recage when we pulled power.

Every crew member was monitoring altitude, one pilot on the radar altitude (RADALT), the other on the barometric backup and aircrewman member backing up RADALT, with the ship's onboard controller, OS2 Lamb , monitoring our descent via SPY radar. We found the ship visually as a speck in our NVGs at three nautical miles, but had to turn outbound to set up a shallow, extended final. We requested a clear-deck landing as we didn't feel that we had the controllability to fight for a trap over the deck.

Creeping toward the back of the ship, oscillating power and altitude as we did so, we had to fight off the black-hole illusion common to small deck landings, by talking back and forth to stay oriented and caged and to keep the aircraft under control. Our altitude fluctuated high enough to consider a wave off, but we had only been able to orient ourselves to the deck at 0.3 DME, and flying this approach again didn't seem worth the risk.

We slid the aircraft back forward and down over the deck, inched into the circle, and set it down smoothly.

Lessons Learned:

Post-mission reconstruction of the many sources of flight data provided by the MH-60R showed that GPS had rapidly cycled in and out several times, precipitating this event. Both of our EGIs reacted poorly and began generating incorrect outputs. The bad EGI data scrambled our flight instruments and the AFCS.

As to why the EGIs didn't kick to INS as advertised, and what caused the initial GPS interruption? The jury is still out.

In the meantime, stay fluent in crew resource management and partial panel. It may save your life.

NOTES:

PUSHING THE LIMITS
PUMA HC MK2, ROYAL AIR FORCE, C FLIGHT, 230 SQUADRON

Flt Lt Tom Woods, July 2011

Five feet isn't a huge distance to have between the tips of your rotor blades and several substantial trees. It is exactly half the minimum horizontal separation allowed in this scenario, however this was the clearest area in the vicinity.

Having discussed the options with the crew we elected to squeeze the aircraft into a landing site which would normally be deemed unsuitable. So I had broken my authorisation, had parked a Puma helicopter in the tightest 'Confined Area' I had ever seen and just to add some excitement to an already interesting morning the intercom decided to completely fail right there and then!

This was the start to one of many casualty evacuations (Casevacs) on Exercise Grand Prix, in Kenya.

To set the scene I should first start with a brief description of the Exercise, the operating environment and the requirement for aviation support in Africa.

Ex Grand Prix takes place in central Kenya, approximately 90 miles north of Nairobi.

It is a continuing commitment that allows the British Army to conduct large scale live-fire training, vital to ongoing Operations the world over. The operating conditions are challenging, for both ground forces and aviation assets. Airfield elevation is 6200ft and the temperature is typically 25-30 Celsius by day, the terrain in the training areas is mostly sun baked dirt interspersed with prickly shrubs and 30-40ft high Kenya Trees. The need for rotary-wing casevac support results from the dangerous nature of live-fire training coupled with several factors, including:

- An almost complete lack of an ambulance/paramedic service in Kenya.
- Incomplete, poorly maintained and dangerous road network.
- Large distances between training areas and medical facilities.

I had been involved in a handful of casevac flights in Kenya previously, one particular occasion remains vivid in my mind. I had been the co-pilot, paired up with a more experienced operator on casevac duty and had been forward based in the field with the exercising troops.

The duty mobile phone awoke us at 3am and we received a '9-liner' (a request for casevac helicopter support), it appeared the casualty had a badly fractured ankle and would need airlifting from the training area to Nairobi hospital at first light. The pick-up was uneventful but as we got closer to Nairobi we were confronted with a growing wall of cloud blocking our intended route. Initially we tried climbing to go over the solid layer of stratus and pick our way through the towering cumulus that was above, it became obvious that this would not be feasible. So we went back, decided to descend and pick our way through the valleys under the inclement weather. I was still flying at this point with lots of direction and encouragement from my Captain.

Going down through a gap in the cloud and into a steep sided valley, the conditions ahead didn't look great so I slowed the Puma and lowered the landing gear, but we decided to push on a little further. It wasn't long after that I remember getting that uncomfortable feeling inside that I usually get when things aren't entirely right. I elected to fly a valley turn-back and the Captain agreed, after this manoeuvre he decided the situation was getting a little tricky and he would take control and I would navigate him to the hospital. We continued to box around the weather, picking our way through valleys in heavy rain and turbulent conditions. It was getting us closer to Nairobi but slowly and our fuel state meant we had to choose whether to keep pushing for Nairobi or to turn back for our Main Operating Base. I'm convinced on any other flight we would have gone home but we had developed task focus and were intent on getting our casualty to hospital. I managed to negotiate a radar service and vectors to either a cloud break or the instrument landing system (ILS) at Nairobi International airport.

I should point out at this juncture that I had not taken this option earlier because the Radar Vector Chart would have required a climb above 10,000ft without oxygen. So the controller vectored us towards the city at approximately 1500ft agl, eventually a small break in the cloud appeared.

Having dived through the gap we made a successful visual join and landed at the airport, where an ambulance was waiting to forward our casualty to hospital.

I will quickly elaborate on the situation I started describing in the introduction to this article, before I link the two.

The casevac began with a '9-Liner' passed by radio, it was an 'Urgent, RTA with spinal injuries'. My co-pilot quickly thumbed through his aide-memoire and stated that 'Urgent' meant the casualty was to be in hospital within 90 minutes. This focused my mind, someone in the training area had been involved in a Road Traffic Accident, had sustained spinal injuries and needed to be in Nairobi hospital within 90 minutes.

The transit alone would take longer than this so there was a real sense of urgency to find the soldier and get him out quickly.

On the way to the accident the intercom cut-out intermittently for 1-2 seconds at a time, fearing the worst I briefed our actions in the event of a total failure. Arriving in the area we surveyed the surroundings, there wasn't anywhere you could describe as a suitable landing site. Scrub, bushes and trees covered the landscape for a mile in all directions. The troops on the ground threw a smoke grenade onto a track which was in the clearest area, this site was the best of a bad bunch and we decided to give it a closer look because the casualty was in a bad way.

After the initial approach to a high hover it was evident that the obstructions would infringe the allowed minima. As the captain, I was faced with the difficult decision: continue and in doing so break the rules, with the view to potentially save a life or scrub the sortie and send ground assets for the soldier. The danger to the aircraft and more importantly the crew had to be weighed up against the risk to the casualty.

I decided, based on all the information available, that it was worth the risk and checked that everyone in the crew was happy to continue. The crewman worked quickly to safely position the helicopter onto the track, with bushes under the rotor disc and a tree in front of the helicopter and one next to the tail rotor. As we landed I breathed a sigh of relief, I also remember being quite taken aback by the sight of a 6ft bush literally right beside my cockpit door. Two soldiers emerged from a nearby vehicle and started a brisk walk toward the helicopter, we assumed this was the local commander coming to brief us on the patient's condition and confirm loading instructions for the stretcher, etc. A stunned silence fell across the aircraft when our crewman announced that one of those two men was actually our casualty!

Our medic conducted a quick assessment of the soldier and suggested that in his opinion he had minor whiplash and didn't need urgent medical attention.

The whole crew was pretty angry about this, but we only had a moment to dwell on it before we were confronted with the next hurdle. The intercom, which you'll remember was playing up earlier, now totally quit. We tried everything we could to fix it but without success. I yelled for the crewman to come forward to the cockpit and confirmed, through the medium of shouting, that we would get out of the confined area as planned but then go back to the Forward Operating Base (FBO) and not the hospital.

As we lifted the co-pilot had swivelled around in his seat looking at the crewman and relaying his instructions to me using a combination of hand signals and verbal directions. We transited back to the FOB where the local medical team was waiting, again the co-pilot used his very effective hand ballet and shouted information to convey the crewman's input and position the aircraft safely. So, two fairly demanding flights, on the first we knew the casualty wasn't in a critical condition but pushed through bad flight conditions to achieve our goal. On the second we pushed the limits based on the information we had been passed, which transpired to be inaccurate and misleading. As it turns out the badly fractured ankle was actually just a sprain and the severe spinal injury was minor whiplash, both of which could have easily been transported by ground assets.

Lessons Learned:

The major lesson I learnt was when you start getting close to the limits, it is wise to take stock for a moment and ask the question: Is this really necessary? Or, what is this actually achieving? If at this stage the risk is not worth the reward then it's probably worth finding an alternative solution.

The second lesson I learnt was how accurate information is absolutely vital to the decision making process. To this end I believe it's pertinent to question/check the information you are passed and keep that information picture updated regularly, especially if you are going to make key judgments based on the weight of that evidence.

<u>Spry says:</u>

An excellent recount from the author. It is difficult to complete accurate risk assessment when given inaccurate information. It would be very easy for me to comment on the rule-breaking by the author, but it was considered rule breaking for an organisational gain, not a personal one. Does that make it right? No. Does it make it understandable? That is a harder question.

Military captains are trained to make difficult decisions at times. In order to make the best decisions possible they must know the rules and fully understand the situation. Decisions must be made with awareness of the required task and possible implications; the foremost of which is safety. The second account particularly demonstrates an evaluation of all the available factors in order to come to a decision with safety in mind. Task focus at the expense of other considerations is a regular occurrence — never let it override safety considerations. There could be more casualties requiring evacuation.

NOTES:

MINIMUM FUEL RESERVES

SEA KING WS-61, ROYAL AIR FORCE, SEARCH AND RESCUE

Name Withheld, June 2012

As a SAR captain, my crew's duty period would normally be for a 24hr shift starting at 0920hrs. My crew will be at RS15 (15 minutes to launch when tasked) until 2200hrs after which we'd enter a more restful period at RS45. The sequence of events outlined below occurred during such a duty shift; it occurred some years ago but the lessons drawn from seeing a series of apparently well considered decisions conspire against us, remain relevant today and when considering flying supervision I have developed a healthy interest in fatigue management.

On the day in question we were much busier than usual with a mixture of some unexpected admin, a demanding role training sortie, completion of some necessary post maintenance flight testing, and finally a SAR Op task to search the river for a bridge jumper. By the time we'd landed from the job it was well into the evening and we'd hardly stopped during the first ten hours of the shift but we still had a few sorties to debrief not to mention some food to prepare for a somewhat late dinner!

After 2200hrs, one or two of the crew retired to their beds while the remainder chose to relax with a bit of TV... then at 2300hrs the job phone rang.

Our task was to collect a MedEvac team and incubator from Leicester, ferry them to Plymouth to stabilise and package a one-day-old baby, then return all pax and equipment to Leicester. The weather en-route appeared fine with good light levels so weight calculations from the pick-up were assessed to determine our maximum fuel load and an RV (rendezvous) time for the landing site was agreed. At this point, I was aware of the fatigue in us all and it's fair to say we were a bit grumpy about going out on what we knew would be an all-nighter.

Upon arrival at Leicester, there was some confusion; the med team were not ready and there was a rumour that the baby may have died. Despite several attempted phone calls, direction was unclear but we were asked to remain rotors turning. After nearly one hour burning-and-turning on the ground, the med team and incubator arrived; they appeared in a hurry so after a recheck of the fuel against remaining distance it was mentioned that reserve margins were tight but were sufficient and we launched.

Routing to the south-west was an uneventful medium level transit in Reversionary Night Flying (RNF) conditions. Fuel was checked regularly against distance/time information and the options of refuel started to be discussed. At around 0330, fuel was again mentioned and as we were approaching Bristol it was noted that, if the airfield had been open, a fuel top-up would have been handy. However, it was not available and as Bristol came and went Chivenor was discussed next: with 24hr fuel from the SAR flight it was a promising option but significantly off-route which would have delayed our landing at Plymouth by a further hour. Mindful that the time delay would have been frustrating for our passengers, and following a further fuel check showing there to be just enough for the final leg, we again continued with the plan.

Upon reaching Dartmoor the weather had deteriorated such that our RNF transit was no longer possible.

We 'goggled down' and continued at 250ft, but in deteriorating visibility our speed was necessarily reduced, then as the ground started to rise it was decided to pull up to safety altitude or VMC on top. Now over SCT cloud, the later necessary descent was discussed but a few of the earlier speed reductions, combined with a notable head wind, presented a more alarming fuel situation and it was at this point that a diversion to Exeter was considered. Unfortunately, although Exeter was intermittently visual through cloud gaps, fuel was not available for another couple of hours so an unplanned diversion would have incurred significant delays. So with almost equal distance between Exeter or pressing on to our destination at Plymouth it was decided to go with the latter.

By about 15 miles to run, fellow captions started to illuminate; intermittently at first, but when steady a rather sick feeling spread through the crew. We were now at 3500ft over complete cloud cover; it was about 0530 and still dark; we were approaching a closed airfield with no usable instrument approach aids and we now had about 10 mins of reliable fuel remaining. Options were to either continue over Plymouth looking for a gap in the clouds but essentially preparing for an internal aids letdown over the sea... or... commence a form of controlled — albeit emergency – descent through the cloud in the hope of a break before Plymouth. It was decided that the former contained too much time risk: at best this would see us to a landing on the beach but the risk of flame-out at some point during our radar procedures could have led to a messy ditching. Therefore, following a double check of our GPS position against obstructions and terrain on the map, we set rad-alt bugs to 500ft for the descent. As we approached 500ft we were still IMC; nothing of the ground was seen but we were still confident of being just 3 miles to the north of Plymouth. With fuel captions on and very little showing on the fuel gauges, we set our rad-alt bugs to 200ft for further descent then fortunately, at around 300ft AGL, we broke cloud almost at the airfield boundary and were able to take a running landing to the first available stretch of tarmac. We all drew a huge sigh of relief.

Lessons Learned:

While our passengers got to work at the hospital, we made a short telephone call to the ARCC to inform them of our fatigue state and an ac from Culdrose continued with the mission while we slept.

In our subsequent analysis as a crew, we recognised that by 0300hrs, about 20 hours from our last sleep, our appreciation of the situation had undoubtedly been impaired; we'd made a series of questionable fuel decisions ignoring all diversion allowances and we'd become too task focussed.

Ultimately, we had been very lucky.

An aviation medicine doctors view :

This is a prime example of "press-on-itis," — a situation wherein the mindset of getting an important job done is so set that information suggesting that a change of plans is required are not given enough weight in decision making (This is a close cousin to 'get-home-itis').

The motivation to provide time-critical, possibly life-saving aid to a seriously ill infant was very strong.

It is entirely understandable how decisions to continue the mission without diversion for refuelling was influenced by this consideration, which probably contributed to the crew's acceptance of the hour on the ground with engines running rather than shutting down and restarting. There is also a tendency to believe that, 'Things will come out okay in the end', in part due to the fact that SAR crew have generally experienced many highly demanding missions which have 'Come out okay in the end'.

It was reasonable to expect this one to do so likewise, and in part based on the fact that the mind does not like to conceive of adverse outcomes, such as mission failure or actual fuel depletion and its consequences. This is especially true when one has a "can do" attitude towards life, and where part of the consequences of failure is a threat to one's life and physical health.

Fatigue promotes "tunnel vision" in which one focuses attention on the most salient parts of the flight environment, paying less attention to items perceived to be of "lesser" importance. In this incident, as fatigue progresses, "getting the job done" becomes of prime importance with fuel status receding in importance. It is notable that they did not ignore it; fuel concerns were addressed several times.

Fatigue also makes it more difficult to perceive when a situation is changing from what is planned, and what is present in the aircrews' minds, even when data is at hand which suggests that a change of plan is necessary. In this instance, it seems that fatigue prevented the crew from having the insight, "This is not going to work. We must divert to refuel."

Fatigue did not cause the situation described above to develop, but it combined with high level of motivation to proceed in a life-saving mission, bad weather, that fact that medical personnel were on board who expected to be delivered as advertised, and perhaps professional SAR pride in always getting the job done. This combination led the crew down the 'garden path' into a very dangerous situation. This is and the other factors mentioned above.

NOTES:

1000 AND 3

AH-1W COBRA, UNITED STATES MARINE CORPS, HMLA-269, MARINE LIGHT ATTACK HELICOPTER SQUADRON 269

CAPT Tyler Boring, October 2015

I was the copilot for the lead aircraft in a section of AH-1W Cobras. We were conducting an ordnance flight in support of JTAC (Joint Terminal Attack Controller) training at the range. The flight was scheduled to land back at New River two hours prior to sunset, and the weather was anticipated to degrade to IFR an hour after sunset. Upon completion of the ordnance event, we had to go to Marine Corps Air Station (MCAS) Cherry Point to de-arm our aircraft. A gun had jammed, which required extensive troubleshooting and maintenance to clear. We delayed as a section and determined everybody's crew day in order to plan for the evening. After maintainers had worked for an hour on our aircraft, we decided to send Dash 2 home as a single while we waited with our aircraft until maintenance was complete.

The weather at MCAS Cherry Point remained VFR, but the forecast at New River was already beginning to degrade (the reported ceiling was at 800 feet). There is a standing order that we can't fly with night vision goggles in IMC conditions.

We were looking at the time and trying to figure out the latest we could take off and still make it into New River without needing the goggles. We anticipated that we'd have until 20 minutes after sunset. We spoke to the pilot of an aircraft that had just arrived from New River. He reported a temperature and dew point spread of one degree approximately 30 minutes prior to sunset.

Maintenance ran right up to the time we had scheduled ourselves to make it back to New River. It was just about sunset, giving us 20 minutes to make a 17-minute flight. There was a three-minute delay holding short of the runway waiting for an aircraft to land. We had our goggles out in the cockpit just in case.

As we were holding short and assessing the time, we still believed we would make it back. Ceilings started at 1000 feet at MCAS Cherry Point, gradually decreasing as we approached New River. New River ATIS was reporting 600 feet as we were approaching course rules from the north east. The weather had a very sharp change in visibility and ceiling as we hit our first reporting point. It became readily apparent we were going to have to use our goggles to get into New River. We decided to continue because we were familiar with the area. We wanted to come in over a river that was obstacle-free and that we could follow all the way into the airfield. We continued to the airfield and landed without event, but in violation of a standard operating procedure.

Lessons Learned:

In debrief we discussed how we had painted ourselves into a corner. We knew the temperature and dew point spread of one degree with sunset approaching. We should have known that the temperature would easily decrease that one degree. When we were estimating the latest time we could land without goggles, we were using a rule of thumb that works well under clear sky conditions. When you look at a solar illumination chart, it shows illumination for clear sky all the way to overcast, and there is a drastic decrease in illumination.

Our "20 minutes after sunset" was more like 15 minutes with the low visibility and overcast ceilings.

Our decision to continue into the airfield was the safest option that we had available. If we had turned around to Cherry Point, we would have been met with numerous towers potentially obscured by the rapidly degrading weather. In the end when minutes start adding up and you start butting up against your timeline, plan on some unexpected minutes. The best option is just to hang it up for the night and fly another day.

NOTES:

MID-PACIFIC INTERNATIONAL MEDEVAC

MH-60 SEA HAWK, UNITED STATES NAVY, HSL-49, HELICOPTER MARITIME STRIKE SQUADRON 49

LT Justin Langan, August 2015

On every Helicopter Aircraft Commander Board, the question inevitably comes up, "When can you deviate from (insert publication here)"? Just months after qualifying, I found myself answering this after knowingly violating two major rules on a medevac flight during RIMPAC 2014. First, I conducted a night NVD landing on a vessel authorized for daytime-only operations. And second, I embarked a medical attendant suspected of not having approved water survival or egress training to assist with the night overwater medevac. Why did I break the rules and take those risks? Well, let me paint the picture to explain.

Our SH-60B detachment was operating on USS Gary (FFG 51) during Group Sail transiting from San Diego to Hawaii to participate in the 2014 Rim of the Pacific (RIMPAC) multinational exercise. We had completed the basic phase of Initial Ship Aviation Team Training (ISATT) just three days prior, and were the only ones in the group of five US and foreign ships whose helicopter detachment had completed the required initial training.

As such, we were the only detachment that could accept operational tasking. After a full day underway, I had recently just hit the rack when at around 0100 my curtains opened and a voice said, "Langan, Langan! Your alert crew has a possible medevac!" My co-pilot, racked out above me in our stateroom, jumped to his feet and started getting dressed. Still in a haze, I climbed out of my rack and stumbled around the room for a few seconds before getting my bearings. Soon I was dressed and headed to Combat Information Center (CIC).

My mind raced back to many of the questions and scenarios that I had prepared for on my HAC board, just two months prior. Is our aircraft ready? What's the patient's condition? Where are we picking him up from? Where are we taking him? What's the distance?

Quickly we started piecing together the details. We were to pick up a Norwegian Sailor from his vessel, Fridtjof Nansen, and transport him plus their English speaking doctor to a big deck Amphib for emergency surgery. The information said the patient was suffering from a ruptured appendix, that he was in critical condition, and that he was to be transferred to USS Peleliu (LHA 5).

As we readied for the mission, it crossed my mind that I'd be undertaking a lot of firsts: first time performing a non-ambulatory medevac, first time flying any medevac as the HAC, first time operating on a foreign ship at night, and my first time landing on an LHA. I was excited yet also nervous. It was quickly obvious that we had two big obstacles to this mission: landing aboard the Fridtjof Nansen and whether or not to transfer their doctor with the patient.

The first obstacle was the Fridtjof Nansen's certifications. According to the HOSTAC (Helicopter Operations from Ships other than Aircraft Carriers), the Fridtjof Nansen was certified for VMC day/night landings of the NH-90 helicopter only. Our SH-60B was only certified for vertrep (Vertical Replenishment) and HIFR (Helicopter In-Flight Refuelling) on the Norwegian ship.

I had never even heard of the NH-90 and did not know if it was comparable in size or weight to the Sikorsky H-60.

As part of the planned RIMPAC exercises, we had received authorization to conduct daytime landings aboard the Fridtjof Nansen, so we knew someone had determined that their flight deck could handle the SH-60B but that did not mean a nighttime landing would be easy. We planned to use NVDs, but were unsure whether their lighting would be compatible. The HOSTAC said they would have a stabilized horizon bar, but would it be like the horizon reference system (HRS) bar we are used to, and would it be NVD compatible? Would their deck lighting be NVD compatible? How would we shoot our approach, since they did not have a TACAN?

Because I was a junior HAC, certainly without much medevac experience, I had limited resources to guide my decision process on whether or not to try for an unauthorized nighttime landing. Sure, my detachment's OIC and Gary's CO wanted this medevac to happen, but I was in the hot seat; it was my decision to make. And yet even as a junior HAC, I knew the answer to my dilemma was ORM. I needed to apply the steps and abide by the principles to do what I could to minimize the risk to the lowest level.

Having authorization that the SH-60B could land on the Fridtjof Nansen helped mitigate that the ship wasn't certified for the SH-60B. But what controls could I put in place to minimize the risks associated with landing there? A good thorough NATOPS brief was a great start. We briefed that we would don NVDs and perform a Self-Contained Approach to the ship using the SH-60B's APS-124 radar. We would execute strict radar altimeter adherence and follow NATOPS procedures for night overwater descent. We would use FLIR to help with alignment if needed. We would have the co-pilot back the pilot up on instruments, being especially ready to call for the wave-off if necessary. We would also take the transition to landing much slower than usual in order to allow our aircrewman to clear the tail and get a better feel for our position over the flight deck.

Our other concern was whether or not to transfer their doctor along with the patient. The patient would need to be transported via litter, and we knew he was in critical condition.

We knew a recent interim change to OPNAVINST 3710.7U says, "a qualified medical attendant who is current in approved water survival training, and has been properly briefed on emergency egress procedures for that aircraft, may be transferred at night with approval from the ship's Commanding Officer." But what about a medical attendant without water survival training? We had to assume the Norwegian doctor lacked any US Navy approved water survival training. The same section of 3710.7U does allow certain commanders to waive the restriction that prohibits night time ship launches/recoveries with passengers, but only in cases of operational necessity. And as far as I knew, we certainly hadn't crossed into the realm of operational necessity for this medevac. Of course there is always the "military exigency may require on-site deviations" caveat, but I did not want to willingly violate the rules just because I could.

So should I take the doctor? My instinct told me yes due to the nature of the emergency and condition of the patient, and both my OIC and the CO of the Gary agreed. I still needed to minimize as much risk as possible through ORM. The biggest control we could think of was to give the doctor a thorough passenger brief, emphasizing egress procedures. We also knew that the takeoff from the Fridtjof Nansen would, in theory, be safer than the initial landing. And we assessed that the landing on the Peleliu would be pretty straightforward, even if I'd never been to an Amphib before. I knew the procedures from the LHA/LHD NATOPS Manual and we knew we could ask for a precision approach as needed. Besides, landing on the Peleliu's giant flight deck would be the safest type of landing we could do with the doctor onboard. The last control we discussed was that the forecasted weather would allow us to maintain altitudes that would keep us in communications and navigation ranges with the various ships during our 120nm transit from the Fridtjof Nansen to the Peleliu.

Having the doctor on board would benefit our aircrewman, in case the patient's condition worsened. The Peleliu might also need the doctor's language skills to communicate with the patient.

I assessed that the risk to the doctor was something I could not completely eliminate, but the benefit of transferring him with the patient outweighed that risk.

Not wanting to delay our initial launch, we agreed in the brief that we'd attempt the landing on the Norwegian vessel and that we would indeed pick up the doctor with the patient. Our detachment's maintenance team readied the aircraft, we preflighted, and launched uneventfully. The landing on the Fridtjof Nansen was smoother than I anticipated, the patient was loaded and the doctor was briefed, and the 120nm transit to the Peleliu was as quick as we could make it. The patient needed morphine during the flight, which the doctor was able to administer. Finally, the landing aboard Peleliu was without incident and their medical team took charge immediately. Later we learned the patient underwent successful surgery onboard the Peleliu and was recovering well.

Lessons Learned:

While most Aircraft Commanders would have made the same decisions I made that night, it was my first time really straying into the gray area between the black-and-white rules and regulations we abide by.

Weighing the risks versus the benefits and using ORM was invaluable in helping me make those decisions. Being a helicopter pilot in the Navy is an inherently dangerous job, but with the right thought process and controls set in place, we minimized the risks in order to increase our chances of having a successful mission and ultimately saved a Sailor's life.

NOTES:

GOTTA LOVE A GOOD AIRSHOW
CH-124 SEA KING, ROYAL CANADIAN AIR FORCE, 423 SQUADRON

Major Scott Young, 2005

I was the lucky Aircraft Captain in charge of getting the airshow asset from Shearwater to Toronto, on target, on time. Festivities were planned starting on the Friday night of the Labour Day long weekend, and with that data point in mind, we began prepping for departure the Monday before. For the journey, we elected to take two Tactical Officers (TACCO), three service technicians, and myself and my co-pilot.

As we were planning our mission from the East Coast to Southern Ontario, we saw a decreasing trend in environmental conditions expected to develop throughout the week. As Tuesday night approached, we realized that we would have to depart IFR, vice a scenic VFR excursion westbound.

On Wednesday morning, we were delayed several hours waiting for the weather to improve before starting our journey. We had pre-planned that the aircrew would flight plan as a team while the technicians loaded the airshow swag onto the aircraft, ensuring that our gear and elementary servicing set was complete and ready to go.

As we waited that morning for the weather to improve, although unspoken, we all had the heavy feeling that we would not make it in time to part of the airshow experience due to the prevailing, albeit typical, East Coast weather patterns. Morning turned into mid-afternoon and planning — both for the delayed flight and aircraft load – came to an abrupt stop. The mindset changed from excitement in showing off the Sea King capabilities in front of thousands of eager onlookers, to disappointment with the coastal weather conditions that had, yet again, placed a damper on the 12 Wing's flight schedule, and mood of its aviators; that would all change late afternoon that fateful Wednesday.

As late afternoon reared its dull, dreary overcast head something magical happened — the forecast improved as did the actual weather conditions, we had our minimums to depart the airfield. As the ceiling lifted, yielding light rain showers, we elected as a team to separate the planning duties to affect a speedy departure.

My co-pilot was charged with conducting the flight planning, and I performed the pre-flight while assisting the rest of the crew to load up the airshow gear and swag. This was it, the big show!

Our departure out of Shearwater was as planned and we entered cloud at just over 200 feet AGL with a right turn enroute to our first fuel stop in Fredericton, New Brunswick.

Upon climbing through 4000 feet Mean Sea Level (MSL), ATC queried us as to where our next destination was. I was operating the radios at the time and found that question quite odd. Did ATC not have our IFR clearance from the handover from Shearwater? Were they not seeing our squawk code? Since I was the non-flying pilot (NFP) I reached over and looked at the flight planning that my co-pilot had calculated. Looking at the tracks on the planning, it became instantly clear that these were not the tracks to get us to Fredericton.

I frantically planned new tracks based on where we were currently heading, west not north as we should have been, and informed ATC we were correcting heading to intercept the appropriate northbound track.

My co-pilot was confused as to what I was doing, and why I just told ATC that we were correcting track. I took control and had him look at his planning. He had planned the off-airways tracks using True tracks, and not Magnetic tracks. He confessed that he had made the faux pas, and we debriefed it and carried on — keep in mind this all transpired in a matter of 2 mins after departing into cloud north of Shearwater.

As we crossed the Bay of Fundy, the skies opened up. We could see blue skies above, and summer campers on the beaches of the New Brunswick coast — things were looking up, or so we thought.

Five miles into New Brunswick, we entered solid IFR conditions again but knew that we not only had minimums at Fredericton, but also a good alternate in Greenwood, Nova Scotia. As we approached Fredericton for the VOR Only approach, it became clear to me that my TACCOs were very silent. Normally jovial gentlemen, they were now sullen, quiet and engaged in conversation and paperwork. I asked what the issue was, as a matter of conversation, and they informed me that if we did not get into Fredericton, we would not have fuel to get back to Greenwood. For the second time on this flight, I grabbed the flight planning and realised that we did not account for the added weight of the aircraft due to the airshow swag, which meant taking on less fuel than we normally would have for a three hour flight. Our only 'out' now, or alternate, just became landing VFR on the beaches of New Brunswick because we did not have the fuel to get anywhere else. I was furious.

I was not upset at my co-pilot, nor at my crew for not informing me earlier. I was upset at myself. I was disappointed in the fact that I had never checked my co-pilot's planning — why would I? He was a seasoned pilot and aircraft captain certified in our community. Fortunately for us that day, we had 'runway environment' on final into Fredericton and landed accordingly. We were all pretty concerned with what had transpired over the last couple of hours and decided to stay the night in Fredericton, get our heads on straight, and thoroughly debrief what had just occurred.

Lessons Learned:

You are likely asking yourself, "So what?" Ever since that afternoon, I habitually do two things before any flight operation.

1. Perform a common sense check on any and all mental math and flight calculations. Even on my own work, I will have another aviator, or honest broker for that matter, check the math. There is no appetite in crewed cockpits or cabins for egos; and

2. I always leave myself an out, an alternate plan – IFR or otherwise — in order to ensure I maintain professionalism and remain legal, but more importantly, to ensure I bring my crew home to their loved ones. I am prepared for conversations in my superior's office regarding the 'hard' talks. I am not prepared, nor should any other aviator for that matter, to talk to a deceased crew member's family regarding 'hard' conversations based on neglect or ego.

It is interesting to point out that we never participated in that Airshow in 2005. A little storm called Katrina made landfall down south and we were tasked to fly down to assist our American brethren.

Gotta love a good airshow...

NOTES:

TRUE CONFESSIONS

MH-60R SEAHAWK, UNITED STATES NAVY, HELICOPTER MARITIME STRIKE SQUADRON 49

LT Anthony Morgana, February 2014

Our detachment was in its seventh week of a southern Pacific deployment in support of Operation Martillo. We were flying Counter Transnational Organized Crime (formerly Counter Drug) operations, attempting to reduce the flow of drugs into the United States. We had a slow start to the deployment with several boardings but no interdictions or disruptions.

One night started out like more of the same: providing eyes in the sky and radar coverage of the operating area. About an hour before our land time, we received a call from control notifying us that a suspect vessel was spotted in the vicinity. Game on.

We gave chase and located the vessel. After identifying it, and with the help of a P-3, we tracked them while our ship was in hot pursuit. The vessel was skirting Panamanian territorial waters. After an hour into the chase, we were given permission from the Panamanian government to enter their national airspace and territorial waters. You could feel the adrenaline pumping through the crew.

To let the vessel know we were there, we descended from 2,000 to 500 feet AGL and flashed our searchlight on them. We maneuvered to maintain forward-looking infrared-radar (FLIR) imagery in case the vessel started dumping bales of drugs.

The moon had just set, so the illumination was dropping; haze further degraded visibility. Meanwhile, our ship was putting the boarding team's rigid hull inflatable boat (RHIB) in the water. We tried to buy some time and keep the suspects from heading straight for a nearby cove that had many islands around it. As we illuminated the vessel, it made erratic maneuvers in an effort to avoid the light.

Despite our efforts, they made it to the cove, and we lost sight of them on FLIR. We tried to find them on radar, FLIR, and visually to no avail. The boarding team was now loaded in the RHIB and waiting for guidance. After what seemed like an eternity of searching the cove and islands, we relocated the vessel. The crew had shut off the motors and were pushing the vessel into a small rock enclosure on the island, trying to mask their position. We maneuvered the helicopter into a 100-foot coupled hover and put our searchlight on them to give the boarding team the location.

Realizing they had been discovered, the suspects frantically began to pull start their engines as our RHIB rapidly closed their position. The vessel got one engine started just as our boarding team arrived on scene. Our team started to chase them. We transitioned from our 100-foot hover to forward flight and climbed to 200 feet. The suspects began to dump bales of drugs overboard.

Our crew of three split up our responsibilities. I kept the search light fixed on the suspects, my copilot flew and maintained standoff, and our aircrewman in the back operated the FLIR. After getting the smugglers on video jettisoning their drugs, the aircrewman got out of his seat and went to the cabin door in his gunner's belt to drop chem lights on the jettisoned bails, marking the location of the contraband to be recovered later.

With our aircrewman at the door, we were down a crew member to provide backup on altitude integrity.

The pilot-at-the-controls became focused on a predominantly outside scan. As the non flying pilot, I was scanning outside to maintain visual on the vessel with the search light. I also looked inside to check instruments and maintain FLIR image. I noticed our altitude rapidly decreasing. Our radar-altimeter altitude hold had disengaged without us noticing. With no reference to the horizon due to a pitch black night, we had entered a nose-low descent approaching 1,500 fpm.

At 150 feet, I called out, "Altitude!" and took the controls. We immediately completed our unusual-attitude recovery procedures, stopping the rate of descent at 50 feet, breaking our briefed SOP hard deck of 100 feet.

Altitude hold is a great tool, but an instrument scan is imperative when there is no reference to the horizon. With an over-reliance on the altitude-hold function, the crew became absorbed in maintaining position on the contact. We wanted to make sure we had video evidence and remained clear of the terrain. But, with the non-NVG compatible search light on, it made the conditions even more difficult to pick out the terrain on NVGs. When we first maneuvered near the cove, the crew was very good at communicating the location of obstacles in reference to the aircraft, but as soon as the chase began, each crew member became focused on their specific tasks.

As the crew transitioned from a coupled hover from 100 feet to 200 feet, we did not readjust our altitude-warning system, leaving it at 90 feet instead of being adjusted to 180 feet as required by our SOP. The missed step eliminated a crucial risk-management control, allowing an increased rate of descent to develop before we caught the unusual attitude and high rate of descent. Fortunately, we caught it when we did. With our altitude-warning system set at 90 feet, the 1,500 fpm rate of descent would have given us only four-seconds to impact.

We had had an opportunity earlier when we fuelled to embark a USCG controller, but after a quick discussion on the ship, we decided not to take him.

If embarked on the helo, the controller could have maintained a hand-held search light on the contact, provided position reports, and dropped chem lights, which would have spread out the workload for the crew. The additional manpower would have allowed the aircrewman to maintain his position at his console, keeping FLIR and backing the pilots up on altitude. Given the opportunity again, I would have taken the controller with me.

Lessons Learned:

With the adrenaline rushing and the workload continuing to increase, a few basic steps were missed, resulting in our crew breaking our hard deck.

I always brief my crew to aviate, navigate, and communicate — in that order.

We lost sight of our priorities and nearly lost the aircraft and our lives.

That simple process was broken in the heat of the mission.

Those who stick to the basics will have the highest success rate and return home safely.

<u>NOTES:</u>

CHAPTER 9

AIRWORTHINESS & FAILURES

"Man wants to fly like a bird, not a bat out of hell."

Lawrence Bell

HOW DO WE LEARN FROM THE THINGS WE DO RIGHT?

APACHE AH1, UK ARMY AIR CORPS, 654 SQUADRON

Lt Col Nick English, January 2014

During January 2014, on an operational mission in Afghanistan I was the aircraft commander and my co-pilot was the handling pilot; when we suffered one of those aircraft failures that is every rotary pilot's worst nightmare — a tail rotor drive failure in flight.

A UK Civil Aviation Authority (CAA) analysis in 2003 of 344 tail rotor failure occurrences found that, while failure in transit accounts for 27 percent of occurrences, they account for 56 percent of fatalities. From their historical analysis, the overall failure rate was about nine per million flying hours.

Through a combination of luck, training and teamwork the aircraft was safely landed (crashed) in the desert, the crew were combat recovered and the aircraft was extracted in less than 24 hours.

What follows is an account of the entire operation from the aircraft emergency to the immediate response and culminating with the aircraft recovery. We sometimes find it difficult to look closely at successful outcomes to find the factors that led us there and then make sure that we reinforce them in our routine operations.

It is just too easy to look for faults. Understanding success will help us to safely develop and reinforce the agile and adaptive performance we need to fight and win.

This particular sortie was a combat Intelligence, Surveillance Target Acquisition and Reconnaissance (ISTAR) mission in support of the US Marine Corps in Northern Helmand as they prepared to withdraw a large number of forces back to Camp Bastion. By mid-morning, it was already our fourth mission of the day and we were extremely comfortable with both the aircraft and the operating conditions. Following a standard low-level departure from Camp Bastion, we climbed away to the east aiming to show presence over an ongoing Afghan National Army operation. Real aircraft failures never manifest in the clean way they do in simulator emergency sorties and, having reached medium level and checked in with the area Joint Terminal Attack Controller (the controller in a Land HQ that controls air fires and deconflicts battlespace) one of our tactical radios started beeping as if it was continuously trying to transmit. That was unusual and annoying so, with some choice words, I turned my attention to isolate the troublesome radio. Seconds later Charlie (the handling pilot) asked me if I could feel a vibration through the floor. My attention was drawn to it, I could feel it through my feet and it felt like 30 mm cannon hydraulic cavitation where the cannon twitches in a feedback loop but settles down when you move it.

As I actioned the gun to investigate this new higher-priority fault, the aircraft suddenly yawed to the right. Charlie instantly (and correctly) identified that we had suffered a tail-rotor failure in flight announcing it initially in a confused voice and, within seconds, with absolute certainty. In the space of 30 seconds I had been diagnosing a radio fault, thinking about a gun vibration, experienced a rapid yaw in the aircraft and my pilot was telling me we had suffered a tail rotor failure. It took about 10 seconds for my brain to process this highly unusual fact. Tail rotors never fail. Nevertheless, the aircraft was definitely not flying properly and Charlie, with his hands on the controls, was absolutely convinced.

We were lucky that in those first 10 seconds, Charlie's immediate reaction to take off power to control the yaw saved our lives. We were flying at maximum all-up mass pulling maximum power and came within seconds of a complete and catastrophic loss of control. Apache has a helmet-mounted display and flight instruments are continuously available to you in front of your eyes. It is like having a head display mounted to your head and always available. As soon as I processed that it was a tail-rotor failure, emergency conditioning kicked in and I was instantly drawn to airspeed — lose your airspeed and you will irrecoverably spin and crash in a burning wreck. As I prompted him, Charlie rapidly recovered the airspeed and dropped the power further resulting in a flight profile that resembled a rapid descent into the heart of the active Taliban insurgency.

It was at this point that our first crucial decision was made. The immediate actions are to enter auto rotation and conduct an engine-off landing but, instead of adopting the expensively conditioned behaviour, we continued to attempt to fly the aircraft. This felt instinctively right and, in retrospect, probably saved our lives. Had we attempted a double engine off landing with no tail rotor into a populated area we would undoubtedly crashed: had we survived it would have been like a scene from Black Hawk Down without much prospect of rescue. Interestingly we displayed an adaptive rather than conditioned behaviour. Despite high stress levels we rapidly and intuitively selected an alternative (and better) course of action. At this point, the world was not looking good: we were heading downwards rapidly and despite having turned away from the threat towards more open terrain we weren't going to get very far. About 28 seconds after the failure, I transmitted a mayday call on the mission primary frequency to my wingman who was in front of us and oblivious to our sudden and rapid change of flight profile.

I remember looking at his tail as I transmitted, feeling real relief that I could just focus on our aircraft as I saw him turn back. Seconds later he relayed our mayday call to US Marine Corps Tactical Airspace.

Control and everyone airborne in South Western Afghanistan was now aware of our predicament. Listening back to the cockpit voice recorder you can hear in our voices that, while we were still flying, it wasn't going to be enough. I knew that we needed to get mass off the aircraft to reduce the rate of descent; it felt that if we could keep flying then at least we might have a chance to think our way out of the problem. Spotting a wadi (Arabic and Hebrew term for valley) coming up, I decided to jettison all the external fuel and stores.

One of the side effects of the fully justifiable quest to make aviation as safe as possible is that we try and learn from every event in training that doesn't go as it might. One of the unfortunate side effects of this is that we tend to focus on negative events more than positive ones. As I went to press the jettison button, I momentarily paused as the thought popped into my head 'I am going to get hung if this isn't a tail rotor-failure and it's something simple I am missing'. Luckily this thought lasted only a second or two before 'I don't care' overtook it. In hindsight, it was a salutary lesson on the unintended consequence of trying to eliminate errors. While our just-culture model absolutely seeks to create a blame-free learning culture, it often doesn't feel like that to those who are having their professional judgement called into doubt and subjected to the magic of hindsight. By relentlessly pursuing learning from errors, we must be careful not to condition doubt into our people that may inadvertently kill them through inaction. Despite being very experienced on type, both as a commander and operationally, it hit me and I delayed a potentially life-saving decision: I wonder what it does to our more junior pilots and commanders? Having dropped the stores on the edge of a wadi and remarkably managing to miss any innocent civilians, the change in performance was marked. We no longer felt like we were imminently crashing and had time to think. I was still not 100 percent convinced that we had suffered a tail rotor failure: the aircraft was still flying, albeit in a horrible left wing low, nose-down configuration and we were still alive.

I think part of me was still hoping that there was a simple failure lurking there that would avoid having to confront the reality of suffering a low survival failure.

At this point my capacity reemerged from somewhere under my seat, I called control to update my mayday, give the position of the stores for denial and nominated UGLY 53 as the on-scene commander. This was relayed by a flight of USMC CH53s returning from an air assault mission to the west that immediately, and without being tasked, started converging on our position.

We now systematically checked that the controls were really responding as they should for a tail rotor failure. I even managed to get my flight reference cards intending to eliminate any hydraulic or control problems. Conscious that I still had nearly 1000 lb of 30 mm ammunition on board and that we needed to be as light as possible if I was going to maintain flight, I elected to fire the ammunition into any safe areas I could find.

I slaved the gun to my helmet, selected 100 round bursts (10 seconds of fire) and started firing into the empty gaps between compounds. It was going well until I spotted a gap in the compounds to the left. As I fired to the left, it became immediately obvious that this was a bad idea. The torque created by the recoil was now working against rather than with the vertical stabiliser and tried to spin us into the ground.

After some pretty vociferous prompting from Charlie, we decided not to try that again. It was at this point that UGLY 53 calmly notified me that my tail rotor was not turning. This crucial piece of information instantly dispelled any doubt — external confirmation that we were indeed in a very bad place. The voice recorder is very telling. Neither of us spoke for about 10 seconds. I vividly remember that this was the point at which the likely consequences for our families and us came sharply into focus.

Not something I would wish to repeat in a hurry.

I was still convinced that we could make Camp Bastion and I had a vague notion of a plan for when we got there.

But to be honest, we had become fixated on just keeping the aircraft in the air. In reality, we were always going to crash from the moment we had the failure and it was almost certainly going to be in the desert. This became abundantly clear as we struggled to maintain height. The drag created by flying with about 30 degrees of yaw and 20 degrees left wing low is immense and continuously tried to slow the aircraft down. As airspeed is lost, the drag gets worse, further compounding the problem. The first time this happened, we were able to remove some power and get the nose right down until the airspeed recovered, essentially pirouetting around the nose which cost us height but avoided departure from controlled flight.

It was at this point that I mentally transitioned from 'get back to Bastion' to 'engine-off in the desert'. I cleared my cockpit of loose articles and locked my harness. We were attempting to adjust our track back towards Bastion when the airspeed started to decay again. By this point, we were only 400 feet above the desert. Charlie managed to get the nose down but the airspeed just didn't respond. After a couple of seconds he said: "I'm losing it, go for the engines".

As we were now 35 degrees nose down, 45 degrees angle of bank and yawing right, I was pretty much looking straight down at the desert and had already concluded that beyond this point lay loss of control and burning wreck. As I pulled the engines back, the low rotor speed warning sounded immediately and we yawed violently left. Charlie managed to flare and level the aircraft but something prompted me to take control. This is not what I practice or brief when I fly as usually the consequence of the commander taking control is loss of your capacity and making the situation far worse. Even after much thought, I still don't know what prompted me to take control from Charlie. Perhaps my mind was playing the sequence of events through and detected an anomaly. Either way Charlie very calmly and confidently replied 'you have control'.

Note to self — practice taking control of an aircraft in about the worst flight condition possible in the simulator before attempting it for real.

In the 20 seconds or so that it took for us to arrive on the ground many things happened very quickly (it felt like five-seconds). We achieved an autorotation configuration and recovered our rotor speed no doubt helped by the 45 degree attitude change. As the ground rapidly approached, a second key bit of adaptive behaviour saved our lives. When I had refreshed back onto Apache following a staff appointment, the simulator flight model had just changed. The dynamics of a tail-rotor failure meant that landing from an engine off configuration was extremely difficult if not impossible. The engine-off manoeuvre taught always resulted in a loss of control and the 'red screen of death'. Unwilling to be defeated, I practiced this again and again until I found a technique that allowed me to beat the simulator at least some of the time. This turned out to be extremely valuable as, with seconds to go, the memory of that technique vividly popped back into my head. Having examined the data recorder, it almost certainly saved our lives; had I flown the technique as taught, we would almost certainly have rolled at high speed on touchdown and distributed ourselves liberally across the desert.

The recovery

As we rolled to a stop upright in the desert, my immediate response of 'holy **** Charlie, we're still alive' says a lot. However, we had just abruptly transitioned from aircraft emergency to escape and evasion. I had realised early on in the tour that Combat Search and Rescue (CSAR) wasn't getting the attention it deserved.

In eight years in Afghanistan there had been very few occasions for anyone to be on the ground and this had affected how seriously crews treated briefing their immediate reactions. I insisted that, instead of just reading through the CSAR information, we would spend a couple of minutes on every brief mentally rehearsing different scenarios until we all knew instinctively what each person in the formation would do. This proved to be absolutely the right thing to do. Our experience of local insurgent reactions meant that we were only likely to have a few minutes before we would have extremely unfriendly company.

As soon as we hit the ground, both Charlie and I went straight into our short term actions. Running on adrenaline, I grabbed my go bag, unclipped my carbine and jumped out. After making both weapons ready I made my colour sergeant from Sandhurst proud and looked for cover and a fire position only to discover we had landed in possibly the flattest bit of Helmand ever. Not even a ripple anywhere nearby. Looking around the other side of the aircraft revealed that we were on the edge of the habitation with nothing but desert behind us. It could have been far worse.

For the first few minutes, Charlie and I quickly ran through our drill of preparing the aircraft for abandonment, removing the crypto and sensitive equipment. As I got out my 112 radio, I discovered a helpful safety equipment fitter had disconnected and tie-wrapped my pre prepared ear-piece when servicing my vest. After cursing a bit while putting it back together, I quickly established comms with my wingman who was orbiting directly overhead anticipating providing suppressive fire or immediate extraction. He then gave me his second game-changing piece of information of the morning — there was no movement converging on us within 500 m. That instantly shifted me down into a more deliberate consideration of what would happen next.

Interestingly Charlie didn't pick up on that useful information and for a while he couldn't work out why I was so calm and I couldn't work out why he was so stressed. Looking back on it, Charlie was unsurprisingly expecting to be mobbed at any time and was expecting to have to fight for his life.

As we had a little time on our hands and weren't going to be running anywhere imminently, I took the opportunity to take some photos of the site and as many relevant bits of the aircraft that I could. Knowing that destroying the aircraft was always going to be an option, I wanted to make sure that I could give any inquiry the best chance possible to find out what went wrong. After about 25 minutes on the ground, the CH53 flight that had responded to our earlier mayday picked us up and gave us a lift back to Bastion.

They didn't really know where to drop us so helpfully took us to the ATC tower where we were able to thumb a lift with SATCO back to the rotary flight line.

Having checked in briefly with the ops room, which was now sharply focused on securing and recovering the aircraft, we retreated to the familiarity of the Apache High Readiness tent.

As I crossed over to my flight line to check in with my Downed Aircraft Recovery Team (DART), I was struck by the precise focused activity that was going on. Equipment was lined up ready to go, weapons and dismounted close combat kit was laid out while still supporting the airborne aircraft. One of my lasting memories of that day will be how the Squadron reacted to the incident — each part knew exactly what to do and meshed perfectly with the others without any overall command present.

The initial assessment team was flown out and on the ground within two hours of the site being secured. They rapidly assessed the aircraft and informed the recovery options being worked up by the Joint Aviation Group and Regional Command (South West).

As the Taliban was showing no interest (or were grossly overmatched by the USMC), the decision was made to recover the aircraft by road at first light. The DART deployed to the aircraft the following morning meeting a combat logistics patrol that had departed by road at first light.

In less than 90 minutes and wearing full combat kit, the team removed the remaining ammunition and fuel and stripped the aircraft for a road move. The aircraft was then lifted onto a trailer using a recovery vehicle and secured for the trip back to Bastion. The recovery operation was completed and the team extracted less than three hours after arriving.

A slick and professional operation they had never had the chance to practice in training.

Just over 24 hours after the tail rotor failed, I had the aircraft back in the hanger at Bastion.

Lessons Learned:

Looking back at the incident, I offer my thoughts as both an aviator and as an operational squadron commander.

From an aircrew perspective, one of the most interesting observations is a question of psychology. We devote a considerable amount of time and money into conditioning behaviour to certain responses: immediate actions are a clear example. In our case, had we responded as conditioned, we would almost certainly have been killed or seriously injured in the resulting crash. So how and why did we deviate from the response that had been drilled into us?

Despite reflecting on this for some time, I'm afraid I don't have a clear answer and it was probably a combination of lots of factors. Experience probably helped but Charlie and I appear to reach the same judgement but with significantly different experience levels.

In terms of emergency training, the situation was novel and to a large extent didn't reflect the simulator modelling although refusal to accept that I couldn't land the sim turned out to be a life saver.

From a psychological perspective, a skilled response can be improved by exposure to multiple variations of the same event. This helps build a bank of possible solutions that the non-conscious mind can process rapidly. It turns out that visualisation and reflection is a powerful tool to compliment simulation; we had mentally rehearsed the evasion drill so many times that it was entirely natural to us.

I suspect that having flown the best part of 150 hours over the previous eight weeks together significantly supported our performance as a crew.

Over my flying career I have always trained and deployed as a formed crew and flight (pair of aircraft). The significant increase in combat performance has always been worth the loss of flexibility. Stress was also probably an important factor.

For the majority of the time that we were still flying, it felt like the induced stress improved our performance, combining with drills to give us the freedom to adapt.

It is entirely possible our final departure from controlled flight was a result of stress-induced control inputs although it doesn't seem to have interfered with flying the engine off. The squadron's reaction to the incident was also extremely interesting. While I had rehearsed in my mind what I would do as the squadron commander if we lost a crew, I hadn't considered the possibility that it might be me. One of the most telling comments was from my second in command who was in the ops room at the point the mayday came in. He rather candidly told me afterwards that one of his first panicked thoughts was, "s***, the boss is dead — that means I am in charge".

Testing the squadron's response to loss of its commander is something that all Army officers would recognise from armoured warfare training but is not something we routinely do in aviation. The tactical success of the recovery operation was largely due to the extremely focused way the squadron responded to the incident. Each of the individual teams responded to both the incident and routine operations in a mutually supporting way and without any central direction. They all knew what my intent was, they trusted each other and the teams acted accordingly. The technicians and ground crew were pumped at the prospect of going onto the ground and getting the aircraft back as fast as possible; they were completely aware of the risks but not phased at all.

Their response was probably due to several factors. I would highlight service culture, training expectation and strong team ethos. When training for operations, we knew that a DART was a realistic prospect or potentially austere operations. The training standard I set for the deployable teams was that they must present no more burden to force protection than any other deployed combat support arm. Being soldiers, they took to this with gusto and this undoubtedly set a high level of expectation of how they would go about the task. The speed that the aircraft was stripped in full combat gear shows just how focused they were. "Train as you fight" was my mantra through our mission specific training and I feel contributed to our robust response.

We tried wherever possible to create common procedures that would stand up both in the UK and in an operational theatre. This is often not the easiest way of doing things in the UK but is essential if you are going to create the standards, expectations and trust that allow you to perform adaptively on operations. Uncomfortably for commanders, this may mean taking increased risk in training. While we talk about as low as reasonably practicable (ALARP)*, we regularly feel under pressure to make it as low as possible. How often do we fly in full combat body armour with weapons in the cockpit? How often do we maintain aircraft and refuel in full PPE? Normalising these tactical frictions and still achieving maximum performance is the purpose of operational training; a commander's skill in risk management is doing it realistically but safely.

Our dominant culture has become one of identifying things that are perceived to have gone wrong and then 'fix' them; we seem to find it extremely difficult to apply the same rigour to learn from things that go right. Two particularly powerful cognitive biases reinforce this culture: hindsight bias and outcome bias. In the case of hindsight bias, we tend to overweight the significance of factors that affected the outcome but we couldn't have known at the time. Outcome bias is more troublesome in the world of aviation leading us to pay far more attention to failure than success. We must strive whenever possible to overcome both of these and identify and reinforce those factors that helped us succeed with the same vigour that we try to eliminate errors. We will know that we have matured into a successful learning organisation when we can do both. Lots of things went right that day and turned an otherwise tragic event into one that most people will never have heard of. Rather than exclusively attempt to avoid errors, we must ruthlessly track down the causes of success and reinforce them. They are often hidden and difficult to find but taking them for granted risks failure later if those successes become eroded. By reinforcing the many things that we do right, we can genuinely build the high performance organisations we need to take risk in combat and win.

Notes:

Lieutenant Colonel Nick English commanded 654 Squadron Army Air Corps from 2012 to 2014 including a tour of Op HERRICK from September 2013 to February 2014. He has 10 years' experience of Apache operations including four tours of Afghanistan and over 1400 hours on type. He is studying for a PhD in Cognitive and Behavioural Psychology specialising in military decision-making. Captain Charlie Russell completed Apache conversion to the role in October 2013 and was on his first operational tour with just over 500 hours on type.

* The term so far as is reasonably practicable (SFARP) is used in the RAAF.

NOTES:

MIRACLE AT SEA

CH-53E SUPER STALLION, UNITED STATES MARINE CORPS, 22ND MARINE EXPEDITIONARY UNIT

CAPT Matthew Dineen, September 2014

In September 2014, my crew and I went to the flight line of Camp Lemonnier in Djibouti, Africa. Like many days before, we were on the flight schedule to fly back out to our ship, the USS Mesa Verde, a San Antonio Class (landing platform/dock (LPD)), after we had conducted training in Djibouti. The pilot who was to be our section leader met us on the flight line as we were loading passengers and cargo, and we conducted our section brief. After some routine delay in loading cargo, we decided to launch my aircraft as a single to the ship. This would ensure we got back to the ship before sunset (which was mandatory when moving passengers over water).

After completing all preflight duties, my crew and I departed with 21 passengers. The flight was about 30 minutes, and I began trying to contact the ship about 15 miles out. Initial attempts to contact the ship were unsuccessful; however, contact was made with the tower liaison officer. Around 5 to 7 miles from the ship, the aircrew called visual with the ship, and I was able to establish radio contact with the Air Boss.

As the aircraft was setting up in the port delta holding pattern, the Air Boss cleared the aircraft to cross the stern and report final for spot five.

I was the flying pilot for the entire flight and set the aircraft up on a standard approach to spot five. After my copilot completed the landing checks with concurrence from the aircrew in the cabin, I made my final voice report to the Air Boss, "Three down and locked, left seat," and was given clearance to land. I descended and decelerated on profile until approximately 60 feet AGL and 10KGS. When the aircraft was on short final, we heard a loud bang. My crew and I began to access secondary indications in the cockpit and cabin. From the left seat, I scanned the instruments from left to right and noticed that all the associated lights indicating a No. 2 engine failure were illuminated. My copilot, in the right seat, saw fluctuating engine performance gauges as he scanned from right to left. At the time I recognized the indications of the No. 2 engine failure I immediately returned the aircraft to its hover attitude and began to pull power to arrest a rapidly building descent and closure rate with the flight deck. Just before the left side of the aircraft hit the LPD, I decided to pull away from the flight deck. This flight-control input allowed the aircraft to hit the water in its most advantageous position, tail first and upright.

I maintained control of the helicopter until touchdown in the water, then I executed my emergency egress procedures. Training took over once we hit the water. I released my cockpit window and with the emergency release handle. The window fell out but was pushed back into the cockpit, barely missing my face as the water rushed in. I was upright in the seat and grabbed the window frame with my left hand for reference. The aircraft began to roll right. After about 90 degrees of roll, the aircraft settled out, and I was able to pull myself free after I released my harness with my right hand. It took two full strokes to get back to the surface. I did not need to use my Helicopter Aircrew Breathing Device (HABD) bottle and pulled the handles to inflate my lobes after I surfaced.

Once I was clear of the aircraft, I immediately began to survey the scene and look for survivors. Most of the passengers were already out of the aircraft, and we began to take count of everyone.

We did a great job of working together to ensure everyone stayed afloat. A few life preservers (LPUs) did not inflate and I made sure that they were paired with a buddy who had a good LPU. Miraculously, the aircraft's raft came out on its own as the tail went into the water. This allowed two of the passengers, one an AH-1W pilot and the other a CH-53E airframes mechanic, to deploy and flip the 20-man life raft upright.

The scene felt very much like aircrew water survival training. People helped pull each other into the raft, and after I got up onto the raft's entry step, I ordered a head count. \

It was one of the most distressing, yet amazing, things that I have ever experienced. The whole time we were getting into the raft I was thinking, "There is no way everyone made it out." As the count progressed, I waited for the number to stop at something other than 25, but it did not.

All 25 Marines and sailors had made it out. After the initial shock and emotion of that realization, we triaged the wounded in the life raft while we waited for the small boats from the LPD. We sent those who were more severely injured back in the first rescue boat. The rest of us were loaded up in the final small boat, and we headed back to the LPD.

As everyone has heard a million times, nothing we do in naval aviation is routine. Being able to react by the book was the key to saving lives.

Lessons Learned:

Egress training works — It is required for pilots and aircrew but should be required for all Navy and Marine Corps personnel who regularly ride in helicopters over water.

Always have a plan — The engine failure occurred at the worst possible time, low and slow in the landing profile, so close to the ship that a standard wave off was not possible.

These are parameters that we — as helicopter, tilt-rotor and VSTOL pilots must accept to do our job.

We brief as a community that we will avoid the ship to minimize danger to the deck crew and enter the water tail first to help absorb impact as we hit the water. This mishap took less than five-seconds from "bang to splash," and we were able to do those two things.

NOTES:

THE GALLOPING HORSE
MH-60S, UNITED STATES NAVY, HSC-8, HELICOPTER SEA COMBAT SQUADRON 8

LTJG Jeffrey Ouimette, October 2015

"Truly superior pilots are those who use their superior judgment to avoid situations where they might have to use their superior skills."

I remember a situation where I had one of those superior pilots. It all started as just another normal instrument flight.

Our plan was to fly an MH-60S to Marine Corps Air Station Miramar's airfield for multiple approaches, navigate the victor airways to MCAS Camp Pendleton, and then return to NAS North Island. Preflight, taxi and takeoff were uneventful and on time, in keeping with the flight schedule. After takeoff, we began our departure procedures and followed the instructions from the air traffic control tower (ATC), climbing to our assigned altitude.

Upon reaching approximately 6,000 feet, I began to feel the aircraft gallop. This sensation of the helicopter moving up and down ever so gently in flight was not uncommon, and I was qualified in model at the time; however, I did not have the experience to know whether or not it was normal.

Since I was the most junior member of the crew and no one else had said anything, I just shrugged it off as something normal with this aircraft.

After about three or four minutes of flying straight and level, I started noticing a change in the aircraft's motion. I looked up and saw what looked like an abnormal blade tip path plane. I have flown plenty of straight and level, with no speed change or control input, but this tip path plane appeared to be bouncing up and down more than I had ever seen before. This, combined with the increased up and down motion, made me feel uncomfortable.

Suddenly, the crew chief called over Intercommunications System (ICS) and asked if anyone felt the excessive up and down motion. I confirmed that I felt the helicopter moving up-and-down and that I noticed the tip path plane had an exaggerated jump. It appeared as if one of the blades was out of track and dipping lower than the others when it passed in front of the nose.

ATC then contacted us and gave instructions to begin our approach into Miramar. The HAC stated over ICS that he also felt excessive motion and had been waiting to see if anyone else noticed to ensure he wasn't feeling something that wasn't there. Deciding to knock it off, he cancelled the approach with ATC and requested to proceed VFR back to Naval Air Station North Island.

As we turned and descended, the galloping motion became more and more noticeable. We were currently abeam MCAS Miramar's airfield looking down the coast. Knowing there would be no safe place to put the helicopter down should the motion get to a point where the aircraft was no longer flyable, the HAC made a time-critical decision: divert. He called ATC and declared an emergency. ATC cleared all the traffic as we proceeded to the runway and landed.

During post-flight inspection, we found nothing wrong with the rotor head, rotor blades, or transmission assembly. A maintenance crew arrived and visually inspected the aircraft, also finding nothing wrong.

Since the HAC was also an FCP, the decision was made to "pro and go" the aircraft back to NAS North Island after talking with the commanding officer.

After completing ground vibration and hover tests, we ran in-flight vibration analysis tests and returned to NAS North Island. Further inspection revealed that one of the blade dampers had a leak that caused the excessive blade motion. If undiscovered and had the aircraft continue to fly, the condition may have led to a catastrophic failure of the rotor system.

Lessons Learned:

Due to the HAC's time-critical decision, the crew returned safely with the aircraft undamaged.

By declaring an emergency and PEL at MCAS Miramar, the HAC avoided passing up a safe airfield for the unknown, even if it was only a few miles away.

The superior pilot didn't fall victim to "get home-itis" or hesitate declaring an emergency. Instead, he used his superior judgment to ensure the safety of aircraft and crew.

NOTES:

DITCHING INTO THE DEEP
MH-53E SEA DRAGON, UNITED STATES NAVY, HELICOPTER MINE COUNTERMEASURES SQUADRON 14, VANGUARD

LCdr. Bill Mellen, June 2005

"Ok guys, this is it, we gotta do this," was the last thing I said before we lost all power to the aircraft. Those words could have been my last ones had I not had the proper training.

I was straight out of Aviation Safety School and just three weeks into my department-head job as the squadron safety officer; I couldn't help but shake my head at the irony of it all.

It was a typically brisk but clear, winter day in Norfolk, with water temperatures reportedly in the high 30s to low 40s.

I begrudgingly donned my dry suit — not thrilled by the prospect of having the suit's rubber seal chafe my neck, like a cheap, rented tuxedo, for the duration of a three-hour, airborne mine-countermeasure (AMCM) sortie.

With a seasoned lieutenant for an aircraft commander (HAC) and a complement of six salty aircrew, I felt the deck was stacked for an easy back-in-the-saddle flight for the old O-4.

Good thing I didn't make a wager.

Scheduled to hunt "mine like" objects in a training minefield 30 miles off the coast, when we reached the training field, I settled our MH-53E into a 75-foot hover as the crew prepared the AMCM gear. We completed our pre mission checklist in the cockpit and awaited the "ready to commence" call from the crew. Instead, we heard, "Sir, do you hear that noise?"

A high-pitched whining sound could be heard over the ICS. I quickly scanned the gauges-indications were normal.

I replied, "Everything looks normal up here. Where is the sound coming from?"

One crewman suspected the No. 3 engine. "No biggie," I thought. After all, this is the mighty 53E, with three engines and power to spare; just transition to forward flight, and, if the engine fails, land as soon as practical. It was time to show the lieutenant how an "old school bubba" greases on a dual-engine landing.

I was awakened from my pretentious stupor by another crewman's remark, "Ah, actually, sir, I think the noise is coming from the main gearbox."

The machine just upped the ante, and this was a winner-takes-all game.

We immediately headed for the beach. As I mentally reviewed the NATOPS procedures for an impending main-gearbox failure, I flew a "low and slow" profile of 100 feet AGL and 80 knots.

Within three minutes, the noises from the back grew deeper and louder; airframe vibrations now accompanied them. I could feel the aircraft laboring to stay in the air. I asked the HAC to check the pressure and temperature gages and to alert me of any abnormal indications. The gages checked within limits, but the aircraft was talking and telling a story whose plot was easy to follow. With numerous mishap accounts fresh in my mind from safety school, I knew the all-too-often abrupt ending.

"This is not good," I remarked to the crew.

Reading between the lines, the HAC directed the aircrew to prepare the cabin for a possible water landing.

Still 28 miles from land, I wondered how much farther I could coax the aircraft to fly. I got my answer moments later when the MGB-chip-detected (Magnetic) light illuminated, followed, in short order, by a hydraulic-pressure caution light.

Completely persuaded that the gearbox was catastrophically failing, I rapidly flared to set up for an immediate, no-hover landing.

"Ditch, ditch, ditch; we're making a water landing guys," I announced over ICS. I asked the HAC to raise the landing gear and to get out a Mayday call on guard frequency.

"I can't believe I'm about to do this," I thought, as I set the aircraft on the ocean.

The tail end settled and immediately began to take on water. The HAC reached up to secure the engines, while I did my best to keep the aircraft upright with the cyclic.

Suddenly, power cut off, and all we heard was the whistle of the blades as they coasted down.

Seeing the water level creep up the chin bubble, I realized I needed to prepare for the inevitable egress. I reached down and pulled the window's emergency release handle, gave the window an elbow, and watched it fall into the water.

"What else?" my mind raced to recall. "Air, that's right, I got air."

I reached across my survival vest and grabbed the helicopter-aircrew-breathing-device (HABD) regulator, put it my mouth, and took a short breath to make sure there would be no surprises (I had been in too much of a hurry on preflight and hadn't bothered to check the bottle pressure). As the rotor blades slapped against the swells and came to a halt, the aircraft began a slow roll. I looked over to the HAC and saw he already was underwater. I held on to my window frame for reference, placed my other hand on the harness release, and braced myself for the big-ticket ride.

I was comforted by how surprisingly close the airframe-roll mirrored that of the 9D5 helo dunker (Helicopter Underwater Escape Training (HUET)). However, my comfort level soon was exceeded by the inrush of water from my window.

It felt like a fire hose had been sprayed in my face. Every part of me desperately wanted to get out of that seat, but the phrase, "Wait until all violent motion stops," rang in my mind, and I stayed strapped in until the rush subsided.

Suddenly, it got dark but calm. Breathing on my HABD bottle, I turned the harness release and fell out of the seat — still holding on to my window frame with the proverbial death grip. As I fought through debris that washed forward from the cabin and filled the cockpit, I pulled myself through the window and made a few strokes.

Next thing I saw was the blue Virginia sky as my head popped out of the water. I soon felt the cold bite of the frigid water; I now was glad to be wearing that cheap, rented tuxedo.

Regrettably, I had opted to leave my dry-suit underliner hanging in the paraloft, because I didn't want to get too warm in flight. I pulled the beaded handles to inflate my survival vest and was granted the luxury of an auto-inflate. Others of the crew were forced to manually inflate their vests when the beaded handles failed them.

I looked around and spotted an orange raft floating 20 yards away —the crew chief had been able to deploy and inflate the raft during egress. I backstroked my way to the raft, where the rest of the crew met me. We all worked to get each other on board. I counted eight smiling—no, make that, giddy—faces and let out a sigh of relief that everyone safely had gotten out. We were cold and wet, but there wasn't a scratch on anyone.

A Coast Guard C-130 crew heard our Mayday and, within minutes, was circling overhead. We established communications with the plane on the PRC-149 survival radio from one of the crewman's vest. Help was on the way. Morale was high in the raft. I almost felt guilty about quenching the festivities by putting on my safety officer's hat and reminding the crew we still were in the ocean and needed to stay focused on our procedures for rescue.

Two Navy H-60 helicopters arrived to hoist us to safety.

Back at the hospital, a crewman asked me if that was the back-in-the-saddle flight I was looking for. "Not so much," I replied.

Lessons Learned:

I learned that the aircraft doesn't lie when it's talking to you, so you better be all ears.

Abnormal noises may be the first and possibly the only indication of malfunction before failure. What's more, it has been said that the NATOPS was written in blood.

Unless you want to write a postscript with yours, know its contents cold; there's no time to cross-reference when things get ugly.

Don't allow the donning of your survival gear to become a mere formality: Dress for survival, not for comfort.

Preflight and thoroughly familiarize yourself with all personal and aircraft survival items; today might be the day you call on them to save your life.

Finally, believe in the emergency-egress training you've been taught. Does it really work? I bet my life on it.

NOTES

STANDBY FOR FREESTREAM

MH-60R SEAHAWK, UNITED STATES NAVY, HSM-75, HELICOPTER MARITIME STRIKE SQUADRON 75 , 'WOLFPACK'

LCDR Justin Eckhoff, June 2014

The freestream recovery of a sonar dome is an emergency procedure (EP) commonly practiced in the MH-60R community. It is usually done in the simulator or without the dome actually in the water. That way you don't have to practice the emergency with a $2.8 million asset, hanging on a thin cable hundreds of feet below the aircraft. Our crew was flying in Lonewolf 710 and encountered this emergency.

Our squadron was onboard USS Nimitz (CVN 68), which was one month into its WestPac deployment.

Lonewolf 710 had just gone through an A-phase maintenance inspection, and our maintainers had installed the airborne low frequency sonar (ALFS) sonar system.

As the functional check pilot conducting the post-phase functional check flight (FCF), I wanted to make sure the ALFS would function should our squadron be tasked to conduct real-world, anti-submarine warfare (ASW).

The weather for the check flight was marginal, with scattered rain showers and patchy fog.

However, we had the minimum visual-meteorological-conditions (VMC) of 1,000-foot ceilings and three miles of visibility to complete all our checks. We made our way through VMC as we cleared the carrier-control zone to find open airspace for the FCF. The ship drove on base-recovery course as she conducted fixed-wing flight operations.

Almost two hours into the flight, we had completed all required checks for the FCF and proceeded to op-check the ALFS. We had a newly installed dome, and the associated NATOPS procedure is to conduct an initial dip of 50 to 100 feet and then to fully seat the dome before conducting further dipping operations. We pulled into a hover at 70 feet and lowered the sonar dome to 90 feet water depth — a total of 160 feet of paid-out cable length (POCL). From the hover, we estimated the seas to be 5 to 7 feet.

After the initial op-check, we recovered the dome with no issues. We departed the hover and flew to the next dip location to conduct a full op-check at a greater depth. On the second dip, we lowered the transducer to 600 feet. We had another good op-check, so the crewman began to raise the dome with the reeling machine.

As the dome was about halfway up, we heard a loud squeal and smelled a strong metallic odor in the cabin. The reeling machine stopped with 307 feet of cable still deployed below the aircraft. Multiple error codes and cautions on the ALFS system were displayed. We were not even sure the transducer was still attached to the cable. Cable angle hover — the automatic-flight-control-system function that keeps the transducer cable centered underneath the aircraft — was disabled when the malfunction occurred and would not reengage.

For the next 20 minutes, the pilot at the controls (PAC) had to manually control the aircraft to maintain position over the oscillating cable. The rest of the crew worked to troubleshoot the emergency. The crewman tried to raise the dome using alternate methods, including auxiliary electric and auxiliary hydraulic modes, but the cable would not reel in.

At this point, the carrier was more than 20 miles away. As the pilot not at controls (PNAC), I started working bingo fuel calculations and communications. Since we were at an altitude of 70 feet, the ship was out of line-of-sight communications range. The squadron CO was airborne in Lonewolf 711, so our crew opted to use his aircraft to relay communications to the carrier about our situation. After 20 minutes of troubleshooting, we determined that we had no method to reel in the remaining cable. As a crew, we decided to execute the freestream recovery EP.

The freestream procedure involves climbing vertically at 100-to-350 feet per minute until the sonar transducer clears the water. Our crew decided to climb to 500 feet, which would give us nearly 200 feet of dome clearance from the water and at least 100 feet of clearance over the carrier flight deck. We slow-climbed to altitude and had the crewman visually verify that the dome was still attached to the cable once it cleared the water. With the dome trailing this far below the aircraft, NATOPs limits kept us to a maximum of 70 knots and 15-degrees angle of bank for the return transit.

We slowly started back to the ship and requested a minimum wind over the flight deck. We also asked for mattresses strapped to the deck on an open area to cushion the landing of the dome. Weather on the return transit deteriorated with ceilings dropping to 500 to 600 feet. The prevailing visibility dropped to one mile with intermittent rain, with winds increasing to 35 knots.

Onboard USS Nimitz, it was the most inopportune time to attempt the emergency recovery. The ship had just cancelled the majority of the fixed-wing cycle due to the weather, yet there was still a C-2 turning on cat 3 prepping to launch. The ship agreed to provide minimum winds over the deck for the recovery and slowed to four knots. Departure cleared the airspace around the CVN to make way for our emergency aircraft. The squadron XO made his way to the tower to assist with communicating with us. Squadron maintainers scrambled to locate and position the mattresses in front of spot 9.

After a slow transit, we made final preparations for landing. Because of the poor weather conditions, we had to orbit for about 15 minutes as the CVN made its way through a squall, disappearing from view at less than a mile on final.

We reviewed the procedures for shearing the cable in the event that we encountered further problems over or near the deck. We also discussed waveoff procedures if we slipped into the clouds or lost sight of the ship. The crewman positioned himself in the open cabin door, so he could spot the dome. With 307 feet of POCL, he lacked sufficient depth perception to judge the height of the dome over the deck. He was able to provide adequate calls regarding the dome's lateral and longitudinal position below the aircraft.

The PAC, in the left seat, flew a slow approach up the stern to spot 9 at 500 feet on the baralt. He skirted the bottom of the cloud deck and kept clearance between the hung dome and the flight deck. At that altitude, only the bow of the carrier was visible. All control inputs were based on calls from the crewman and non flying pilot who could see just the tower below him. The PNAC provided conning inputs to keep the aircraft clear of the tower and antennae, while the crewman conned the dome into position over the mattresses.

The two single mattresses were side by side and looked no bigger than a postage stamp from 400 feet above the deck. However, with timely and accurate conning by the crewman and PNAC, and control inputs by the PAC, we managed to hit the target. We lowered the dome directly onto the mattresses.

Once the dome was grounded, maintenance crews rushed in and pulled the cable to the starboard side of the deck. We slowly descended and landed forward of spot 9, between the 1- and 2-wire.

Post-incident analysis of the aircraft revealed that the sonar cable fell out of the guides on the reeling machine, and the cable became pinched between the reel and the housing, causing the reeling machine to seize during flight.

The excess tension during the seizure caused the cable to break, leaving the dome attached to the aircraft only because the cable was being pinched in place. As a crew, we were fortunate that the $2.8 million dome assembly didn't depart the aircraft. The dome was inspected and reinstalled in a matter of days.

Lessons Learned:

Both the PAC and the PNAC were former MH-60R FRS (Fleet Replacement Squadron) instructors and had practiced manually controlling the aircraft with cable angle secured to keep the cable position centered. The task is not particularly difficult, but without sufficient experience, errant pilot inputs can induce excessive oscillations putting the dome and aircraft at risk. Just like learning to hover for the first time, it requires small inputs and patience to keep the dome stable.

Cushioning the dome on a mattress or two sounds straightforward, but doing so from 400 feet requires solid conning commands from the non flying crew and responsive inputs from the pilot. With a freestream conducted from higher altitudes, you might want to enlarge the area with more mattresses.

CRM is not an abstract concept to which we simply give lip service. During the emergency and afterwards in the debrief, we commented how comfortable we were with the plan that evolved during the procedure, including bingo, wave-off criteria, communications and contingencies. Each member was clear on their tasks and we effectively backed-up each other throughout.

Our success started well before the flight by briefing clear expectations of crew responsibilities during emergencies, and then sticking to those expectations during the flight.

NOTES:

ENGINE OUT

MH-60S SEAHAWK, UNITED STATES NAVY, HSC-8, HELICOPTER SEA COMBAT SQUADRON 8

LT Robert Steiner, April 2014

The aircraft descended toward runway 23 at San Clemente Island, just above safe single-engine speed. This was not a usual profile for an MH-60S, and this was no routine landing. Usually, a landing at San Clemente Island is for extra fuel after a long training flight before heading home to NAS North Island.

Under the glare shield glowed the yellow No. 1 ENG OUT caution light. As the main mounts touched down, the glow disappeared, but spinning red lights still illuminated the taxiway as the crash crew stood by.

They followed the aircraft down the runway from along the taxiway.

Here's how I got there. The day had started like any other. I came in early to finish the last-minute preparations for the flight, staple the smart packs together, read the aircraft discrepancy book, and put the finishing touches on the brief. The mission was close-air-support (CAS) training, 70 miles to the west, off the coast of San Diego.

Today was to be a valuable day of training for HSC-8.

Laser ranges are scheduled far in advance, and the next opportunity for training like this was uncertain. With the federal budget still undecided, no one knew how many hours we would fly in the next fiscal quarter. It might be the last opportunity for our pilots to train toward their anti-surface warfare level III (ASUW3) qualification. Today would also be more valuable because we were operating with a real joint-terminal-attack controller (JTAC) on the ground, directing our simulated AGM-114K Hellfire missile shots.

As the 75-minute brief came to an end and the final questions were wrapped up, the crews finished their NATOPS brief. The plan was set, the mission cards were burned, the crews were ready, and we headed to the flight line. A captive-air-training missile (CATM) was mounted to the starboard side of each aircraft, an important part of our close-air-support training mission. It would give us indications in the cockpit from our laser rangefinder designator (LRD), allowing the Hellfire missile's seeker-head to know exactly where it needed to direct the ordnance.

Flying in Dash 2, we received clearance from tower for takeoff, taxied onto the pad, and made a final check of the engine instruments. Everything was ready, and as lead called "10 seconds" over the radio for our dual aircraft takeoff, the aircraft commander pulled in power early to beat the lead aircraft off the ground. His intent was to avoid the main rotor downwash from the aircraft ahead of us. The ground shrank beneath us, and we headed in tight formation down the channel out of San Diego Bay. We switched radio frequencies and prepared for our transit to San Clemente Island.

"Diablo, this is Loosefoot 11 and flight," we called. No response.

"Don't worry, I'm sure we will be in comms once we make it over that ridge," we said to the other aircraft over our squadron's tactical frequency. One of the disadvantages of helicopters that always fly low and behind terrain is the lack of radio reception.

The island came into view on the forward-looking infrared (FLIR) and combat checks were complete.

Time to get things started.

"Diablo, this is Loosefoot 11 and flight," we called.

"Loosefoot flight, this is Diablo, standby for SITREP (Situation Report). There's a concentration of simulated enemy troops located along a ridgeline near small buildings with heavy armored vehicles and small arms, perfect targets for Hellfire missiles. Proceed direct Holding Area Sally and stand by for 9-line."

The mission commander scribbled down instructions from the JTAC onto his kneeboard and prepared a plan. The section attack brief would be given, and we'd be ready for target acquisition. We pushed toward the battle position where we would release our simulated attack on the enemy.

Every second is valuable when the ordnance needs to hit the target at a precise moment.

"Twenty-two seconds to push time," came over the radio.

"I concur," I announced, "push time of three five four two."

We headed inbound to the target, sensors aimed and laser's armed. "Ten-seconds," came over the radio. Time to laser the target.

"Spot, solid box, no constraints, rifle away, time of flight sixteen-seconds." No missile came off the rail on this flight, but all the indications were there for a good shot.

"Impact, terminate. Loosefoot flight pull right." The island slid across the windscreen, and the target disappeared from my mission display.

The pilot at the controls looked down and inquisitively alerted the crew to an advisory on his display. "Ng is in the twelve-second range," he said, as he switched his scan to the engine instruments to diagnose the issue.

We levelled off at safe single-engine airspeed. Our compressor turbine was pegged at maximum; something was obviously wrong. For a split-second my stomach dropped, and then instinct kicked-in as my eyes scanned the rest of the instruments.

Nothing else was out of the ordinary, and we agreed that we had indications of a digital-engine-control malfunction.

The next step was to pull the No. 1 engine power control lever (PCL) out of the fly detent to bring the overspeed condition into control. We concurred on the No. 1 engine PCL, and I pulled it halfway back to the six o'clock position, reducing fuel flow to our engine. Ng was still in the red range, and our torque indications dropped below 20 percent.

"Not enough," I thought. My helicopter aircraft commander (HAC) thought the same. He said, "Pull it back a little bit more."

I slowly slid the PCL back nearer to the idle detent. "Ng is in the green," I announced. "Let's turn north along the west side of the island for a precautionary landing at San Clemente Island NALF."

We were in a safe flight regime with a single engine. We called our lead aircraft, made them aware of the situation and told them that we had it under control. They slid back and perched above us as we headed north. "It looks like you have smoke coming from your No. 1 engine," we heard over the radio.

"Fantastic," I sarcastically thought. We started a slow climb away from the water and terrain to a higher altitude and finished the checklist for our malfunction. As we gained altitude, we noticed the oil pressure drop from 50 to 30 psi. It would soon be in the precautionary range.

"Time to shut off No. 1 engine," HAC announced to the crew.

The crew chief didn't miss a beat and spoke up: "I've got it, sir. Page two, tac two, Engine Shutdown in Flight Procedure!"

We began to execute the steps, and as I pulled the PCL to the OFF detent, the engine spooled down, temperature indications began to drop. The No. 1 ENG OUT caution light illuminated.

"There isn't smoke coming from the engine anymore," we heard over the radio. It's not every day you pull a PCL to the OFF position at 1,000 feet above the ground. " ... mente tower, this is Loosefoot 613 and flight declaring an emergency."

I heard half of the transmission over the radio as I switched to tower frequency. Close behind us was our skipper in the other aircraft, backing us up and making radio calls for our landing.

As we got closer to the airfield, our HAC maintained a calm demeanor, set up the plan and announced it to the crew. "All right guys, we are flying just fine right now. We have a road right below us in case anything else happens, we have our clearance to land, and we will be making a running landing at safe single-engine airspeed."

I referenced my preflight calculations and updated them based on our weight. I replied, "We have a safe power margin above 30 knots."

As we approached the runway, the fire truck and ambulance stood by at the approach end of the runway, ready for the worst but hoping for the best. The crash crews probably didn't know what was happening in our aircraft. We rolled on final and settled into ground effect, almost safe on deck.

After landing, it turned out that the malfunction had caused a rupture somewhere in the oil system. The smoke coming from the engine was oil burning near the hot engine exhaust. The drop in oil pressure was due to the leak, and oil was slicked across the port side of the aircraft just below the engine cowling. The engine-oil sight gauge was empty, and oil was pooled in the lowest part of the compartment. If we had not recognized the overspeed when we did, it could have been much worse.

Lessons Learned:

Handling a situation like this, although nerve racking at the time, brings a sense of confidence. It also shows the importance of crew resource management (CRM), training and the value of simulators. Exposure to emergency procedures that you cannot duplicate in the aircraft is invaluable training. In a time of budget uncertainty, making the most out of our limited simulator hours is critical to proficiency. Although faced with an emergency, the entire crew knew their roles. We immediately acted as a team.

NOTES:

LIVE HOISTING, LIVE RESCUE

SH-60B, UNITED STATES NAVY, HSL-49, HELICOPTER MARITIME STRIKE SQUADRON 49

LT Patrick Kelley-Hauske, April 2014

An aircraft commander must anticipate and prepare for all possible contingencies during a mission. I learned this lesson as a newly designated SH-60B aircraft commander, when an unexpected turn of events occurred during a search-and-rescue (SAR) jump currency flight. We had adequate controls in place to prevent a mishap but learned much for future SAR training and, in particular, operational missions.

We had been scheduled for day and night SAR jumps with an aircraft from a sister squadron. We discussed the safety aspects of aircraft separation and the rescue procedures in case an aircraft could not recover its swimmers. Because we did not have a surface vessel acting as a safety boat, each aircraft provided rescue capability for the other. We also discussed a recent change to HSL-49 operating procedures, which stated live hoisting should be done at 40 feet AGL. Although the lower hover altitude allowed for much more expeditious and safer hoisting, the crew chiefs preferred to remain at 70 feet AGL to avoid large rotor-wash interference.

This altitude criteria was an important decision point during the brief as it represented a deviation from my previous experience during live hoists. Two weeks earlier, I had flown a SAR-jumps currency flight where the same factors were taken into consideration, and we conducted all live hoists at 40 feet AGL. In this case, I went against my better judgment and allowed my crew chiefs to talk me out of the proper procedure.

We assessed that our swimmers had the experience to correctly rig themselves and prevent inadvertent free fall, and that the higher altitude was safer if we had a sudden, single-engine malfunction. Although the crew chiefs had vast experience in live hoisting, it was my responsibility as the aircraft commander to execute the flight in accordance with squadron guidance.

The day portion of the flight went as planned. The aircraft was flying well and the weather was cooperating. After refuelling and returning to the SAR jump area, we made our first automatic approach for the night, live-hoisting evolution. I was in the left seat and at the controls. My copilot, a senior H2P, was backing me up on altitude during the descent, as well as hover checks once we established a coupled hover. After a steady hover was established, we cleared our crew chief to lower the first swimmer into the water. We had a steady left crosswind and continually corrected for right drift.

The crew chief reported that the second swimmer was ready, and I granted permission to begin lowering. The swimmer gave the appropriate hand signals passing through 20 feet above the water and again at 10 feet. The crew chief conned us into a better position.

As the swimmer approached the surface, the right drift correction as well as the height above water resulted in him swinging underneath the aircraft, causing a failure of our radar altimeter (radalt). As designed, the coupled-hover function of the H-60 automatic flight control system (AFCS) will secure if radalt-hold is lost and automatically switch over to barometric-altimeter (baralt) hold. Baralt is not as accurate as radalt, and when the altitude-hold transfers, it immediately causes altitude deviations.

In our case, we rapidly descended 10 feet. As the pilot at controls, I increased collective to correct. For the swimmer below, this sequence of events can be violent. The altitude loss most likely will dunk swimmers in the water, and depending on the pilot's correction, they may be yanked back out of the water. Being pulled from the water can be particularly harmful because of the water resistance and possible cable entanglement, which can lead to severe injury. Our crew chief was experienced in this scenario from many prior practice jumps. When he recognized the altitude loss, he immediately anticipated a pilot correction. He tried to shear the rescue hoist to avoid injury to the swimmer. He broke the shear-wire securing the switch; however, we had steadied out the aircraft before he could actuate the shear system.

With the swimmer signalling OK, we checked that radalt-hold was reengaged. We decided as a crew that it was safe to continue the evolution. As we were once again conned into position via the crew chief's calls, the swimmer again swung underneath the aircraft and into the beam of the radalt, again causing it to fail. The aircraft again dropped 10 feet. The crew chief sheared the hoist.

With our aircraft no longer SAR-capable, we marked the position of the survivors and transitioned to forward flight. We alerted our playmate, who subsequently recovered both uninjured personnel from the water. With all personnel accounted for, we headed home, landed and debriefed.

Lessons Learned:

We had many takeaways that apply to live hoisting.

The first is the justification behind the 40-foot hover altitude for live hoisting. While everyone is familiar with the inadvertent free-fall hazard during hoisting, our crew chief had confidence in the experience level of the swimmers, and we trusted they would properly hook up to the hoist. As we learned, the rescue swimmer may fall due to no fault of his own from a sheared hoist.

We also learned the hard way the need to conduct live hoisting at 40 feet AGL as published by the standardization board.

We gained experience on how to better respond to the NATOPS warning regarding the injury to the swimmer if radalt-hold fails. NATOPS warns not to make any large or abrupt control inputs; however, it may be advisable to briefly stabilize the aircraft at the altitude you descend to, rather than correcting to the original altitude. Stabilize the aircraft, communicate to the crew chief when steady, and reset to hoisting altitude once the swimmer is OK and not at risk of sudden jerking motions or cable entanglement.

Finally, this event illustrates to aircraft commanders the necessity of a backup plan in case of an actual SAR. While engine or transmission failures are certainly possible, a radalt-hold failure is much more likely. It can easily result in a stranded swimmer as well as survivors. Requesting additional assets is important, even for simple rescues under ideal conditions. You may suddenly find yourself not SAR-capable because of the actions of your experienced crew.

NOTES:

SPRAG CLUTCH FAILURE

AH-64E, UNITED STATES ARMY, ARMY AIRCRAFT ACCIDENT PREVENTION

Name withheld by request, September 2019

The mishap crew was part of a battalion aerial gunnery qualification in preparation for an upcoming combat training center rotation. The battalion assets arrived at their aerial gunnery training area and began conducting operations two days later. The unit conducted briefings, crews were designated and appropriate risk assessments and mission briefings were executed. The mishap crew was slated to conduct a two-ship flight to engage in night aerial gunnery of Table VII, VIII and IX. The mishap crew was designated as "Gun 1."

Prior to departure, the crew experienced a few maintenance delays that required a ground run and maintenance operational check. Following a two-hour weather delay, the two aircrews had the weather to depart and execute the gunnery operation. Due to time constraints, the crews determined they could execute only the Table VII. They were re-briefed by the mission briefing officer and updated their weather.

Ready to execute one table, the mishap crew started and ran-up the aircraft on the parking pad.

As the aircraft rose and hover taxied aft to exit parking at an altitude of 17 feet above ground level (AGL), it experienced a rapid main rotor (MR) RPM decay followed by a massive torque spike. The aircraft lost tail rotor authority while descending due to MR droop. The aircraft struck the ground left-side low with a rearward momentum and came to rest. The aircrew was not injured.

Crew

The pilot in command (PC) had 436 hours in mission, type, design, series (MTDS) and 1,078 hours total time. The pilot (PI) had 424 hours in MTDS and 1,793 hours total time.

Lessons Learned:

The aircraft experienced a material failure of the sprag clutches, resulting in rapid MR RPM decay followed nearly immediately by a massive torque spike.

It is believed the near simultaneous slippage of the No. 1 and No.2 sprag clutches released the drivetrain input. When the clutches reengaged, it created a massive shock to the drivetrain and resulted in the aircraft engine droop, main transmission damage and loss of tail rotor authority.

The mishap crew took immediate actions to get the AH-64E on the ground with no crew injuries and exited the aircraft.

This situation demonstrates that even when units take all actions within the scope of the known to reduce the risk to aircraft and crew, unforeseen events can still occur. For aviation personnel, aircrews and supporting personnel, it is important to ensure you understand the dangers of aviation operations.

There are no guarantees that mechanical systems will not fail. It is imperative that aircrews train thoroughly and know their emergency procedures while using simulator training to inject those situations into missions so crews maintain their "edge."

Supporting personnel have that same implied task; train hard in your skillset and tasks so you become the resident expert. Use your knowledge to counsel those less experienced and impart lessons learned from your experiences. The ability to react to unforeseen events requires acknowledging they do occur in our operational environment. Prepare the best you can so when they do occur, you can react without hesitation and fly the aircraft.

NOTES:

CHAPTER 10

FURTHER READING

There are a six other books in the *Lessons From The Sky* series. The goal of these books is to save as many lives as possible, and so there's something there for every pilot — fixed wing or rotary, military or civilian, private pilot or commercial:

51 Lessons From The Sky (U.S. Air Force)
61 Lessons From The Sky (Military Helicopters)
71 Lessons From The Sky (Civilian Helicopters)
72 Lessons From The Sky (Cessna 172)
81 Lessons From The Sky (General Aviation)
101 Lessons From The Sky (Commercial Aviation)
Top Gun Lessons From The Sky (U.S. Navy)

I WOULD REALLY APPRECIATE if you could post a review (or simply a rating) online. Your review may help save the life of another pilot.

Blue skies.

GLOSSARY

This is a list of initials, acronyms, expressions, euphemisms, jargon, military slang, and sayings in common or formerly common use in the various militaries reported in this book.

Many of the words or phrases have varying levels of acceptance among different units or communities, and some also have varying levels of appropriateness (usually dependent on how senior the user is in rank).

Many terms also have equivalents among other service branches that are comparable in meaning. Many acronyms and terms have come into common use from voice procedure use over communication channels, translated into the NATO phonetic alphabet, or both.

Numerical

100 nm - Nautical Miles

1000-3 - 1000ft cloud ceiling 3 mile visibility rule

10Z - all weather maps, radar, and satellite images all have their time expressed in "Z". The Zulu term stems from military usage while

Coordinated Universal Time (UTC) is the civilian term for this 24-hour clock. 10Z refers to 10am time.

1300L - Lima Time Zone UTC +11 hours

20Gs – 20 x gravitational force equivalent, commonly called a g-force, is a measurement of the type of force per unit mass – typically acceleration this causes a perception of weight, with a g-force of "1 g" equal to the conventional value of gravitational acceleration on Earth, g, at around 9.8 m/s2

2100L - Lima Time Zone UTC +11 hours

2P - 2nd Pilot

38 Gp - No 38 Group RAF is a group of the Royal Air Force. It was formed on 6 November 1943 from nine squadrons as part of Fighter Command.

3P - 3rd Pilot

A

AAR - Air-to-Air Refuel

ABF - attack by fire

AC - aircraft commander

ACTC - Air Combat Training Continuum

ADB - aircraft discrepancy book

AFC - automated flight control system

AFCS - automatic flight control system

AFRCC - Air Force Rescue Coordination Center

AFSOC - Air Force special operations command

AGL - Above Ground Level

AH-64 Apache - twin-turboshaft attack helicopter with tandem cockpit for a crew of two with nose-mounted sensor suite for target acquisition and night vision systems.

AI - Attitude Indicators

Air Boss - the air officer (along with his assistant, the miniboss) is responsible for all aspects of operations involving aircraft

Aircrewman - US Naval rating (known as Aviation Warfare Systems Operator or AW prior to 2008) is an enlisted rating

Airprox - a near collision between two or more aircraft

ALARP* - as low as reasonably practicable

ALFS - airborne low frequency sonar

ALM - Air Loadmaster

AMC - Air Mission Commander

AMCM - airborne mine-countermeasure

AMSL - Height above mean sea level

AMU - Aircraft Maintenance Unit

Anderson Air Force Base - located approximately 4 miles (6.4 km) northeast of Yigo near Agafo Gumas in the United States territory of Guam.

AoB (Angle of Bank)

Apache AH1 - first designated WAH-64 by Westland Helicopters then given the designation Apache AH Mk 1 (also written as "Apache AH1") by the UK Ministry of Defence.

ARCC - Aeronautical Rescue Coordination Centre

ASI - Air Speed Indicator

ASO - aviation safety officers

ASW - anti-submarine warfare

ATC - Air Traffic Control

ATIS - Automatic terminal information service

ATM - aircrew training module

AWACS - Airborne Warning And Control System

AWR - Aircrewman Tactical Helicopter

AWS - area weapons system

AWS - Aircrewman Helicopter

AWT - attack weapons team

B

BARALT - Barometric Altitude

BINGO - An order to proceed and land at the field specified, utilizing a bingo profile. Aircraft is considered to be in an emergency/fuel critical situation. Bearing, distance, and destination shall be provided. US Navy definition from NAVTOPS

BRC - Base Recovery Course

BT-11 - Restricted training airspace (bombing range)

C

C-2A Greyhound - twin-engine, high-wing cargo aircraft, designed to carry supplies, mail, and passengers to and from aircraft carriers of the United States Navy

CADS - centralised aviation data service

CAG - Carrier Air Group, outdated, but CAG is still used as a nickname for the Air Wing Commander

CAL - confined area landings

CALA - combat arms loading area

Camp Bastion - Now Camp Shorabak is a former British Army airbase, located northwest of the city of Lashkar Gah in Helmand Province, Afghanistan.

Capt. - captain is a senior officer rank

CAS - close-air-support

Casevacs - casualty evacuations

CASEX - Combined Anti Submarine Exercise

CAST/HRST - Navy Helicopter Rope Suspension Training including rappelling with descending devices and fast-roping and special patrol insertion/extraction

CAT - catapult

CAT 2 - catapult no 2

cat-shot - catapult shot

CATM - captive-air-training missile

CCA - carrier controlled approach

CDO - command duty officer

CE - crew chief

CFIT - Controlled Flight Into Terrain. A mishap where an airworthy aircraft, under pilot control, inadvertently flies into terrain, water, or an object. This does not include incidents where there is intent to land, object/wire strikes, or the aircraft departs controlled flight.

CFS - Central Flying School

CG - Coast Guard

CH53 - Sea Stallion is a family of heavy-lift transport helicopters designed and built by Sikorsky Aircraft.

Chinook - Boeing CH-47 Chinook is an American twin-engined, tandem rotor, heavy-lift helicopter

CIC - Combat Information Center

CIVSAR - civilian search and rescue

COD - Carrier onboard delivery is the use of aircraft to ferry personnel, mail, supplies.

Columbo - International Airport is the main international airport serving Columbo, Sri Lanka.

COMPTUEX - Composite Training Unit Exercise, is a rehearsal each US Navy Carrier Strike Group performs before departing for deployment

CP - Co Pilot

CQ - carrier qualifications - CQ is performed for new pilots and periodically for experienced pilots to gain/maintain carrier landing currency.

CRM - Crew resource management

CRRC - combat rubber raiding craft

CSAR - Combat Search and Rescue

CTAF - Common traffic advisory frequency

CTOC - Counter Transnational Organized Crime

CV - Aircraft carrier

CV-22B Osprey - a multi-mission, tiltrotor military aircraft designed as a vertical takeoff and landing (VTOL), and short takeoff and landing (STOL) aircraft. It combines the functionality of a conventional helicopter with the long-range and high-speed cruise performance of a turboprop aircraft.

CVN - aircraft carrier nuclear propulsion

CVW CQ - Carrier Air Wing carrier qualification flights

CWS - control wheel steering

D

DA - density altitude

DART - Downed Aircraft Recovery Team

Davy-Jones' locker - an idiom for the bottom of the sea: the state of death among drowned sailors and shipwrecks.

de rigeur - required by etiquette or current fashion

DECU - digital electronic control unit

DEN - Domestic Events Network

det - detachment

DFC - Duty Flight Commander

DFSOR - Defence Flight Safety Occurrence Reporting

Dstl - Defence Science and Technology Laboratory (UK)

DVE - Degraded Visual Environment. The Army defines DVE as an environment of reduced visibility of potentially varying degree, wherein situational awareness and aircraft control cannot be maintained as comprehensively as they are in normal Visual Meteorological Conditions (VMC) and can potentially be lost. This description of DVE is applicable to all regimes of flight.

DZ - Drop Zone

DZSO - Drop Zone Safety Officer

E

E-2 - Northrop Grumman E-2 Hawkeye all-weather, carrier-capable tactical airborne early warning (AEW) aircraft.

EADS - Eastern Air Defense Sector

ECS - environment control system

EGI - Embedded GPS Inertial Navigation System

EMT - emergency medical technician

EP - emergency procedures

ETL - effective translational lift

EVLA - emergency low visibility approach

F

FACSFAC - Fleet Area Control and Surveillance Facility

FADEC - a system consisting of a digital computer, called an electronic engine controller (EEC) or engine control unit (ECU)

FARP - forward arming and refueling point

FAST - The Fatigue Avoidance Scheduling Tool

FBO - fixed-base operator

FCF - functional check flight

FDNF - Forward Deployed Naval Forces

FE/s - Flight engineer/Flight engineers

FLIR - Forward-looking infrared camera

Flt - Flight, an independent Flight is a military administrative structure which is used to command flying units where the number of aircraft is not large enough to warrant a fully fledged squadron.

FOB - Forward operating base

fpm - feet per minute

Fragged targets - fragmented number of targets

FRIES - fast rope insertion / extraction system

FRS - Fleet Replacement Squadron

FRS CQ - Fleet Replacement Squadron Carrier Qualifications

FRZ - Flight Restricted Zone

FSCE - fire support coordination exercise

FSCX - fire support coordination exercise

FSII - fuel without icing inhibitor

G

GPS - Global Positioning System

Group Sail - training to improve interoperability and coordination in preparation for an upcoming deployment.

GUAMEX - multi-national anti-submarine warfare (ASW) exercise with the Japanese Maritime Self Defense Force and the Royal New Zealand Air Force.

H

H2P - helicopter second pilot

HA/DR - humanitarian assistance / disaster relief

HABD - Helicopter Aircrew Breathing Device

HAC - helicopter aircraft commander

Haddon Cave - Loss of RAF Nimrod MR2 XV230 and the Haddon-Cave Review - led by London barrister Charles Haddon-Cave QC, who was widely recognised as a leading UK lawyer in the aviation field, having served on the defence team for the 1985 Manchester air disaster and having also represented survivors in the inquiry into The Herald of Free Enterprise ferry disaster.

The Haddon-Cave Report, was published on 28 October 2009 with 90 recommendations.

Haiti - Caribbean country that shares the island of Hispaniola East of the Dominican Republic.

HCO - helicopter control officer

HECO - hurricane evacuation coordinating officer

helo - helicopter

HEMS - Helicopter Emergency Medical Service

HIFR - Helicopter In-Flight Refueling

HIGE - hover in ground effect

HIT - health indicator test

HLS - helicopter landing site

HM1 - SAR medical technician

HMLA - Helicopter Marine Light Attack Helicopter Squadron

HOCAS - hands-on collective and stick

HOGE - hover out of ground effect

HOSTAC (Helicopter Operations from Ships other than Aircraft Carriers

HRS - horizon reference system

HSC - helicopter sea combat squadron

I

ICAWs - Integrated Caution and Warnings

ICS - Intercommunications System

IFF - Identification Friend or Foe transponder system

IFR - Instrument Flight Rules

ILS - instrument landing system

IMC - Instrument meteorological conditions

INS - Inertial Navigation System

IP - Impact Point

IP - Instructor Pilot

IPP - Integrated Power Package

IR - Infra Red

ISATT - Initial Ship Aviation Team Training

ISTAR - Surveillance Target Acquisition and Reconnaissance

ITG - initial terminal guidance

J

JBD - jet blast deflector

JO - Junior Officer

JTAC - Joint Terminal Attack Controller

K

KGS - Knots Ground Speed

KIAS - Knots-Indicated Air Speed

KTAS - knots true airspeed

L

LFA - Low Flying Area

LHS - Left Hand Seat

LLL - low light level

LP - Landing Point

LPD - landing platform/dock

LPU - life preserver unit

LRD - laser rangefinder designator

LS - landing site

LSE - landing signalmen enlisted (guiding helicopters to the designated flight deck)

LSO - landing safety officer

Lt Col - Lieutenant colonel is a rank of commissioned officer.

Lt. - Lieutenant is a commissioned officer rank in many nations' navies. It is typically the most senior of junior officer ranks.

Lt. Cmdr. - Lieutenant commander is a commissioned officer rank in many navies. The rank is superior to a lieutenant and subordinate to a commander.

Lyneham Ops - RAF Lyneham which was the home of all Lockheed C-130 Hercules transport aircraft of the Royal Air Force (RAF) until they were relocated to RAF Brize Norton. The RAF station closed in 31 December 2012.

LZ - landing zone

M

MAD - Magnetic Anomaly Detector

MAG - Marine Aircraft Group

Maj - Major is a military rank of commissioned officers.

MCAS - Marine Corps Air Station

MDG - maneuver description guides

Medal of Honor - the United States of America's highest and most prestigious personal military decoration that may be awarded to recognize U.S. military service members who have distinguished themselves by acts of valor.

METL - methods for executing aviation

MFD - multi-function display

MH - Maritime Helicopter

MH-60R Seahawk - twin turboshaft engine, multi-mission US Navy helicopter based on the US Army UH-60 Black Hawk.

MIL - military power

MISR - maritime intelligence, surveillance, and reconnaissance

MOC - maintenance operations center

MSH - minimum safe height

MSL - Mean Sea Level

MSR - Main Supply Route

MTDS - mission, type, design, and series

MTS - Multi-Spectral Targeting System

N

N1 - Compressor speed

N2 - Power turbine speed

nap of the earth flight - a type of very low-altitude flight course used by military aircraft to avoid enemy detection and attack. Using geographical features as cover, exploiting valleys and folds in the terrain by flying in, rather than over them.

NAS - Naval Air Station

NASNI - Naval Air Station North Island

NATOPS - The Naval Air Training and Operating Procedures Standardization program (pronounced NAY-Tops) prescribes general flight and operating instructions and procedures applicable to the operation of all U.S. naval aircraft and related activities.

Nav - Navigator

NAVEX - Navigation Exercise

Ng - gas generator turbine speed

NH-90 - NHIndustries NH90 is a medium-sized, twin-engine, multi-role military helicopter

NHS - National Health System

NM - Nautical Miles

NMAC - Near Mid Air Collision

NMCI - Navy Marine Corps Intranet

NOE - nap of the earth flight - a type of very low-altitude flight course used by military aircraft to avoid enemy detection and attack. Using geographical features as cover, exploiting valleys and folds in the terrain by flying in, rather than over them.

NOLF - Naval outlying landing field

Northern Helmand - Helmand was part of the Greater Kandahar region of Afghanistan.

NOTAM - A notice to airmen is a notice filed with an aviation authority to alert aircraft pilots of potential hazards along a flight route or at a location that could affect the safety of the flight.

Nr - % rotation speed or the rotor

NSI - night systems instructors

NTRP - Navy tactical reference publications

NVDs - night-vision devices

NVG - Night Vision Googles

NVS - Night Vision Systems

O

O&I - operations and intelligence

OAT - outside air temperature

OBOGS - Onboard Oxygen Generation System

Odiham - Royal Air Force Odiham is a Royal Air Force station situated a little to the south of the historic village of Odiham in Hampshire, England. It is the home of the Royal Air Force's heavy lift helicopter, the Chinook.

ODO - operations duty officer

OGE - Out of ground effect

OIC - officer in charge

Op - Operational

Op HERRICK - Operation Herrick was the codename which all British operations in the War in Afghanistan were conducted from 2002 to the end of operations in 2014.

Operation Unified Response - the United States military's response to the 2010 Haiti earthquake.

OPFOR - opposing force

OPNAV - a formally documented lawful order that is issued by the Chief of Naval Operations

OPTEMPO - Operational Tempo. The Pace Of An Operation Or Operations; Includes All Of The Activities The Unit Is Conducting; Can Be A Single Activity Or Series Of Operations

ORM - Operational Risk Management

OTA - operational training area

Otterburn Training Area - The Otterburn Army TrainingEstate (ATE) is a military training area near Otterburn, Northumberland, in northern England.

P

PAC - pilot at the controls

Pacific - the Pacific Ocean is the largest and deepest of Earth's oceanic divisions.

PAN - radio message PAN-PAN-PAN is the international standard urgency signal for a boat, ship, aircraft, or other vehicle uses to declare that they have a situation that is urgent, but does not pose an immediate danger to life

PAR - Precision approach radar

PC - Air wing Plane Captain - squadron personnel who prepare aircraft for flight

PC - Pilot in Command

PCL - power control lever

PF - Pilot Flying

PFLs - Practice forced landing

PI - The PI will complete all tasks assigned by the PC (Pilot in Command)

PIM - path of intended movement

PIO - Pilot Induced Oscillation

PM - Pilot Monitoring

PNAC - pilot not at controls

PNF - Pilot Not Flying

POC - Point of Contact

POCL - paid-out cable length

Port Au-Prince - the capital and most populous city of Haiti.

PPE - Personal protective equipment

PZ - Pick Up Zone

Q

QHIs - Qualified Helicopter Instructors

QHTI - Qualified Helicopter Tactics Instructor

R

R5306A - Restricted training airspace

RA - Resolution advisory

RAD ALT - radar altimeter

RAF - Royal Air Force

RAF Akrotiri - Royal Air Force Akrotiri is a large Royal Air Force station, on the Mediterranean island of Cyprus.

RAF Bruggen - The former Royal Air Force Station Brüggen, in Germany was a major station of the Royal Air Force until 15 June 2001.

RAF Lyneham - RAF Lyneham was the Royal Air Force's principal Transport hub

RAM - ram air, which allows for outside air cooling for flight critical systems

RHIB - rigid hull inflatable boat

RIMPAC - the Rim of the Pacific Exercise, is the world's largest international maritime warfare exercise

RLG - relief landing ground

RM - Royal Marines

RNAF - Royal Norwegian Air Force

RNF - Reversionary Night Flying

Rothbury - a town and civil parish in Northumberland, England used as a Navigation guide.

RSD - rapid securing device

RTA - Road Traffic Accident

RTS - Release-to-Service

RV - rendezvous

RWAI - Rotary Wing Air Intercept

S

SA - situational awareness

Safed - inserted safety pin

SAR - Search and Rescue

SATCO - Senior Air Traffic Controller

SCT - Scattered (3 to 4 oktas)

Seeb - International Airport is the main international airport serving Seeb, Oman.

Senior Master Sgt. - Senior master sergeant (SMSgt)

SERE - Survival, Evasion, Resistance and Escape

Seventh Fleet - a numbered fleet (a military formation) of the United States Navy, headquartered at Yokosuka, Kanagawa Prefecture, Japan.

SF - Special Forces

SFARP* - so far as is reasonably practicable

SFRA - Special Flight Rules Area

SH - Support Helicopter

Singapore Slings at Raffles - The Singapore Sling, widely regarded as the national drink, was first created in 1915 by Raffles (the famous Singapore hotel) bartender Ngiam Tong Boon.

SITREP - Situation Report

SOF - Supervisor of flying

SOP - standing operating procedure

SPIE -special patrol insertion/extraction

SPSS - Self-Propelled Semi-Submersible

sqn - Squadron

Sqn Execs - squadron executives

Sqn Ldr - Squadron Leader

SSC - surface search and control

STANO - standards officer

Stornoway - Royal Air Force Station Stornoway is a former Royal Air Force station near the burgh of Stornoway, on the Isle of Lewis, in the Western Isles of Scotland.

SWD - specific weapons delivery

SWTI - special weapons and tactics instructor

T

TA/RA - TCAS will issue traffic advisories (TA) and resolution advisories (RA), when appropriate

TAA - Tactical Assembly Area

Tac AT - Tactical Air Transport

TACAN - Tactical air navigation system

TACCO - tactical coordinator

TACCO - Tactical Officers

TACFORM - tactical-formation

TACREPO - tactical reposition

TC 3-04.45 - Training Circular (United States Army Training and Doctrine)

TCAS - Traffic Collision Avoidance System

TERF - terrain-flight

terra firma - dry land; the ground as distinct from the sea

TFR - Terrain Following Radar

TGT - turbine gas temperature

TOI - target-of-interest

TOT - Turbine outlet temperature

TQ - torque

trapped, sidelined - explaining the aircraft landed trapped with a tail hook and was moved away from the operations on deck

TS - Transport Support

TTP - Tactic technique and procedure

U

USMC - United States Marine Corps

V

V/STOL - vertical and/or short take-off and landing

VC10 tanker - The Vickers VC10 is a mid-sized, narrow-body long-range British jet airliner designed and built by Vickers-Armstrongs - converted by the RAF for Inflight-refuelling.

VERTREP - Vertical replenishment

VFR - visual flight rules

VIDS - Vertical Instrument Display System

VMC - visual meteorological conditions

VOR - Very high frequency omni-directional range is a short-range radio navigation system for aircraft

VRC squadrons - Fleet Logistics Support Squadron

VRS - Vortex Ring State

Y

Yellow shirt - different flight deck crews wear coloured jerseys to visually distinguish their functions (USN)

ACKNOWLEDGMENTS

I wish to thank a few people who helped my flying career, whether they realise it or not, our fun conversations or the serious chats we had and the discussions around flying, made this book possible.

As I worked through the list of everyone who has influenced my aviation career, it is incredible to see the number of people I will always be grateful to. Thank you.

Neville Swan (first gliding instructor)
Craig McNeal (first power flying instructor)
Aaron Shipman
Aaron 'AJ' Jeffery
Aaron Pearce
Aaron Marshall
Adam Eltham
Aiden Campbell
Alan Beck QSM
Alistair Blake
Amiria Wallis
Anastasios Raptis
Andrew Gormlie
Andrew Hope
Andrew Lorimer
Andrew Love
Andrew Sunde

Andrew Telfer
Andy Mackay
Andy Stevenson MNZM
Angelo Cruz
Ben Lee
Ben Marcus
Ben Pryor NZGM
Benjamin James
Bevan Dewes
Bill Reid
Bradley Marsh
Brett Emeny
Brett Nicholls
Bruce Lynch
Bryn Lockie
Carlo Santoro
Carlton Campbell
Chantel Strooh
Charles J Cook
Chris Barry
Chris Bromley
Chris Pond
Chris Satler
Chris Sperou OAM
Christina Harvey
Christoph Berthoud
Conor Neill
Cosmo Mead
Craig Piner
Craig Rook
Craig Speck
Craig Steel
Craig Walecki
Damien Campbell

Daniel Campbell
Darren Crabb
Daryl Gillett
Dave Blackwell
David Brown
Dave Campbell
Dave Cogan
Dave Hayman
Dave Rouse
David Lowy AM
David Morgan
David Saunders
David Wilkinson
Dennis Eckhoff
Derry Belcher
Desmond Barry
Don Lockie
Donovan Burns
Doug Batten
Doug Brown
Doug Burrell
Dwight Weston
Enya Mae McPherson
Eric Morgan
Eva Keim
Flo Smith
Frank Parker
Gareth Wheeler
Gavin Conroy
Gavin Trethewey
Gavin Weir
Gene De Marco
Geoff Cooper
George Oldfield JP

Giovanni Nustrini
Graeme 'Spud' Spurdle
Graham Lake
Graham Nevill
Graham Orphan
Grant Armishaw
Grant 'Muddy' Murdoch
Greg Quinn
Guy Bourke
Harvey Lockie
Hayden Leech
HH Prince Faisal bin Abdulla bin Mohammed Saud
Ian Lilley
Ian 'Iggy' Wood
Imogen Ling
James Aldridge
Jamie Wagner
Jason Alexander
Jason Haggitt DSD
Jay McIntyre
Jed Melling
Jill McCaw
Jim Rankin DSD
Jock MacLachlan
Joe Oldfield
John Duxfield ARCOM
John Gemmell
John Lamont
John Martin
John McCaw
Jonathan Bowen
Joseph D'Ath
Josh Camp
Juan Ferandoes

Jurgis Kairys

Karl Stol

Keith McKenzie QSM

Keith Skilling

Keith Stephens

Kenny Love

Kermit Weeks

Kevin Langley

Kevin Vile

Kirsty Coleman

Kishan Bhashyam

Kris Vette

Lawrence Acket

Liberio Riosa

Lionel Page

Liz King (Mother Goose)

Lloyd Galloway

Loïc Ifrah

Louisa 'Choppy' Patterson

Malcolm Clement

Martin Schulze

Mark Helliwell

Mark Lowndes

Mary Patterson

Matt Hall

Matt Ledger

Maurizio Folini

Melissa Andrzejewski (nee Pemberton)

Michael Bach

Michael Jeffs

Mike Clark

Mike Foster

Mike Harvey

Mike Jorgenson

Mike Read
Mike Slack
Nando Parrado
Nathan Graves
Nick Cree
Nick Tarascio
Nigel Cooper
Nigel Lamb
Nina Hayman
Paul Andronicou
Paul 'Huggy' Hughan
Paul 'Simmo' Simmons AM CSM
Pete Meadows
Pete Pring Shambler
Peter Harper
Peter Jefferies
Peter Thorpe
Phil Freeman
Phill Hooker
Pip Borrman
Ray Burns
Ray Richards
Reuben Muir
Rex Pemberton
Richard Button
Richard Hectors
Richard Hood
Rev. Dr Richard Waugh QSM
Richie McCaw ONZ
Rick Watson
Rob Fox
Rob Fry
Rob Mackley
Rob Neil

Rob Owens
Rob Weavers
Robert Burns
Roy Crane
Roy Cunningham
Ruan Heynike
Ruth Nisbet
Ryan Brooks
Ryan Francis
Sam Elimelech
Scott 'Macka' McKenzie
Sean Perrett
Shaun Clark
Shaun Roseveare
Simon J Gault
Simon Lockie
Simon Mundell
Simone Moro
SQNLDR Les Munro CNZM DSO QSO DFC JP
Steve Ahrens
Steve Wallace
Stephen Boyce
Stephen Death
Steve Gibson
Steve Newland
Steve Jurd
Steven Perreau
Stu Wards
Tasos Raptis
Tee Jay Sullivan
Tim Marshall
Sir Tim Wallis
Todd O'Hara
Tracy Dixon

Wayne Fowler
Wayne Ormrod
Wayne Thompson
Vaughan Davis
Yoshihide 'Yoshi' Muroya

ABOUT THE AUTHOR

With a passion for aviation passed on from his father who worked in the National Airways Corporation (NAC) office in Auckland, New Zealand. Fletcher often heard about the NAC DC3 Kaimai Ranges crash, this had made an impact on his father as he knew one of the flight attendants killed in the accident.

As a teenager, Fletcher knew the youngest instructor on his first gliding course who was sadly killed in a glider crash some months after that course.

Over his flying carrier, and during his adventures filming extreme aviators around the world, the deeper Fletcher read into understanding the situations pilots got into, and the more he understood the factors might lead to poor decision making in the skies above.

Coupled with twenty years of experience working with global entrepreneurs through EO (Entrepreneurs Organisation), training them to experience share between each other and to learn from any mistakes, Fletcher selected and compiled these stories to help us learn from others. To ensure current and future pilots will be safe in the skies.

www.fletchermckenzie.com

Printed in Great Britain
by Amazon